DATE DUE

FEB 1 9			
MAY -9			
FEB 2 5			
APR 2 5			
MAR 26			
APR 0 2			
OCT 08			
OCT 09			

Demco, Inc. 38-293

Milton's Imperial Epic

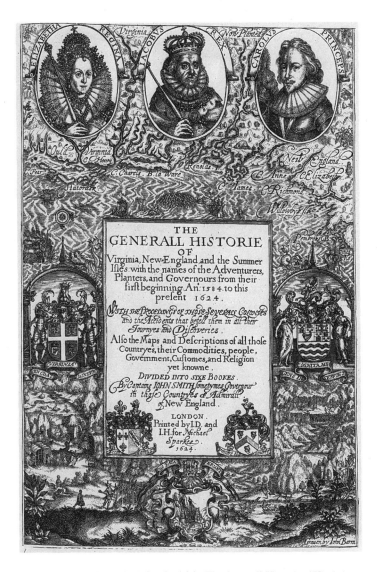

Title page of Captain John Smith's *The Generall Historie of Virginia,
New England, and the Summer Isles,* London, 1624, by
permission of the Huntington Library, San Marino, California.

MILTON'S IMPERIAL EPIC

Paradise Lost and the
Discourse of Colonialism

J. MARTIN EVANS

Cornell University Press

ITHACA AND LONDON

First published 1996 by Cornell University Press.

Printed in the United States of America

∞ The paper in this book meets the minimum requirements
of the American National Standard for Information Sciences—
Permanence of Paper for Printed Library Materials. ANSI Z39.48–1984.

Library of Congress Cataloging-in-Publication Data

Evans, J. Martin (John Martin), 1935–
Milton's imperial epic : Paradise lost and the discourse
of colonialism / by J. Martin Evans.
p. cm.
Includes bibliographical references and index.
ISBN 0-8014-3211-1
1. Milton, John, 1608–1674. Paradise lost. 2. Milton, John, 1608–1674—
Political and social views. 3. Imperialism—Great Britain—History—
17th century. 4. Epic poetry, English—History and criticism. 5. Imperialism
in literature. 6. Colonies in literature. I. Title.
PR3562.E89 1996
821'.4—dc20   95-30018

Contents

Acknowledgments

This book is the product of many years of teaching and research at Stanford University. During the course of its preparation I have received helpful advice from numerous friends and colleagues, in particular from Professors John Bender, George Dekker, Suvir Kaul, Stephen Orgel, and Jay Fliegelman, who read early drafts of several chapters, and from Professors David Kennedy, John Leonard, Herbie Lindenberger, and David Riggs, who read the final draft of the entire manuscript. I am also grateful to the anonymous reader for Cornell University Press whose comments and suggestions strengthened my argument at several crucial points, and to my research assistant, G. E. Light, for his valuable assistance in preparing the manuscript for the press. Finally, I would like to record my gratitude to Professor Paul G. Stanwood for permission to incorporate into chapters 1 and 3 material from my paper "Milton's Imperial Epic," which recently appeared in his edition of the proceedings of the Fourth International Milton Symposium, *Of Poetry and Politics: New Essays on Milton and His World,* and to the Deans of Humanities and Sciences at Stanford University, who made available to me the necessary resources to see this study through to a conclusion.

J. M. E.

Abbreviations

AIQ	*American Indian Quarterly*
AQ	*American Quarterly*
CMHS	*Collections of the Massachusetts Historical Society*
CW	*The Works of John Milton.* Ed. Frank A. Patterson et al. 18 volumes. New York: Columbia University Press, 1931–38
ELH	*Journal of English Literary History*
JAS	*The Journal of American Studies*
MAFS	*March of America Facsimile Series*
MS	*Milton Studies*
NEQ	*New England Quarterly*
NQ	*Notes and Queries*
PAPS	*Proceedings of the American Philosophical Society*
WMQ	*William and Mary Quarterly*

All quotations from Milton's prose and poetry are from the Columbia edition of the complete works cited above.

Milton's Imperial Epic

Introduction

> The subject of an epick poem is naturally an event of great importance. That of Milton is not the destruction of a city, the conduct of a colony, or the foundation of an empire.
>
> —Samuel Johnson, "The Life of Milton"

Just over thirty years ago my former colleague George F. Sensabaugh published a book titled *Milton in Early America* in which he explored the impact of the poet's writings on antebellum American culture. In a very real sense the present volume may be described as a complement to his, for its subject is early America in Milton, specifically the impact of America's colonization on *Paradise Lost*. The idea that Milton's epic might have something to do with the discovery and settlement of the New World first occurred to me while I was preparing an edition of Books 9 and 10 for the Cambridge Milton in 1972. Satan, I noticed, was greeted by his followers in Hell as a "great adventurer" newly returned "from the search / Of Forrein Worlds" (10.440–41), while his victims were explicitly compared with "th'American" discovered by Columbus "wilde / Among the Trees on Iles and woodie Shores" (9.1116–18). The Fall, I concluded, could thus be seen as an act of imperial conquest by "history's first colonist."[1]

At the time, I did not pursue the implications of this idea any further, partly because they would have taken me far beyond the limits of the project at hand and partly, I suspect, because the interpretive context within which I was then working was not especially conducive to such speculations. During the past twenty years or so, however, the critical landscape has been transformed by a series of theoretical developments that have made it possible to interrogate both canonical and noncanonical texts in ways that would have been

1

almost unimaginable only two or three decades ago. The result has been an extraordinary expansion in our understanding of discursive relationships, and in particular in our understanding of the complex transactions between literary texts and the ideologies of the cultures that produced them.

In the case of Renaissance texts relating to the conquest of North and South America, this enlargement of our critical vision has been particularly fruitful. For, appropriately enough perhaps, the years between the bicentennial of the Declaration of Independence and the quincentennial of Columbus's arrival in Hispaniola have seen a steady stream of pathfinding studies devoted to the discursive consequences of the Discovery and its aftermath. Following the publication of Hugh Honour's survey of European images of America in 1975 and Fredi Chiappelli's massive anthology of essays on the impact of the New World on the Old in 1976, both of which were directly associated with the bicentennial celebrations, an increasing number of influential scholars has explored the imaginative repercussions of the voyages of discovery.[2] In 1979, Wayne Franklin published his seminal discussion of the various modes of colonial discourse employed by discoverers, explorers, and settlers respectively. Tzvetan Todorov's suggestive account of European reactions to American alterity was translated into English in 1984. Peter Hulme's illuminating analysis of colonial encounters in the writings of Columbus, Shakespeare, and Captain John Smith appeared in print two years later. In 1991, Stephen Greenblatt crowned his earlier investigations of Renaissance colonialism in such essays as "Learning to Curse" and "Invisible Bullets" with his comprehensive study of the role of wonder in the chronicles of exploration. In the same year Eric Cheyfitz anatomized the poetics of imperialism in works ranging from *The Tempest* to *Robinson Crusoe.* Jeffrey Knapp's provocative study of England, America, and literature from *Utopia* to *The Tempest*, tracing "the problem of an island empire, colonialism as a special solution to the problem, and poetry as a special model of both problem and solution," came out in 1992. And in 1993, Anthony Pagden, building on the foundational work of J. H. Elliott, published his broad-ranging history of European encounters with the New World from the Renaissance to the early nineteenth century.[3] Although none of these books was specifically concerned with the relationship between *Paradise Lost* and the colonization of America, their cumulative insights enabled me to think about that relationship in terms that were far more responsive to the dynamics of cultural mimesis than any I could have employed back in 1972.[4]

At the same time, I began to read as many of the primary colonial texts available during Milton's lifetime as I could identify, beginning with the translations of French and Spanish sources upon which England was largely dependent for its information about the New World until the publication of Richard Hakluyt's *Principal Navigations, Voyages, Traffiques, and Discoveries of the English Nation* in 1598, and continuing with the promotional and descriptive tracts that accompanied England's colonial activities in Virginia, New England, and the West Indies in the seventeenth century.[5] Throughout the book I shall refer to this body of writing collectively as "the literature of colonialism," but I should make it clear at the outset that by using such a blanket term I do not mean to suggest that Renaissance accounts of America constitute a unified and coherent literary tradition comparable to that of the epic or the romance. On the contrary, they consist of an incredibly heterogeneous collection of works written in a bewildering variety of forms ranging all the way from the letter and the journal to the biography and the sermon, and informed by an equally bewildering variety of political, moral, and religious viewpoints running the entire gamut from the fiery denunciations of Bartolomé de Las Casas to the grandiose fantasies of Sir Ferdinando Gorges.

Yet different as they are in genre, provenance, date, and purpose, the texts that comprise the literature of colonialism share not only a set of recurring themes—the nature of the colony, the status of the colonized, the character of the colonizers, for example—but also a common body of linguistic practices, descriptive tropes, narrative patterns, and conceptual categories. In short, they partake of a common discourse, and the more widely I read in them, the more connections I noticed between this discourse on the one hand and Milton's "great Argument" (1. 24) on the other. Over and over again the rhetorical and argumentative strategies deployed by the promoters and agents of European imperialism seemed to find an echo in the text of *Paradise Lost*. Milton's epic, I gradually became convinced, constitutes a significant exception to K. G. Davies's claim that "after Hakluyt . . . and some would say *The Tempest*, no major English literary work of the seventeenth century comes to mind that breathes an Atlantic air or takes the American empire for its theme."[6]

To begin at the most obvious level, the poem contains a number of quite explicitly colonial terms. God, for instance, is "the sovran Planter" (4.691), a periphrasis that links him with the royal patron of England's first transatlantic colony; Satan is an "adventurer" (10.440), hoping like the investors in the Virginia Company to reap a handsome profit from the labors of his surrogates in the terrestrial paradise; and Earth is consistently described as the "New World" (2.403, 867, 4.34, 113, 391, 10.257, 377), a term which had been synonymous with America ever since the publication of Vespucci's *Mundus Novus*. Of the four figures from recent history named in the poem, moreover, three were inseparably connected with the colonial enterprise—Columbus (9.1116), Montezuma (11.407), and Atabalipa (11.409). Most notably of all, the word "empire" itself reverberates throughout the entire narrative, sometimes in such close proximity to the word "empyreal" that it is tempting to suspect a conscious pun.[7] From his "Impereal Throne" (7.585) God rules over an "Eternal Empire" (7.96, 609) and creates the world as "th'addition of his Empire" (7.555). Having fallen because he "doubted [God's] empire" (1.114), Satan plans to create a "nether Empire" (2.296) so that he can at least share "Divided Empire" (4.111) with his adversary. In Heaven he and his angels held "Imperial Titles" (5.801) and in "th'infernal Empire" (10.389) he assumes "Imperial Sovranty" (2.446) over the "Imperial Powers" (2.310) with whom he plans to found a "growing Empire" (2.315). "Honour and Empire" (4.390) prompt him to invade the garden of Eden, which itself overlooks a "neather Empire" (4.145), and hand it over to Sin and Death, the new governor-generals of the diabolic "Empire" (10.592).

Still more significantly, Milton seems to have conceived the principal sites and characters in the poem in essentially colonial terms. Both Hell and the garden of Eden function as cosmic outposts of Heaven, designed to serve in the first case as a receptacle for its outcasts and in the second as an extension of its imperial power. At various junctures of the story, Satan, Adam and Eve, Raphael and Michael all perform actions that replicate those of the discoverers or settlers of the New World. And elsewhere in the poem the first three of these characters behave in ways that would have reminded Milton's readers of the American Indians. Indeed, the poem as a whole reenacts on the cosmic stage many of the central events that took place during the conquest of the New World: the voyage of discovery, the initial encounter with naked innocents, the delivery of the *requerimiento,* the establishment of the colony, the search for gold, the cultivation of the land, the conversion of the natives, the dispossession of the indigenous population, the triumphant return home. *Pace* Dr. Johnson, the conduct of a colony and the foundation of an empire are central concerns in Milton's version of the Genesis narrative.

Having reached this conclusion, however, I was faced with the problem of describing the relationship between the colonial and the biblical elements in the poem without resorting to a crudely allegorical reading of a story that Milton certainly believed to be the literal truth. I found at least the beginnings of a solution in Peter Hulme's account of another seventeenth-century work that combines colonial with noncolonial themes, *The Tempest.* According to Hulme, Shakespeare's American fable, as Leo Marx once called it, is a palimpsest "on which there are two texts, an original Mediterranean text with, superimposed upon it, an Atlantic text written entirely in the spaces between the Mediterranean words."[8] By the same token, *Paradise Lost* might well be described as a palimpsest containing an ancient biblical text with, superimposed upon it, a modern colonial narrative written in the spaces between the biblical words. The story of "Mans First Disobedience, and the Fruit / Of that Forbidden Tree" (1.1–2) contains within it the story of Europe's discovery and settlement of America. From Satan's arrival in Hell to Adam and Eve's expulsion from the garden of Eden, Milton's version of the Genesis myth resonates with the complex thematics of Renaissance colonialism. If Spenser was "our originating and preeminent poet of empire," as Stephen Greenblatt has proposed, then Milton, in this as in so many other respects, was his heir and successor.[9]

Quite apart from the internal evidence I shall be presenting in support of this thesis, three external considerations seemed to point in the same general direction. In the first place, as David Quint has recently reminded us, the very form in which Milton chose to cast the biblical story brought with it a heavy freight of imperial ideology. In Quint's own words, "to enter the [epic] genre at all was again to evoke ideological categories and patterns of thought that had proved surprisingly tenacious across two millennia."[10] Inasmuch as virtually every epic from the *Iliad* and the *Odyssey* to *The Faerie Queene* and the *Lusiads* is about the foundation or destruction of empires, it would have been surprising indeed if a work that so forcefully asserted its relationship to that tradition did *not* address the theme of imperial conquest.

In the second place, the particular story that Milton set out to tell was, by the middle of the seventeenth century, redolent with colonial overtones. For as we shall see later, the first three chapters of Genesis constituted one of the standard proof-texts upon which the promoters of Virginia and New England based their arguments for settling the New World. The conception of God as a planter and of Adam as the prototypical *colonus,* the association of Eden with the paradisal landscapes of America and of Adam and Eve with the noble savages who inhabited them, were all familiar commonplaces in the colonial literature that appeared in print during the years preceding the composition of *Paradise Lost*. To write a poem based on the Genesis narrative was to engage a text that was already thoroughly impregnated with the ideology of European imperialism.

Finally, as Robert Fallon has pointed out, Milton's experience as a member of Oliver Cromwell's government must have made him even more aware than most of his contemporaries of England's colonial role in the world of seventeenth-century geopolitics.[11] When he began work on *Paradise Lost* in the late 1650s, he had been privy for almost a decade to the inmost councils of the various executive bodies that effectively constituted the English government during the interregnum. As Secretary for Foreign Tongues he had almost certainly heard Cromwell rehearsing the arguments for his disastrous attempt to drive the Spanish out of Hispaniola in 1654, and he may even have had a hand in translating the Lord Protector's rationale for his Western Design in the following year. Whatever Milton's private opinion of his employers' international policies may have been, and there is no evidence to suggest that he disapproved of them, the conduct of colonies and the foundation of empires had occupied a significant fraction of his attention during the waning years of the Protectorate.

In exploring the way in which these issues made their way into the text of *Paradise Lost*, I am not going to argue that Milton was intimately acquainted with this or that specific document—this is not intended to be a source study of the kind that Robert Cawley undertook in *Milton and the Literature of Travel*. Although it is quite probable that the poet had read some of the works I shall be citing, my concern is not so much with the question of direct influence as with the much more complicated and elusive process of cultural mimesis whereby a literary text articulates the complex of beliefs, values, anxieties, hopes, and prejudices, in a word the ideology, of the society that generated it.

The theoretical difficulties attendant on such a project are formidable. If Milton had not necessarily read many of the works I cite, how could the images and themes they enunciate have found their way into *Paradise Lost* as I claim? Precisely what kind of relationship does the poem have with the colonial texts I put alongside it? For a practitioner of what has come to be known as the new historicism, the answer to this kind of question is to be found in the nature of ideology itself, a force so powerful and all-pervasive that it informs virtually all the cultural products of the historical moment in which it achieved its dominance. The homologies and analogies which the new historical critic discloses between apparently unrelated texts are thus the result of a common cultural origin rather than any direct interconnection.

The argument that follows is predicated on a version of this theory but with one important difference. For although the new historicist model of intertextuality may offer a more accurate and more flexible description of discursive relationships than the positivist system of sources and influences was able to provide, the concept of a dominant ideology has only limited relevance to a period as turbulent and disjunctive as the mid seventeenth century. So far as the colonization of the New World is concerned, at any rate, official opinion in England was so divided, and changed so frequently, that it hardly makes sense to speak of an established ideology of colonialism at all. In reality, the royalist and puritan regimes entertained radically different attitudes toward different colonies at different times. In the years leading up to the Civil War, for instance, the government of James I was generally supportive of Virginia, whereas the government of Charles I regarded New England with a mixture of distrust and genuine animosity. After the Civil War, on the other hand, the Commonwealth government of Cromwell was justifiably suspicious of Virginia, actively hostile to Maryland, and only lukewarm in its support of New England. Indeed, seventeenth-century English colonial policy resembles not so much a seamless network of harmonious and widely accepted principles as a disorderly patchwork of conflicting and unstable hopes, fears, and prejudices. The diversity of colonial literature I noted earlier merely reflects the diversity of the ideologies it embodies.

While I shall assume that the parallels I note between *Paradise Lost* and the literature of colonialism derive from a common source in the culture of seventeenth-century England, therefore, I shall not assume that this source consisted of a monolithic ideology. On the contrary, I shall operate on the premise that it consisted of a common *discourse* by means of which the colonial writers of the sixteenth and seventeenth centuries expressed their ideological differences. Instead of placing a single "congeneric"[12] text beside *Paradise Lost* as a new historicist might do, I shall consequently draw on a multiplicity of texts from every sector of the ideological spectrum. Milton's epic, I shall argue, interacts continuously not with any dominant set of assumptions or principles but with an agglomeration of deeply ambivalent cultural responses to the colonization of the New World.

Like any attempt to identify a new matrix within which to read a well-known work, my argument is vulnerable, of course, to the obvious objection that I have ignored all the other contexts that are relevant to its interpretation. In my desire to demonstrate the relationship between *Paradise Lost* and seventeenth-century colonial discourse, I necessarily run the risk of underestimating, or at least of understating, the poem's links to such crucial phenomena as the hexaemeral tradition, which I investigated in *"Paradise Lost" and the Genesis Tradition*, and the history of the classical, medieval, and Renaissance epic, which Francis Blessington and Charles Martindale have recently reevaluated.[13] My intention here, however, is not to displace these other discursive milieux but to supplement them with an additional context that has not received as much attention as it deserves. If I pay relatively little attention to theological or generic issues in the pages that follow, it is not because I think they are unimportant. It is because they have already been exhaustively investigated by other scholars, and I saw little to be gained by going over ground that has been so recently and so thoroughly cultivated by my fellow Miltonists.

As its title suggests, *Milton's Imperial Epic* is addressed primarily to students of *Paradise Lost*, though I hope that specialists in seventeenth-century British and colonial American history may also find it of interest. The latter will already be familiar with most, if not all, of the material I present in the opening chapter, but I thought it advisable to provide the former with at least a general overview of English attitudes to the colonization of America before proceeding to the literary analysis contained in the rest of the book. Needless to say, my principal objective throughout has been to cast fresh light on Milton's imperial epic rather than on the colonial history I believe it recapitulates.

1

The Colonial Idea

The complex origins of the colonial idea in England, the immense and contradictory elements that contributed to its growth and that led to the planting of mainland colonies of Englishmen in the New World show . . . that the pristine image of a new Eden had already been criss-crossed with darker shades of doubt and selfishness.

—Howard Mumford Jones, *O Strange New World*

There were many reasons for pondering the relationship between the Old World and the New as Milton turned his attention back to his long delayed plans for an epic poem in the late 1650s.[1] To begin with, the Commonwealth's war with Spain had rekindled anti-Spanish sentiment, and writers in tune with the mood of the times were busy turning out works based on the so-called "black legend" of Spanish brutality in South America. In 1655, Cromwell himself issued, possibly with the aid of Milton, *A Declaration Against Spain* reminding his fellow-countrymen of "the Innocent Blood of so many Millions of Indians, so barbarously Butchered by the Spaniards, and of the Wrong and Injustice that hath been done unto them."[2] In the following year Milton's nephew, John Phillips, produced an English translation of the original source of the black legend, Bartolomé de las Casas's *Brevíssima relación de la destrucción de las Indias*, complete with a series of vivid illustrations by R. Gaywood (modeled on Theodore de Bry) detailing the atrocities committed by the early Spanish colonists.[3] Dedicated to his uncle's employer, Oliver Cromwell, it was, in the words of one historian, "an open cry to the English people to challenge the supremacy of Spain in the New World."[4] And in 1658, Sir William Davenant, the erstwhile governor-designate of Maryland, catered to prevailing English taste with his sensational masque on the same subject, *The Cruelty of the Spaniards in Peru*, which staged a purely imaginary victory over the brutal Spanish colonists by a troop of English soldiers and their Peruvian allies.[5] For anyone as sensitive as Milton was to contemporary events, the conquest of America was an inescapable feature of the political landscape.

Still more to the point, Cromwell's "Western Design" and the conflict with Spain it precipitated served as a vivid reminder that England, too, was a major colonial power.[6] Indeed, the crucial first phase of English empire-building in the New World coincided more or less exactly with Milton's lifetime. The year before he was born the first English settlers dispatched by the Virginia Company of London arrived in Chesapeake Bay. The establishment of the Plymouth colony took place when he was eleven, the widely publicized Virginia massacre when he was thirteen, and the great Puritan migration to Massachusetts Bay and the West Indies while he was in his twenties. He was thirty-five when the second Virginia massacre occurred, forty-four when Massachusetts declared itself to be an independent commonwealth, forty-six when Cromwell acquired Jamaica. By the time he had reached his fifties, England was the dominant colonial power in North America with between twenty-five and thirty thousand settlers in New England and thirty-six thousand or so in Virginia.[7]

What is more, by the time he began work on *Paradise Lost* Milton had come into contact with numerous men who had promoted, or emigrated to, the colonies. Ralph Hamor, the author of *A True Discourse of the Present Estate of Virginia*, grew up in the house next to the Milton family home on Bread Street.[8] Several of the poet's Cambridge contemporaries emigrated to New England, and his longtime friend Samuel Hartlib produced a treatise on the Virginian silk worm.[9] Sir Henry Vane, to whom he addressed an admiring sonnet in 1652, was a former governor of Massachusetts. And Roger Williams, the notorious champion of religious liberty and Indian property rights, gave him conversation lessons in Dutch during the early 1650s.[10] It is hardly suprising, then, that Milton's writings are liberally sprinkled with references to the colonization of America.

Not that Milton needed large numbers of close friends actively involved in the settlement of the New World in order to be vividly aware of its progress. For in seventeenth-century England "this glorious businesse," as the preacher William Crashaw called it, was deeply imprinted in the national consciousness, inscribed there by dozens of promotional pamphlets, controversial tracts, personal histories, and economic analyses.[11] From 1609 to 1624 the London bookstalls were inundated with sermons and treatises either prophesying or proclaiming the success of the English plantation in Virginia.[12] Beginning with the publication of *Mourt's Relation* in 1622, there followed a steady stream of works recording the early history of New England, detailing the political and religious controversies going on there, and proclaiming the progress of the gospel among the Indians.[13] Then in the mid 1650s came a spate of tracts reporting on the power struggle between the Catholic proprietor, Lord Baltimore, and his Puritan adversaries in Maryland.[14] Whether or not he had a personal stake in the success of the American colonies, Milton could hardly avoid being aware of events taking place on the other side of the Atlantic.

With the exception of a handful of works by New England dissidents such as Samuel Gorton and John Childe, most of the literature I have just mentioned took a wholeheartedly positive view of England's transatlantic activities. Titles such as *Good Newes from Virginia, The Glorious Progress of the Gospel,* and *Wonder-Working Providence* accurately reflect the insistently upbeat tone of English colonial discourse in this period. Yet just beneath the surface of even the most optimistic evaluations of England's possessions in the New World there runs a powerful undercurrent of barely repressed anxiety concerning the settlement of North America. Again and again the promoters complain that Virginia and New England have been unjustly slandered by various unnamed detractors. The Council for Virginia promised readers of *A True Declaration of The estate of the Colonie in Virginia,* for example, that the work would provide "a confutation of such scandalous reports as have tended to the disgrace of so worthy an enterprise." And in the body of the treatise the anonymous authors went on to claim that "the honor and prosperity of this so noble an action, is eclipsed by the interposition of clamorous and tragicall narrations" spread abroad by "the scum of men," who, having been disappointed in their piratical "dreames of mountaines of gold, and happy robberies," have returned to England "to discredit the land, to deplore the famyne, and to protest that this their comming awaie, proceeded from desperate necessitie."[15] In the dedicatory epistle to *The New Life of Virginea*, Alderman Robert Johnson likewise lamented that "not only the ignorant and simple minded are much discouraged, but the malitious and looser sort (being accompanied with the licentious vaine of stage Poets) have whet their tongues with scornfull taunts against the action it selfe, in so much as there is no common speech nor publicke name of anything this day ... which is more vildly depraved, traduced and derided by such unhallowed lips, then the name of Virginia."[16] A year later, the Virginian minister Alexander Whitaker suggested in *Good Newes From Virginia* that "the calumnies and slanders, raised upon our Colonies" were inspired by the Devil himself and blown abroad by "Papists, Players and such like."[17] In 1620, the Council for Virginia again complained that "ill disposed mindes" were attempting "to staine and blemish that Countrey, as being barren and unprofitable."[18] And as late as 1656, John Hammond was still protesting that numerous "blackmouthed babblers" were describing the plantation as "an unhealthy place, a nest of Rogues, whores, desolute and rooking persons; a place of intolerable labour, bad usage and hard Diet."[19]

Nor were these criticisms confined to Virginia. Just two years after the establishment of the Plymouth settlement, the Council for New England felt compelled to defend the young colony against what it called "the injurious aspersions that have beene laid upon it, by the malicious practises of some that would adventure nothing in the beginning."[20] And in his address to the reader of *New Englands Prospect*, William Wood revealed that he was moved to undertake his treatise "because there hath been many scandalous and false reports past upon the country, even from the sulphurious breath of every base ballad-monger."[21] A stanza or two from "A Proper Newe Ballett Called the Summons to Newe England" may serve to illustrate the kind of criticism he probably had in mind:

> Lett all that putrifidean secte,
> I meane the counterfeite electe,
> All zealous banckrupps, puncks devout,

> Preachers suspended, rable rout,
> Lett them sell all, and out of hand
> Prepare to goe for Newe England,
>   To build newe Babel strong and sure
>   Now calld a 'Church unspotted, pure.'
>   .   .   .
> Loe! in this Church all shal be free
> T'enjoy all Christian libertie:
> All thinges made common; t'avoide strife
> Each man may take anothers wife,
> And keepe a handmaid too if neede
> To multiplie, encrease and breede.
>   And is not this foundacion sure
>   To raise a Church unspotted, pure?[22]

Few, if any, of these reported slanders were ever printed—like the heresies of the early Christian church they owe their preservation to the writers who endeavored to refute them—but they clearly constituted a powerful critique of England's activities across the Atlantic. To judge from the available evidence, there existed throughout the first half of the seventeenth century a vehemently anticolonial and largely oral subculture which threatened to discredit the whole enterprise. As a result, whether they are excusing the failure of the New World to live up to expectations in some regard or defending Virginia and New England against some allegedly unjustified criticism by their detractors, seventeenth-century English descriptions of America are relentlessly defensive. From Daniel Price's *Sauls Prohibition Staide . . . with a reproofe of those that traduce the Honourable Plantation of Virginia* (1609) to John Hammond's *Leah and Rachel . . . With A Removall of such Imputations as are scandalously cast on those Countries* (1656), justification is the keynote.

It is not difficult to understand why a seventeenth-century English Protestant might have harbored deeply ambivalent feelings about his country's American colonies. To begin with, their history had hardly been a happy one. After a disastrous beginning, which cost many of the adventurers their investments and hundreds of planters their lives, Virginia had sided with the king during the Civil War and only with the very greatest reluctance had accepted the authority of the

Commonwealth commissioners dispatched by Cromwell in 1651. As John Hammond remarked, England's first plantation was "whol for monarchy, and the last Country belonging to England that submitted to obedience of the Common-wealth of England."[23] Maryland, despite several attempts to reverse Lord Baltimore's policy of religious toleration, was still a haven for English Catholics, "a receptacle for Papists, and Priests, and Jesuites" as the anonymous author of *Virginia and Maryland* called it in 1655.[24] Thanks to the internal disputes which had convulsed it during the 1630s and 1640s, New England, which might have been expected to command respect on both political and religious grounds, was regarded in many quarters as "a Nursery of Schismatickes"[25] and had in any case lost a great deal of its ideological *raison d'être* now that the reform of the church had been accomplished in England itself. As Cotton Mather put it later, with the successful overthrow of Charles I there "ensued such change of Times, that instead of Old England's driving its People into New, it was itself turned into New."[26] As a direct consequence, many of the colony's most energetic and well-educated settlers returned across the Atlantic to serve in the revolutionary government or in the reformed English church.[27] In comparison with the events that were taking place in the new Puritan Commonwealth at home, the affairs of the Massachusetts Bay Colony had become, in David Cressy's words, a mere "side-show."[28]

Compared with the Spanish possessions in Peru and Mexico, moreover, none of the English colonies had yet brought significant economic benefits to the mother country. Virginia, to be sure, was a fertile source of tobacco, and New England of timber, but no gold or silver mines had been found, no shortcut to the Pacific had been discovered, no fortunes had been made overnight. As a result, English accounts of North America seem to be haunted by the memory of Spanish achievements to the South. In his attempt to explain "how it came to passe there was no better speed and successe" in early Virginia, for example, Captain John Smith writes with one eye constantly over his shoulder on England's Catholic competitors. Some readers, he declares, may find his story disappointing "because not stuffed with Relations of heapes and mynes of gold and silver, nor such rare commodities, as the Portugals and Spanyards found in the East and

West Indies." But it was the Spaniards' good fortune to land in an area where the people "had the use of gold and silver . . . so that, what the Spaniard got was chiefely the spoyle and pillage of those Country people, and not the labours of their owne hands." "Had those fruitfull Countries been as salvage, as barbarous, as ill peopled, as little planted, laboured, and manured, as Virginia," he concludes, "their proper labours it is likely would haue produced as small profit as ours."[29]

Smith's allusion to the Spaniards' exploitation of the Indians brings us to an even more fundamental source of uneasiness in English colonial discourse. For although the historians of Sir Humphrey Gilbert's, Sir Walter Raleigh's, and Sir Francis Drake's voyages were careful to emphasize the comparative benevolence with which the Elizabethan explorers treated the Indians, both they and their successors still had to face a profoundly disturbing question: how could the inhabitants of Europe occupy the New World without infringing on the property rights of the indigenous population? As the preacher Robert Gray put it in his promotional tract, *A Good Speed to Virginia,* "by what right or warrant can we enter into the land of these Savages, take away their rightfull inheritance from them, and plant our selves in their places, being unwronged or unprovoked by them?"[30] The issue surfaced as soon as any serious efforts were mounted to establish an English settlement in North America. Sir George Peckham, for instance, devoted a substantial portion of his *True Report* of Sir Humphrey Gilbert's unsuccessful voyage to Newfoundland in 1583 to proving "that we may justly trade and traffique with the Savages, and lawfully plant and inhabite their Countries."[31] But despite Peckham's attempt to dispose of it, the question persisted. Even as dedicated an imperialist as Captain John Smith could still remark in 1631 that "many good, religious, devout men have made it a great question, as a matter in conscience, by what warrant they might go to possess those countries, which are none of theirs, but the poor savages."[32] The extraordinary amount of energy expended on answering this question during the first few decades of the seventeenth century reveals how deeply it troubled the consciences of promoters and planters alike.

In addressing the same problem, the Spanish had relied principally on two arguments: they were entitled to their possessions in

America first because Christopher Columbus had discovered the New World on behalf of the Spanish crown, and second because in the papal bull *Inter Caetera*, Pope Alexander VI had granted all the land over a hundred leagues west of the Azores to Spain. But neither of these arguments, of course, was relevant to the English case. In the eyes of Protestants, the papal decree was *ipso facto* null and void. And although some English writers echoed the first argument by tracing the right of the English crown all the way back to the Cabots' voyages in the late 1400s,[33] by the mid seventeenth century the argument of ownership by discovery had come to seem at best questionable, at worst downright ridiculous. The Kentish preacher Thomas Gage, for instance, observed in the dedicatory epistle to his journal *The English-American* published in 1648 that "to bring in the title of First-discovery, to me it seems as little reason, that the sailing of a Spanish ship upon the coast of India, should intitle the King of Spain to that Countrey, as the sayling of an Indian or English Ship upon the coast of Spain, should intitle either the Indians or the English unto the Dominion thereof."[34] Clearly some alternative rationale had to be constructed to justify the dispossession of the Indians, and the English promoters were not slow to provide it.

At its most extreme it took the form of wishing away the native inhabitants altogether, of erasing the Indians from the American landscape by declaring that those parts of the New World settled by the English were to all intents and purposes empty. Invoking the doctrine of *vacuum domicilium*, according to which unoccupied land belonged to the first people to settle on it, Richard Eburne declared that "when finding a Country quite void of people, as no doubt in America yet there are many, we seize upon it, take it, possesse it, and as by the Lawes of God and Nations, lawfully we may hold it as our owne, and so fill and replenish it with our people."[35] And Samuel Purchas amplified the argument in *Virginia's Verger* published the following year. As men, he wrote:

we have a naturall right to replenish the whole earth; so that if any Countrey be not possessed by other men . . . every man by Law of Nature and Humanitie hath right of Plantation and may not by other after commers be disposessed, without wrong to human nature. And if a country be inhabited in some parts therof, other parts remaining unpeopled, the same reason giveth liberty to other men which want convenient habitation to seat themselves, where (without wrong to others) they may provide for themselves . . . and thus Virginia hath roome enough for her own . . . and for others also which wanting a home, seeke habitations there in vacant places."[36]

In New England, where the remarkable paucity of native inhabitants offered more plausible grounds for this claim, the Indians' absence was attributed to a providential act of genocide: an epidemic virus left behind by English fishermen between 1616 and 1618 had exterminated most of the local population just in time to make room for the Pilgrims. There was enough land in New England for all the inhabitants of the British Isles, declared Captain John Smith, since "it seems God hath provided this Country for our Nation, destroying the natives by the plague, it touching not one Englishman."[37] As a result, confirmed Sir Ferdinando Gorges, "the greater part of that land was left desert, without any to disturb or oppose our free and peaceable possession thereof; from whence we may justly conclude that God made the way to effect his work according to the time he had assigned for laying the foundation thereof."[38]

A variant of this argument, proposed as early as 1609, acknowledged the existence of the Indians but suggested that their migratory way of life precluded the possibility of their possessing or asserting property rights. In the first official sermon in support of the English settlement in Virginia, William Symonds thus insisted that there is a crucial difference between "a bloudy invasion" such as the Spanish inflicted on South America and "the planting of a peaceable Colony in a waste country, where the people doe liue but like Deere in heards."[39] The idea was developed in more strictly legal terms by Robert Gray. "Some affirme, and it is likely to be true," he wrote, "that these Savages have no particular proprietie in any part or parcell of that Country, but only a generall residencie there, as wild beasts have in the forrest, for . . . there is not *meum* or *tuum* amongst them: so that if the whole lande should bee taken from them, there is not a man that can complaine of any particular wrong done unto him."[40] And the argument was repeated twenty years later by John

Winthrop, who asserted: "As for the natives of New England, they inclose no Land, neither have any setled habytation, nor any tame Cattle to improve the Land by, . . . soe as if we leave them sufficient for their use, we may lawfully take the rest, there being more than enough for them and us."[41]

What is more, Elizabeth's original charter to Raleigh and Gilbert had given them the right to have, hold, occupy, and enjoy "all remote and heathen lands not in the actual possession of any Christian Prince," and the formula was repeated in both of James I's patents to the Virginia Company.[42] The implication was clear: the heathen savages had no property rights. As Gray put it, "this earth which is mans fee-simple by deede of gift from God is the greater part of it possessed and wrongfully usurped by wild beasts, and unreasonable creatures, or by brutish savages, which by reason of their godless ignorance, and blasphemous Idolatrie, are worse than those beasts which are of most wilde and savage nature."[43] Clearly it was the moral duty of the civilized English to undo that act of usurpation and return God's gift to his chosen people.

Elsewhere in the same tract, Gray elaborated a rather less extreme argument. Far from dispossessing the Indians by force, he explained, the English colonists intended to occupy only those lands which the Indians voluntarily ceded to them. For "they are willing to entertaine us," he insisted, "and have offered to yeelde into our handes on reasonable conditions, more lande then we shall bee able this long time to plant and manure: and out of all question upon easie composition with them, wee may have as much of their Countrey yeelded unto us, by lawfull graunt from them, as wee can or will desire."[44] Smith, too, attempted to quiet "tender consciences" by assuring them that "for a copper knife and a few toys, as beads and hatchets, they will sell you a whole country: and for a small matter, their houses and the ground they dwell upon; but those of the Massachusetts have resigned theirs freely."[45] The flagrant disproportion between the property the colonists thus acquired and the price they paid for it evidently did not trouble him in the slightest.

When the Indians of Virginia made it unambiguously clear in 1622 and again in 1644 that they did not desire the presence of the English colonists, however, more radical arguments became necessary. The first of them derived from the fact of the massacre itself. In his report of the slaughter, the secretary of the Virginia Company, Edward Waterhouse, proposed that the English should, quite literally, beat their plowshares into swords:

> Our hands which before were tied with gentlenesse and faire usage are now set at liberty by the treacherous violence of the Savages not untying the Knot, but cutting it: So that we, who hitherto have had possession of no more ground then their waste, and our purchase at a valuable consideration to their owne contentment, gained; may now by right of Warre, and law of Nations, invade the Country, and destroy them who sought to destroy us: whereby wee shall enjoy their cultivated places, turning the laborious Mattocke into the victorious Sword . . . and possessing the fruits of others labours.[46]

When the Indians violated the natural law by "the late barbarous Massacre," agreed Purchas, their disloyal treason "confiscated whatsoever remainders of right the unnaturall Naturalls had, and made both them and their Countrey wholly English." The bodies of Raleigh's lost colony, slaughtered by the Indians, he continued, "have taken a mortall immortall possession, and being dead, speak, proclaime and cry, This our earth is truly English, and therefore the Land is justly yours O English."[47] As Louis B. Wright wryly remarks, there was a corner of a foreign field that was forever England long before Rupert Brooke wrote his patriotic sonnet.[48]

Nor were these arguments merely theoretical. Both in Virginia and in New England the English settlers put them into brutal practice. In Virginia the uprisings of 1622 and 1644 were put down so savagely that only eleven of the twenty-eight tribes described by Smith survived the century. In New England the Pequot wars of 1637, vividly reported by Phillip Vincent and John Underhill, exterminated an entire tribe.[49] By 1653, Edward Johnson could report with evident satisfaction that within the space of twenty-one years "the wondrous work of the great Jehovah" had reduced the Massachusetts from thirty thousand to three hundred.[50] In what Stephen Greenblatt has called "an eerily prescient" prophecy, the Chesapeake Indians had told Thomas Hariot back in 1585 that they believed "there were more of [the English] generation to come, to kill theirs, to take their places."[51] By the time Milton published *Paradise Lost* that is precisely what the English had done, not only in Virginia but in large tracts of New England as well. If Providence had failed to wipe the slate clean, the colonists almost succeeded.

In order to justify this kind of violence against the native population, the promoters frequently sought biblical precedents. And in the Old Testament history of Israel's entry into the promised land they found precisely what they were looking for, an account of violent dispossession sanctioned by God himself. The comparison first appeared in Sir George Peckham's *True Report* in which he justified the use of force against the Indians on the grounds that "the like hath bene done by sundry Kings and Princes, Governours of the children of Israel," notably by Joshua, who drove the Canaanites out of the promised land.[52] Early in the seventeenth century the parallel was taken up and elaborated in the sermon that William Symonds delivered to the Virginia Company in 1607. His text came from Genesis 12.1–3:

> Now the Lord had said unto Abram, Get thee out of thy country, and from thy kindred, and from thy father's house, unto a land that I will shew thee.
>
> And I will make of thee a great nation, and I will bless thee, and make thy name great; and thou shalt be a blessing.
>
> I will bless them that bless thee, and curse him that curseth thee; and in thee shall all families of the earth be blessed.

This promise, Symonds argued, was applicable not only to the seed of Abraham but to the English, the chosen people of the latest age. Virginia was theirs by manifest destiny.

Within days of Symonds' sermon Robert Gray preached in London on a closely related text, Joshua 17.14–18:

> And the children of Joseph spake unto Joshua, saying, Why hast thou given me but one lot, and one portion to inherit, seeing I am a great people? . . .

> And Joshua answered them, If thou be a great people then get thee
> up to the wood country, and cut down for thy self there in the land of
> the Perizzites and of the giants, if mount Ephraim be too narrow for
> thee. . . .

> But the mountain shall be thine; for it is a wood, and thou shalt cut it
> down: and the outgoings of it shall be thine: for thou shalt drive out
> the Canaanites though they have iron chariots, and though they be
> strong.

The implications were inescapable. God's design for the chosen
people, Gray argued, "is much like that plot which we have now in
hand for Virginia."[53] Just as the children of Israel expelled the
Canaanites from their native land, so, if necessary, the English could
drive the idolatrous savages out of their territories in the New World.

Shortly afterwards, a third Old Testament text was pressed into the
service of the Virginia Company's American venture. Urging his fellow investors not to abandon the enterprise, Robert Johnson remarked that "it had been extreame madness in the Jewes (when
having sent to spy the land that flowed with milke and honey, and ten
for two returned backe with tydings of impossibilitie to enter and
prevaile,) if then they had retyred and lost the land of promise."[54]
The allusion here is to chapters 13 and 14 of the Book of Numbers
in which the representatives of the tribes of Israel dispatched by
Moses to survey the land of Canaan advise against entering it. As
Johnson points out in another passage, only Caleb and Joshua urged
the chosen people to take possession of it: "And now in discribing
the natural seate and disposition of the countrie it selfe," he wrote,
"if I should say no more but with Caleb and Joshua, The land which
we have searched out is a very good land, if the Lord love us, he will
bring our people to it, and will give it us for a possession, this were
enough."[55]

In subsequent English promotional literature written to encour-
age the colonization of Virginia, the association of America with
Canaan became almost as commonplace as the equation of the New
World with the garden of Eden, though the original purpose of the
equation was often either forgotten or ignored. In *Good Newes from
Virginia*, for example, Alexander Whitaker assured his readers that

God had promised the English success in their colonial endeavours, and "if God do promise Abraham that his seed shall inherit the Land of Canaan: Abrahams posteritie shall after many daies in the appointed time be planted *peaceably* in the land of Canaan."[56] The fact that Abraham's posterity occupied the land of Canaan in a way that was anything but peaceable seems to have escaped the pious cleric's attention entirely.

With the exception of Thomas Morton, who appealed to any man of judgment "whether it be not a Land, that for her excellent indowments of Nature may passe for a plaine paralell (*sic*) to Canaan of Israell,"[57] writers on New England were rather more cautious in their use of the biblical precedent. Opponents of the colony had evidently pointed out that there was a crucial difference between the two immigrations: whereas the Jews had received divine authorization to dispossess the native population, the English were acting purely on their own initiative. "It is the conceit of some men," wrote John White, "that no man may undertake this taske without an extraordinary warrant, such as Abraham had from God, to call him out of Mesopotamia to Canaan." In order to explain how the English could colonize North America without such a warrant he was forced to admit that "Abraham's example is nothing to this purpose because the case is different."[58] Probably for the same reason, Robert Cushman also rejected the biblical parallel. God no longer summons his people to dwell in a particular area, he argued, "neither is there any land or possession now, like unto the possession which the Iewes had in Caanan, being legally holy and appropriated unto a holy people the seed of Abraham . . . but now there is no land of that Sanctimonie, no land so appropriated; none typicall: much lesse any that can be said to be given of God to any nation as was Canaan."[59]

But despite these objections, the association of America with Canaan persisted in colonial discourse. Attempting to explain why the English had encountered so many obstacles in their attempts to settle the New World, Richard Eburne explained two years after the publication of *Mourt's Relation* that "wee find, when God would bring his owne people the children of *Israel* into that good Land, the land of *Canaan*, which so oft and so solemnly he had promised to them and to their Fathers, he did it not without letting them passe and feel some perils by the way."[60] Indeed, in order to reinforce the parallel, more than one writer went so far as to create a *literal* relationship between the two episodes by tracing the ancestry of the Indians back to the biblical Canaanites, the unfortunate inheritors of Noah's curse on the offspring of Ham in Genesis 9.25: "And [Noah] said, Cursed be Canaan; a servant of servants shall he be unto his brethren." Originally proposed in 1580 by Juan Suarez de Peralta in his unpublished treatise *Tratado del descrubimiento de las Indias*, the connection between the Canaanites and the Indians was firmly established in the early seventeenth century by William Strachey, who declared that the natives of Virginia were the direct descendants of Ham. "Both in the travels and Idolatry of the family of Cham," he wrote in his *Historie of Travaile into Virginia Britannia*, "this portion of the World (westward from Africa upon the Atlantic Sea) became both peopled, and instructed in the forme of prophane worshippe."[61] By 1630 the idea had evidently spread to New England. "Some conceive the Inhabitants of New-England to be Chams posterity," noted John White in *The Planters Plea*, "and consequently shut out from grace by Noahs curse, till the conversion of the Jewes be past at least."[62]

White's allusion to conversion brings us to another source of uneasiness that began to make itself felt with increasing intensity as the century wore on, namely England's relative failure to convert the Indians to the reformed religion. In the original Virginia patent of 1606, James I had commended the settlers for "so Noble a worke, which may by the providence of Almightie God hereafter tend to the glorie of his Divine Majestie, in the propagating of Christian Religion to such people as yet live in darknesse, miserable ignorance of the true knowledge and worship of God, and may in time bring the Infidels and Savages (living in those parts) to humane civilitie and to a settled and quiet government," and in the charter of 1609 he again gave priority to "the Conversion and Reduction of the People in those Parts unto the true Worship of God and Christian Religion."[63]

James's evangelical intentions inform the writings of virtually all the promoters of the Virginia plantation. To take just one example, in his *Nova Britannia* Robert Johnson gave pride of place to "this high and acceptable worke," extolling in rapturous terms the advancement of "the kingdome of God, and the knowledge of the truth, among so many millions of men and women, Sauage and blind, that never yet saw the true light shine before their eyes."[64]

In Puritan New England the conversion of the Indians played an even more important role, at least in theory, for once the reform of the church had been accomplished back in the old country, the enlargement of Christ's kingdom in America offered the colony a new sense of mission, which it eagerly pursued. As the dedicatory epistle to Thomas Shepard's *Cleare Sunshine of the Gospell* put it in 1649, "a long time it was before God let them see any farther end of their comming over, then to preserve their consciences. . . . But when Providence invited their return, he let them know it was for some farther Arrand that he brought them thither."[65] "These godly persons who fled into America for shelter from Prelaticall persecution," agreed I. D. in an appendix to *The Glorious Progress of the Gospel*, "doe now appeare to be carried there by a sacred and sweet providence of Christ, to make known his name to those poor soules, who have been Captives to Satan these many Ages."[66]

According to several writers, indeed, the course of religion was destined to move westward long before the course of empire. The idea was first promulgated by Edward Haye, who noted in his report of the voyage of Sir Humphrey Gilbert that "the course of Gods word and religion from the beginning hath moved from the East, towards, and at last unto the West."[67] It was then enthusiastically endorsed by several seventeenth-century advocates of English missionary efforts in the New World. "From the first planting of Religion among men," declared John White, "it hath always held a constant way from East to West."[68] Hugh Peter and Thomas Weld elaborated on the theme as follows: "God meanes to carry his Gospel westward in these latter times of the world; and have thought, as the Sunne in the afternoon of the day, full declines more and more to the West and then sets: so the Gospel (that great light of the world) though it rose in the east, and in former ages hath lightened it with his beames, yet in the latter ages of the world will bend Westward, and before its setting brighten these parts with his glorious lustre also."[69]

As the century wore on, however, it became increasingly obvious that the divinely appointed westward movement of the Gospel was not proceeding according to plan either in Virginia or in New England, and the contrast between the success of Spanish missionizing activities in South America and the failure of English efforts in the North became an ever deepening source of embarrassment. "I would to God," wrote Richard Eburne, "there were among us, us Protestants, that professe and have a better Religion then they the Papists, one halfe of that zeale and desire to further and disperse our good and sound Religion, as seemes to be among them for furthering and dispersing theirs."[70] "Nay, what a scorne would it be to the Religion we professe," added John White, "that we should refuse to purchase the propagation of it at so easie a rate, when the Popish partie charge themselves with such excessive expenses; for the advancement of idolatry and superstition?"[71] And in 1641, William Castell and a group of seventy Anglican ministers formally presented to the Long Parliament a petition "for the Propagating of the Gospel in America and the West Indies" in which they lamented "the small prosecution that hath hitherto been made of it, either by us or others, having as yet never been generally undertaken in pity to men's souls, but in hope to possess land of those infidels, or of gain by commerce, may well make this and all other Christian kingdoms confess that they have been exceeding remiss in performing this so religious, so great, so necessary a work."[72]

Puritan New England was particularly sensitive on this score, and during the next twenty years or so a steady stream of testimonials were produced attesting to the alleged progress of the gospel in the New World. In response to the publication in 1642 of a tract by Thomas Lechford urging the colonists to turn their attention to the spiritual plight of the Indians, a work entitled *New Englands First Fruits* was published in 1643 "by the instant request of sundry Friends, who desire to be satisfied in these points by many New England Men who are here present, and were eye or eare-witneses of the same."[73] It was followed in 1647 by John Wilson's *Day-Breaking if Not the Sun-Rising of the Gospel with the Indians in New England*, in 1648 by Thomas Shepard's *Cleare Sunshine of the Gospell Breaking forth Upon the Indians in New-England*, and in 1649 by Edward Winslow's *Glorious Progress of the Gospel Amongst the Indians in New-England*.

Spurred on by these declarations, in 1649 Parliament finally incorporated the "Society for Promoting and Propagating the Gospel among the Heathen in New-England," which issued in 1651 Henry Whitfield's *The Light appearing more and more towards the perfect Day* and in 1652 his *Strength Out Of Weaknesse; Or a Glorious Manifestation Of the further Progresse of the Gospel among the Indians in New-England.*[74] These tracts were followed in turn by John Eliot's *Tears of Repentance* in 1653, *A Late and Further Manifestation of the Progress of the Gospel amongst the Indians in New-England* in 1655, and *A further Accompt of the Progresse of the Gospel amongst the Indians in New-England* in 1659.

In all these works, English readers were not only alerted to the extraordinary difficulties involved in the conversion of the Indians as a result "of their infinite distance from Christianity, having never been prepared thereunto by any Civility at all . . . the difficulty of their Language to us and of ours to them . . . [and] the diversity of their owne Language to itselfe" but also assured that despite all appearances to the contrary the ministers of God's word in New England were energetically and successfully bringing the native inhabitants into the Christian fold.[75]

In fact, of course, the conversion of the Indians was often merely a pretext for territorial conquest and commercial exploitation. As William Castell sourly observed, the colonization of America had "as yet never been generally undertaken in pity to men's souls, but in hope to possess land of those infidels, or of gain by commerce."[76] This fact, too, was clearly an ongoing source of anxiety in English colonial discourse. At first the promoters insisted that the profit motive should play absolutely no part in their enterprise. Edward Haye, for example, invited every prospective colonizer "to examine his owne motions: which if the same proceed of ambition or avarice, he may assure himselfe it commeth not of God, and therefore can not have confidence of Gods protection and assistance." But as the need to raise funds to defray the expenses of colonization became more pressing, the desire for gain was slowly permitted to emerge into the open, always provided that it remained subordinate to the religious goal. "The use of trade and traffique (be it never so profitable) ought not to be preferred before the planting of Christian faith," cautioned Sir George Peckham, but it could, by implication, constitute a secondary consideration. After warning adventurers against "that bitter root of greedy gaine," Robert Johnson thus went on to ask: "But are

wee to looke for no gaine in the lewe of all adventures?" "Yes undoubtedly," he answered, "there is assured hope of gaine . . . but look
it be not chiefe in your thoughts." Only Captain Smith had the
temerity to admit openly that although the settlers had "made Religion their colour," their real aim "was nothing but present profit."
"For I am not so simple," he wrote, "to think that any other motive
than wealth will ever erect in Virginia a Commonweale."[77]

Other writers blamed the pursuit of wealth for the slow progress of
England's colonial ventures. Among the reasons for the disasters
which overtook the plantation in Virginia during the early seventeenth century Patrick Copland singled out the possibility that the
adventurers had "too much affected [their] gaine." Sir Francis
Bacon argued forcefully that "the principal thing that hath been the
destruction of most plantations hath been the base and hasty drawing of profit in the first years." More often, however, mercantile and
religious considerations were both acknowledged as valid and necessary. In a metaphor which neatly synthesized the two motives, Joseph
Caryl informed the missionary John Eliot that "this game of soules is
a Merchandize worth glorying in upon all the Exchanges . . . And of
this the ensuing Discourse presents you with a Bill of many particu-
lars, from your spirituall Factory in New England."[78]

For all these reasons—the revived memories of Spanish atrocities
in South America and the West Indies, the disappointing results of
English colonizing efforts in Virginia and New England, the American colonies' behavior during the Civil War and its aftermath, the
anxiety generated by the dispossession of the Indians, the slow
progress of missionary efforts, and worries over the role of the profit
motive—the conquest of the New World stirred deeply ambivalent
feelings in the collective consciousness of seventeenth-century England. The remainder of this book will be concerned with the various ways in which this ambivalence makes itself felt in the text of
Paradise Lost. In response to the moral, political, and religious ten-
sions generated by the settlement of America, I argue, Milton's colonial images repeatedly split into incompatible fragments. In Chapter
2, for instance, I examine how the concept of the plantation itself
breaks down into two opposing colonial sites: the demonic settlement in the sterile wastes of Hell where Mammon and his fellow

devils mine for gold, and the fertile landscape of Eden where the naked inhabitants are overwhelmed by nature's burgeoning abundance.

In Chapter 3 I suggest that the figure of the colonist splinters into four quite distinct components: Raphael, the divine missionary who brings to Adam and Eve the authentic word of God and instructs them in the history of the ancient rivalry of which their world is the focal point; Satan, the diabolic deceiver who enslaves the inhabitants of the New World by cheating them out of their territory and replacing them with his own destructive plenipotentiaries; Adam, the indentured servant placed in the paradisal garden by "the sovran Planter" and destined for release from his labors after a fixed period of obedient toil; and finally Michael, the representative of imperial authority who drives the rebellious natives out of their original home into the alien wilderness.

In Chapter 4 I consider the various surrogates for the Indians themselves: on the one hand, Satan and his angels, exiled from their native Heaven and desperate to avenge themselves on the newcomers who have come to occupy their "room"; on the other, Adam and Eve, who welcome God's emissary as a visitor from Heaven, and willingly submit themselves to the sovereign authority he represents.

And finally in Chapter 5 I analyze Milton's contradictory stance as a colonial narrator, at times recording at second hand a story he has heard from an unimpeachable eyewitness, at times offering a first hand account of events he has seen with his own eyes, yet always serving as an intermediary between the decadent world of his readers and the distant paradise he is describing.

Clearly, the fragmentation of these various images precludes a naive uniplanar reading of the poem. We cannot, for instance, simply equate God with James I, Eden with Virginia, and then read the text as a straightforward political allegory about the colonization of America. My point is both simpler and more complicated. Milton's imperial epic, I want to suggest, not only breathes an Atlantic air but plays out in mythic form some of the deepest and most disturbing contradictions in England's experience of the New World.

2

The Colony

Now the reasons for plantations are many: Adam and Eve did
first begin this innocent worke to plant the earth to remaine to
posterity.

—John Smith, *Advertisements for the
Unexperienced Planters of New England*

For most of Milton's lifetime, English colonial policy was a curious
amalgam of disparate and sometimes contradictory aims.
Broadly speaking, however, the arguments that were advanced for
settling North America can be divided into two general categories
which I shall call the purgative and the expansive. Purgative arguments were based on the widespread belief that England's population had grown so dramatically during the sixteenth century that the
country was bursting at the seams. The vast continent across the Atlantic, on the contrary, appeared to be only sparsely populated, and
as such it offered precisely the kind of *lebensraum* that the nation believed it needed. "What a number in every town," Richard Eburne
wrote in 1625, "yea in every parish and village, doe abound, which
for want of commodious and ordinary places to dwell in, doe build
up Cotages by the highway side, and thrust their heads into every
corner, to the grievous overcharging of the places of their abode for
the present, and to the very ruine of the whole Land within a while,
if it be not looked unto; which if they were transported into other regions, might both richly increase their owne estates, and notably ease
and disburden ours."[1] Despite the claim that emigrants might be
able to live more prosperously "in other regions," the main burden
of Eburne's proposal is clearly the improvement of conditions in
England itself. The argument looks inward, not outward.

Occasionally the case for colonization was presented in terms that transformed the deportation of England's surplus population into a purely natural process. Robert Johnson, for example, compared overcrowded countries to "plants and trees that be too frolicke, which not able to sustaine and feede their multitude of branches, doe admit an engrafting of their buds and scions into some other soile, accounting it a benefite for preservation of their kind, and a disburdening their stocke of those superfluous twigs that suck away their nourishment."[2] And John Cotton invoked an analogy from the insect world. Just as bees "when the hive is too full, seeke abroad for new dwellings," he explained in his farewell sermon to the Massachusetts Company, "so when the hive of the Commonwealth is so full, that Tradesmen cannot live one by another . . . in this case it is lawfull to remove."[3] Colonization, then, was essentially a way of redistributing the world's human resources in a more equitable manner. As Patrick Copland explained to the residents of Virginia, "our Countrey aboundeth with people; your Colony wanteth them."[4]

Expansive arguments, on the other hand, focused not so much on the social problems afflicting England as on the opportunities presented by America. To the investors of the Virginia and New England Companies, for example, the New World offered an almost limitless reservoir of natural resources waiting to be exploited, while devout Protestant churchmen saw the colonies as a providential opportunity to expand the community of right-thinking Christians. Indeed, the first reason that Richard Hakluyt offered for western planting was "inlarginge the glorious gospell of Christe, and reducinge of infinite multitudes of these simple people that are in errour into the right and perfecte way of their salvation."[5] Far from being a relatively inexpensive means of relieving the country's overcrowded towns and cities, the colonization of America thus came to be portrayed as a commercial and religious crusade whose primary goal was to expand English trade and the Christian community. As Richard Eburne summed it up, the establishment of English plantations in the New World tended "notably to the glory of Almightie God, the enlargement of the Kings maiesties Dominions, and the manifold and inestimable benefit of this whole Land."[6]

Both the purgative and the expansive visions of America, I now want to suggest, find elaborate expression in *Paradise Lost*, the former in Milton's representation of Hell, the latter in his portrayal of the garden of Eden.

This nether Empire (2.296)

As we have seen, exponents of the purgative rationale for colonizing America were generally more concerned with the health of their native land than with the precise nature of the site to which they proposed to ship its human surplus, and as a result their writings contain relatively little information about living conditions in the New World itself. Not the least remarkable feature of Milton's account of Hell in *Paradise Lost* is that it offers a fully articulated vision of the kind of colony that the purgative rationale implies. Located not in its traditional position at the center of the earth but in the remotest recesses of the universe, "As far remov'd from God and light of Heav'n / As from the Center thrice to th'utmost Pole" (1.73–74), the infernal colony embodies in concrete form the physical and moral consequences of the arguments advanced by Eburne, Cotton, Copland, and others for deporting England's excess population across the Atlantic.

Before we examine its specific characteristics, it is worth noting that, according to Satan at least, the reason for the devils' conflict with God may have had something to do with the social phenomenon upon which the whole purgative argument was based. The creatures with whom God intends to replace the fallen angels, the Devil tells Sin toward the end of Book 2, have been created: "more remov'd, / Least Heav'n surcharg'd with potent multitude / Might hap to move new broiles" (2.835–37). John Broadbent dismisses the idea that the celestial kingdom was overpopulated as "flippant speculation" on Satan's part, and so indeed it may be.[7] Nevertheless, the Devil's explanation for Adam and Eve's physical location accurately reflects the fundamental assumption underlying the purgative rationale for empire-building. For according to virtually every writer who considered the subject, the first consequence of overpopulation was unemployment, and unemployment, as Sir Thomas More had argued in the first major English text to be written in response to the discovery of the New World, led in turn to social unrest and criminal behavior. In his *Discourse on Western Planting*, Richard Hakluyt the elder consequently argued that it was necessary to "deliver our commonwealth from multitudes of loiterers and idle vagabonds . . . which, having no way to be set on work, be either mutinous and seek alteration in the state, or at least very burdensome to the commonwealth, and often fall to pilfering and thieving and other lewdness, whereby all the prisons of the land are daily pestered and stuffed full of them . . . Whereas if this voyage [to Virginia] were put in execution, these petty thieves might be condemned for certain years in the western parts."[8]

Although Hakluyt's proposal was not put into practice on a significant scale until many years later, the image of America as a transatlantic "Bridewell" was a powerful element in English perceptions of the New World for most of the seventeenth century.[9] In tract after tract America was represented as a vast penal colony in which the nation's unemployed malcontents, criminals, dissenters, and heretics could conveniently be confined at a safe distance from civilized society. So when Satan suggests that a society that is "surcharg'd with potent multitude" is likely to experience internal "broiles" he is articulating the standard justification for establishing precisely the kind of penal colony he himself now occupies.

What is more, his prior expulsion from Heaven is described in language that clearly echoes the most graphic of the metaphors commonly used to describe the purgative process. For according to Samuel Purchas, the colonists were "Englands excrements" and Virginia "a Port Exquiline for such as by ordure or vomit were by good order and physicke worthy to be evacuated from This Body." "Without some such evacuation," he argued, the body politic "either breeds matter for the pestilence and other Epidemicall Diseases, or at least for Dearth, Famine, Disorders, over-burthening the wealthier, oppressing the poorer, disquieting both themselves and others, that I mention not the fatall hand of the Hangman."[10] Even those who disapproved of the practice availed themselves of the same metaphor. "It seemes to be a common grosse errour," complained John White, "that

Colonies ought to be Emunctories or sinckes of States; to drayne away their filth."[11] As these passages reveal, the New World was perceived by many Renaissance Englishmen as little more than an enormous cesspool into which "the very excrements of a full and swelling State" could be conveniently discharged.[12] Seen from this point of view, the colonial enterprise was essentially a form of social hygiene.

Read in this context, Milton's account of the devils' rebellion and fall has unmistakably purgative overtones. After their defeat in the "Intestine War" (6.259), the rebellious angels are forcibly discharged through a "mural breach" (6.879) down into "the wastful Deep" (6.862) far below. And when Satan finally reaches dry land for the first time, his arrival is accompanied by the following simile:

> as when the force
> Of subterranean wind transports a Hill
> Torn from Pelorus, or the shatter'd side
> Of thundring Aetna, whose combustible
> And fewel'd entrails thence conceiving Fire,
> Sublim'd with Mineral fury, aid the Winds,
> And leave a singed bottom all involv'd
> With stench and smoak.
>
> (1.230–37)

As one critic has commented, "we are given the impression of a cosmic defecation."[13] In his fall from Heaven to Hell the Devil seems to pass through the digestive tract of the entire universe. Metaphorically, at least, the "Infernal Pit" (1.657) is a sewer.

Literally, of course, it is a "prison" (1.71, 2.59, 434), an enormous "dungeon" (1.61, 2.317, 1003) in which the "rebellious" (1.71) outcasts of Heaven are punished with "penal Fire" (1.48) for seeking "alteration in the state." As such, it immediately poses the major problem associated with the purgative strategy, namely that a colony consisting chiefly of felons, revolutionaries, and heretics was likely to be a violent and lawless society, fiercely resistant not only to the edicts of the authorities back home but also to the rule of its own governors. As John White pointed out, if England planted colonies that were populated exclusively by "men nourished up in idlenesse, unconstant, and affecting novelties, unwilling, stubborne, enclined to faction, covetous, luxurious, prodigall, and generally men habituated to any grosse evill" then it could look for "nothing else but the ruine and subversion of all at last." And indeed, the early years of the Virginia colony bore out his observation to the letter. Thanks to what Edward Winslow called the "bestial, yea, diabolical affections" of the planters themselves, the colony was almost torn apart by internal dissension as Wingfield, Ratcliffe, Newport, and Smith struggled for power. "Every man would be a commander," observed the authors of *A True Report* in 1610, "every man underprizing another's value, denied to be commanded."[14] As Samuel Purchas summed it up several years later, "Division, that taile-headed Amphisboena and many-headed monster, deformed issue of that deformed old Serpent . . . hath from time to time thrust in her forged venemous tongue . . . whence suspicions, iealousies, factions, . . . and other furious passions have transported men from Virginia's good and their owne."[15] The purgative policy, in short, was a recipe for anarchy.

As the self-appointed ruler of God's penal colony, Satan is consequently only too well aware of the danger of faction. Indeed, it is the first subject he addresses when he opens the "great consult" (1.799) in Pandemonium at the beginning of Book 2. In a remarkably successful attempt to head off any challenge to his own leadership he argues that the sheer desperation of the devils' situation renders the role of "Leader" (2.19) so unenviable that no one else could possibly be interested in competing for it:

> where there is then no good
> For which to strive, no strife can grow up there
> From Faction; for none sure will claim in Hell
> Precedence, none, whose portion is so small
> Of present pain, that with ambitious mind
> Will covet more.
>
> (2.30–34)

The price of reigning in Hell is too high for anyone but Satan to pay.

In New England, with its far more ideologically self-conscious and morally self-disciplined immigrant population, the factions tended to be intellectual rather than personal, but the basic impression of divisiveness was much the same. Thanks to its distinctively theocratic character, wrote John White, the plantation appeared to many Englishmen to be nothing more than "a nursery of faction and rebellion," "a seminary of faction and separation." The Antinomian and other controversies that broke out during the 1630s and 1640s did nothing to dispel this impression, with the result that by 1647 the colony was widely regarded as "a Colluvies of wild Opinionists, swarmed into a remote wilderness to find elbow-roome for our phanatick Doctrines and practices."[16]

From this intellectual kind of faction Milton's Hell is not entirely exempt either. Even though it ends in "concord" (2.497), the great debate among Moloch, Belial, Mammon, and Beelzebub discloses fundamental disagreements about the proper foreign policy for the colony to pursue, while the devils' sterile debate about "Providence, Foreknowledge, Will and Fate, / Fixt Fate, free will, foreknowledge absolute" (2.559–60) reaches no conclusion at all. Read in the light of the violent theological disputes between the Puritans and their various adversaries that erupted during the 1630s and 1640s, the "Vain wisdom" (2.565) of Satan's followers would have had a distinctly contemporary ring for any of Milton's readers familiar with the recent history of New England.

Faction, however, was by no means the only vice that plagued England's settlements during their formative years. In one of the most scathing critiques of English colonial policy in Virginia to be published in the seventeenth century, Sir Francis Bacon insisted that "it is a shameful and unblessed thing to take the scum of people and wicked condemned men to be the people with whom you plant; and not only so, but it spoileth the plantation, for they will ever live like rogues, and not fall to work, but be lazy." His observation was based, no doubt, on the frustrating experience of men like Captain Smith, who complained over and over again of the settlers' disinclination to labor either for their own good or for that of their fellows. In Patrick Copland's words, "most of them at the first, beeing the very scumme of the Land, . . . neglected Gods worship [and] lived in idlenesse." The authors of *A True and Sincere declaration* do not appear to have been exaggerating when they blamed the problems af-

flicting Virginia "upon the Idlenesse and bestiall slouth" of its colonizers.[17]

In Milton's Hell the representative of this particular vice is obviously Belial, "To vice industrious, but to Nobler deeds / Timorous
and slothful" (2.116–17). Despite its apparent reasonableness, his
suave rebuttal of Moloch's call for "open Warr" (2.51) against the
heavenly kingdom exemplifies the moral indolence of those who
prefer bondage with ease to strenuous liberty. For Belial proposes, in
effect, that the fallen angels do absolutely nothing. In the context of
the devils' council, the great classical and Christian virtue of patience
degenerates into a cowardly reluctance to take any action at all. As
Milton comments, Belial advocates only "ignoble ease, and peaceful
sloath" (2.227).

The third major vice of the first English colonists, virtually all the
writers of the time concurred, was greed. Inspired by the Spanish experience in Central and South America, the early settlers in Virginia
seem to have been obsessed by dreams of instant wealth in the form
of gold mines. Thanks to their "guilded refiners with their golden
promises," wrote Captain Smith, "there was no talke, no hope, no
worke, but dig gold, wash gold, refine gold, loade gold, such a bruit
of gold, that one mad fellow desired to be buried in the sands least
they should by there (*sic*) art make gold of his bones." Despite the
colonists' failure to locate any mines, the hope of finding one persisted for many years. "There bee many rockie places in all quarters,"
observed Alexander Whitaker in 1613, "and more then probable
likelihoods of rich Mines of all sorts." As late as 1651, Edward Bland
was assuring his fellow countrymen that " 'tis very probable that
there may be Gold and other Mettals amongst the hils" of Virginia.
Occasionally a lonely voice was raised in protest. Captain Smith repeatedly denounced what he called "these great guilded hopes of the
South Sea Mines."[18] In 1625, Samuel Purchas incorporated into his
description of Virginia a passionate diatribe against the evils of gold
mining loosely based on Ovid's famous account in the *Metamorphoses*
of the invention of mining:

Precious perils, specious punishments, whose originall is neerest hell,
whose house is darknesse, . . . never produced to light but by violence,

and convinced, upon records written bloud, the occasioners of violence in the World; which have infected the surface of their native earth with deformity and sterility . . . her bowels with darknesse, damps, deaths, causing trouble to the neighbour Regions, and mischiefe to the remotest! Penurious mindes! Is there no riches but Gold Mines? . . . Are not Myners the most miserable of Slaves, toyled continually, and unto manifold deaths tired for others, in bringing to light those Treasures of darknesse, and living . . . in the suburbs of Hell, to make others dream of Heaven? Yea Paradise, the modell of heaven, had in it no Mineralls, nor was Adam in his innocency . . . employed in Mines, but (in those happy works which Virginia inviteth England unto) in Vines, Gardening, and Husbandry.[19]

Milton's description of the activities of Mammon and his followers in Book 1 of *Paradise Lost* has traditionally been associated with the Ovidian passage that Purchas evidently had in mind here, and indeed his reference to miners who have followed Mammon's example and "Ransack'd the Centre" (1.686) for the wealth concealed there clearly alludes to the men of the iron age in the *Metamorphoses*. But in their condemnation of mining as an incestuous assault upon our common mother, and their exclusive focus on gold rather than iron, Milton's lines have more in common with Purchas's excursus on gold mining than with Ovid's. For just as human "Myners" in the New World dig out "Treasures of darknesse" from the "bowels" of the "native earth," so the fallen angels foreshadow the unnatural crimes of men who rifle "the bowels of thir mother Earth / For Treasures better hid" (1.687–88). Spying a nearby hill whose surface "Shon with a glossie scurff, undoubted sign / That in his womb was hid metallic Ore" (1.672–73), Mammon's crew: "Op'nd into the Hill a spacious wound / And dig'd out ribs of Gold" (1.689–90). Milton's judgement on their labors clearly echoes Purchas's: "Let none admire / That riches grow in Hell; that soyle may best / Deserve the precious bane" (1.690–92).

As the texts I have been citing may suggest, with the exception of faction most of the colonial vices identified by men like John Smith, Francis Bacon, and Samuel Purchas were associated principally with the English settlements in Virginia. Not long after the accession of Charles I, however, New England too came under attack, albeit on rather different grounds. In an effort to forestall the charge of separatism, John White reminded prospective colonists that "nature hath as much force, and founds as strong a relation betweene people and people, as betweene person and person: So that a Colonie denying due respect to the State from whose bowels it issued is as great a monster as an unnaturall childe."[20] But despite his efforts, the settlement on Massachusetts Bay soon came to be suspected of denying "due respect" to the English state and church. As a result, in 1634 the Privy Council, fearing that the emigrants to New England included "divers persons known to be ill affected and discontented, as well with the civil as ecclesiastical government" of their native land, began to impose severe restrictions on emigration. For the rest of Charles's reign prospective settlers were required to take the oaths of supremacy and allegiance before they set sail for America. Then in 1637 the recently established Commission for Foreign Plantations under the leadership of Archbishop Laud issued a proclamation announcing that because the emigrants included "many idle and refractory humours, whose only or principal end is to live as much as they can without the reach of authority," the king had decided to curb "such promiscuous and disorderly departing out of the realm."[21] Writing over twenty years later, Sir Ferdinando Gorges recollected with evident satisfaction:

> It was specially ordered by the king's command, that none should be suffered to go without license first had and obtained, and they take the oaths of supremacy and allegiance. . . . The reason of that restraint was grounded upon the several complaints, that came out of those parts, of the divers sects and schisms that were amongst them, all contemning the public government of the ecclesiastical state. And it was doubted that they would, in short time, wholly shake off the royal jurisdiction of the Sovereign Magistrate.[22]

So far as the royalist government was concerned, New England represented above all else a potential challenge to the authority of the English church and state.[23]

In *Paradise Lost* the challenge to "the sovran Planter" is not merely potential. From the very outset, Hell is a rebellious colony, populated by malcontents united only by their implacable hostility to the ruler of their homeland, and for the first two books of the poem Satan and his followers play out the government's recurring nightmare of a colony that rejects the authority of its parent state. Moloch, for example, articulates precisely the kind of mindless hatred for his native land that many writers feared would develop in England's colonies if they were populated exclusively by dissidents and outcasts. Taken together with Mammon's description of life before the devils' rebellion, which makes Heaven sound like an Anglican cathedral, Moloch's determination to "disturb his Heav'n, / And with perpetual inrodes to Allarme, / Though inaccessible, his fatal Throne" (2.102–4) encapsulates the worst fears of the Commission for Foreign Plantations.

None of the characteristics of Hell that I have described so far were exclusively colonial, of course. Political faction, theological dispute, greed, sloth, and disobedience were all in ample supply in the Old World as well as in the New during the seventeenth century, and every individual example I have discussed could equally well be accounted for in non-colonial terms. But this particular combination of vices reflects contemporary critiques of English colonial policy so precisely that anyone familiar with the history of Virginia and New England would have recognized in Milton's underworld a grotesque image of the kind of colony that the purgative process might be expected to produce.

In one crucial respect, however, Milton's description of Hell also enacts the basic premise of the expansive conception of empire-building. For according to one of the most sophisticated proponents of English expansion, John White, the process of colonization was a continuous one, analogous to the proliferation of the human race itself. "Replenishing wast and voyd Countries," he argued, was warranted by God's command to Adam in the opening chapter of Genesis to replenish the earth and subdue it. And just as marriage was the mechanism by which individual human beings fulfilled this obligation, so colonization was the vehicle through which nation-states accomplished the same purpose. For "that order that God annexed to marriage in his first institution, viz. that married persons should leave father and mother and cleave each to other, is a good warrant of this practice. For sometime there will be a necessitie, that yong married persons should remove out of their fathers house, and live apart by themselves, and so erect new families. Now what are new families, but pettie Colonies: and so at last removing further and further they overflow the whole earth. Therefore, so long as there shall be use of marriage, the warrant of deducing Colonies will continue."[24] Mandated by the book of Genesis itself, colonial expansion was the very engine of social reproduction and growth, and it was only natural, therefore, that each new colony should eventually become the staging area for the creation of another one.

And this, of course, is precisely what happens in the case of Hell. What began as a penal colony founded to accommodate the outcasts from Heaven rapidly becomes a center of colonial exploration in its own right. With its administrative headquarters in Pandemonium, which as several critics have noted bears a remarkable resemblance to the seat of the imperialistic Catholic church, the devils' prison turns into a springboard for further colonization. Shortly after the debate in Pandemonium, a group of Satan's followers thus embark:

> On bold adventure to discover wide
> That dismal world, if any Clime perhaps
> Might yield them easier habitation.
>
> (2.571–73)

Like John Smith in Virginia, they travel "along the Banks" (2.574) of the local rivers in search of a more accommodating site for their settlement, but like Martin Frobisher they encounter only a "frozen Continent / . . . dark and wilde, beat with perpetual storms" (2.587–88).[25] In lines that look forward to Keats's description of America in "Lines to Fanny," Milton describes their expedition as a journey into the heart of darkness:

> Thus roving on
> In confus'd march forlorn, th'adventrous Bands
> With shuddring horror pale, and eyes agast
> View'd first thir lamentable lot, and found
> No rest: through many a dark and drearie Vaile

> They pass'd, and many a Region dolorous,
> O're many a Frozen, many a fierie Alpe,
> Rocks, Caves, Lakes, Fens, Bogs, Dens, and shades of
>   death,
> A Universe of death, which God by curse
> Created evil, for evil only good,
> Where all life dies, death lives, and Nature breeds
> Perverse, all monstrous, all prodigious things,
> Abominable, inutterable, and worse
> Than Fables yet have feign'd, or fear conceiv'd.
>
> (2.614–27)

As a result, the new colony is never established, and, as we learn later in Book 10, the devils soon withdraw to their demonic headquarters "Far to the inland" (10.423), leaving "desert utmost Hell / Many a dark League" (10.437–38). In a movement presaged by Sin's unnatural hell-hounds who return "when they list into the womb / That bred them" (2.798–99) the would-be colonists retreat to the security of their parent city. The expansive enterprise, it seems, has failed.

At the same time, however, a second, and far more ambitious imperial "adventure" (2.474) is under way. Satan has left in search of the "new world" (2.403) which he hopes to annex to his own, and unlike the devils' abortive sortie into the outlying regions of Hell this voyage of discovery will be successful. Just as "God himselfe had built a bridge for men to passe from England to Virginia," according to William Crashaw, so, thanks to their father's exploits, Sin and Death will construct "a Bridge / Of length prodigious" (10.301–2) linking Hell with its new possession.[26] Almost before we have time to adjust our perceptions, the erstwhile exile thus becomes an explorer, and his penitentiary an imperial palace. In a famous essay on Satan, A. J. A. Waldock complained that Milton's Hell combines two basically incompatible functions. "As a locality [it] has to serve a double duty," he wrote. "It is a place of perpetual and increasing punishment in theory; and it is also, in the practice of the poem, an assembly ground, a military area, a base for operations."[27] The point is well taken, and to the best of my knowledge it has never been convincingly refuted. Yet troubling as it may be from a purely logical point of

view, the inconsistency that Waldock identifies in Milton's representation of Hell is firmly anchored in historical reality. The "double
duty" that the infernal colony performs accurately reflects the fundamental contradiction between the two most influential English ra-
tionales for settling North America.

A Wilderness of sweets (5.294)

Nowhere is the colonial theme in *Paradise Lost* more evident than
in Milton's treatment of the garden of Eden. As the epigraph for this
chapter reveals, John Smith regarded the biblical garden as the
model for all subsequent plantations, and John White, too, based his
justification of colonialism on the text of Genesis. "Colonies (as
other conditions and states in humane society)," he wrote, "have
their warrant from Gods direction and command; who as soone as
men were, set them their taske, to replenish the earth, and to subdue
it, *Gen* 1.28."[28] It would have seemed only natural, then, to represent
the garden of Eden as a prototypical colony, and this is precisely what
Milton did in *Paradise Lost.*

Within the poem's political economy, for example, Adam and
Eve's earthly paradise stands in much the same relation to Heaven as
a colonial outpost to the state that founded it. The Creator who
"planted" (4.210) it as "th'addition of his Empire" (7.555) has in-
vested a portion of his ontological capital in the garden's occupants,
and he expects them to yield a handsome rate of return. After multi-
plying in sufficient numbers, the human race is destined to travel
back to its homeland where it will occupy the places left empty by
Satan and his followers. The purpose of God's second colony, then,
is essentially expansive; it has been established in order to fill the "vacant room" (2.835, 7.190) in Heaven.

Individual features of Adam and Eve's "happy rural seat" (4.247)
have been traced to a wide variety of literary and historical sources—
Spenser's Garden of Adonis in Book 3 of the *Faerie Queene*, Dante's
earthly paradise in the *Divine Comedy*, Renaissance English country
gardens, and Ovid's Golden Age in the *Metamorphoses*, to name only
a few.[29] But the characteristics which set Milton's Eden apart from all

other descriptions of unfallen nature derive, I believe, from a rather more recent imaginative construct. Contemporary representations of America, I shall argue, were largely responsible for shaping the poet's unique vision of the biblical garden.

Ever since Columbus declared that "the Terrestrial Paradise is in the place I have described,"[30] the New World had been associated in one way or another with the garden of Eden, and English writers were particularly fond of the comparison. According to Francis Higginson, for instance, New England was "our new paradise," and the same idea inspired Thomas Morton to one of his most eloquent paragraphs:

> And when I had more seriously considered of the bewty of the place with all her faire indowments, I did not thinke that in all the knowne world it could be paralel'd. For so many goodly groues of trees; dainty fine round rising hillucks: delicate faire large plaines, sweete cristall fountaines, and cleare running streames, that twine in fine meanders through the meads, making so sweete a murmering noise to the heare (*sic*), as would even lull the sences with delight a sleepe, so pleasantly doe they glide upon the pebble stones, jetting most jocundly where they doe meete; . . . contained within the volume of the Land, Fowles in abundance, Fish in multitude, and discovered besides: Millions of Turtledoves on the greene boughes: which sate pecking of the full ripe pleasant grapes, that were supported by the lusty trees, . . . which made the Land to mee seeme paradice.

It is hard to believe that Morton was writing about the very same landscape that only a few years later would be described by Puritan apologists as a "howling desart."[31]

Not to be outdone, William Bullock claimed that Virginia, with its "many fair Navigable Rivers, Rivelets and Springs, imbrodered with fresh Marshes and Medows, very delightfull to the prospect, sending forth exceeding sweet and pleasant savours that perfume the Ayre," was so beautiful that it "may well deserve the name of the New-Paradice (*sic*)." Edward Williams, after suggesting that the colony was "preserved by Nature out of a desire to show mankinde fallen into the Old age of the Creation, what a brow of fertility and beauty she was adorned with when the World was vigorous and youthfull," concluded that Virginia could legitimately "entitle her self to an affinity with Eden."[32]

By locating the biblical garden in "the New World" (2.403, 867; 4.34, 113, 391; 10.257, 377), Milton reverses the traditional equation—Eden resembles America rather than vice versa. As a result the fundamental similarities which led generations of explorers to construct an image of the New World as a terrestrial paradise can now be deployed to give the state of innocence a contemporary geographical identity. Indeed, if "in the Beginning all the World was America," as John Locke was to claim, then it is hard to see how the portrayal of prelapsarian nature in *Paradise Lost* could have failed to conjure up visions of the newly discovered continent across the Atlantic.[33]

So when Satan comes within sight of Eden and is greeted by "gentle gales / Fanning thir odoriferous wings" which "dispense / Native perfumes, and whisper whence they stole / Those balmie spoiles" (4.156–59), he is replicating the experience of innumerable European explorers who, even before they had set foot in the New World, "smelt so sweet, and so strong a smel, as if we had bene in the midst of some delicate garden abounding with all kinde of odoriferous flowers."[34] When he comes upon a "Silvan Scene" of "Cedar, and Pine, and Firr" (4.139–40), he is seeing the very same trees which English promoters had listed among the most valuable commodities that New England and Virginia had to offer.[35] And when at last he views a "blissful Paradise" (4.208) irrigated by "crisped Brooks" (4.237), filled with "Flours of all hue" (4.256) growing on "palmie hilloc[s]" (4.254) or in "irriguous Valleys" (4.255), and "purple Grape[s]" (4.259) hanging on "the mantling Vine" (4.258), while "Birds thir choir apply" (4.264) and "vernal aires" (4.264) breathe forth "the smell of field and grove" (4.265) in a climate of "eternal Spring" (4.268), he is witnessing a scene that virtually duplicates the pastoral idyll in Thomas Morton's *New English Canaan*.

All these resemblances, of course, may simply reflect the fact that the explorers' descriptions of America and Milton's description of the garden have a common source in the long-standing *topos* of the earthly paradise. But there is one crucially important aspect of Milton's Eden which cannot be explained by the paradisal tradition: as Adam and Eve tell their Creator, their home is "For us too large"

(4.730). They mean, of course, not that Eden is too big but that it is too productive, too generous.[36] It is a place where "thy abundance wants / Partakers, and uncropt falls to the ground" (4.730–31). In *"Paradise Lost" and the Genesis Tradition,* I called attention to the extraordinary emphasis Milton has placed on the "wanton growth" (4.629) of the garden, which will yield more fruit than Adam and Eve can possibly hope to consume.[37] As I remarked, Milton's treatment of prelapsarian nature is perhaps "the most strikingly original feature" of his entire portrayal of the state of innocence.[38]

At the time I was able to account for the exuberant vitality of the plants only in metaphorical terms as an image of Adam and Eve's psychological and moral condition. The theme of overabundance, I now believe, has in addition a historical explanation. For no aspect of the New World was more frequently held up for the reader's admiration and astonishment than its almost supernatural fertility. From Columbus's *Journal* with its extravagant praise of the "beautiful variety" of the trees, fruits, and plants in Hispaniola to John Hammond's *Leah and Rachel* with its mouth-watering description of the meats, fish, and vegetables available in Virginia, European colonial literature is virtually unanimous in its enthusiasm for the natural bounty of the New World.[39] Samuel Purchas's comprehensive tribute to the fecundity of the area around Chesapeake Bay is representative:

> The soile is blessed, euery Element bestowing a rich portion on her. The fire hath treasures laid up to maintaine her fewell unto prodigality . . . for many yeeres. Her store of waters you haue heard, but not her watery store of fishes unto incredibility in kinds, goodnesse, numbers. The Aire is no lesse luxuriant in the Fowles of Heauene. But the Earth (fruitfull Mother of Mankind) she is prodigiously prodigall, in fatnesse of the soile; talnesse, sweetnesse, strength, varietie, numberlesse numbers of her Trees.[40]

And what was true of Virginia was also true of the Massachusetts Bay colony to the north. As William Cronon observes, "there was one European perception that was undoubtedly accurate, and about it all visitors were agreed—the incredible abundance of New England plant and animal life, an abundance which . . . left more than one vis-

FIGURE 1. "The Indies" from the Gobelins tapestries, 1687 (after Albert Eckhout). Reproduced by permission of the Centre National Des Arts Plastiques.

itor dumbfounded."[41] Compared with the ever more limited resources of the Old World, the fruitfulness of the New, depicted in such works as the Gobelins tapestry (fig. 1), seemed to be little short of miraculous.

The theme of natural abundance makes its first appearance in Milton's writings not in *Paradise Lost,* of course, but in Comus's great hymn to Nature's fecundity in *A Masque Presented at Ludlow Castle:*

> Wherfore did nature powre her bounties forth
> With such a full and unwithdrawing hand,

Covering the earth with odoours, fruits, and flocks,
Thronging the Seas with spawn innumerable,
But all to please and sate the curious taste?
And set to work millions of spinning Worms,
That in their green shops weave the smooth-hair'd silk
To deck her Sons, and that no corner might
Be vacant of her plenty, in her own loyns
She hutch't th'all-worshipt ore, and precious gems
To store her children with.

(lines 709–719)

The extraordinary thing about this passage, it seems to me, is the relatively exotic character of the two specific phenomena upon which Comus elaborates. For neither the "spinning worms" that produced "the smooth-hair'd silk" nor the mines that produced "th'all-worshipt ore" were native to seventeenth-century England (or to seventeenth-century Wales for that matter). Both gold mines and silkworms, however, were well-known features of the Virginian landscape as it was represented in the writings of the colony's promoters. As we saw earlier, the prospect of finding precious metals in the mountains of Appalachia never ceased to tantalize the early planters. Still more to the point, numerous authors asserted that Virginia could become a rich source of silk production. Almost at the top of Thomas Hariot's list of "merchantable commodities" in *A briefe and true report*, for instance, is "worme silke." "In many of our journeys," he wrote, "we found Silke-worms fair and great, as bigge as our ordinary Walnuts. Although it hath not beene our hap to have found such plenty, as elsewhere in the countrey we have heard of, yet seeing that the countrey doth naturally breed and nourish them, there is no doubt but if arte be added in planting of Mulberie trees . . . there wil rise as great profit in time to the Virginians, as thereof now to the Persians, Turks, Italians and Spanyards." As it turned out, moreover, it was not even necessary to plant mulberry trees, for according to several later reports the local environment produced them in ample quantities. "No Country affoordeth more store of Mulbery trees, or a kind with whose leafe [silk worms] more delight, or thriue better" declared Ralph Hamor in 1615. His observation was confirmed by Edward Waterhouse, who claimed that there were "whole woods of many miles together of Mulberry trees of the best kindes, the proper food of the Silke-worme."[42] In short, Virginia contained an abundance of "silke-wormes, and plenty of Mulberie-trees, whereby Ladies, Gentlewomen and little children . . . may be emploied with pleasure in making Silke, comparable to that of Persia, Turkey, or any other."[43] For Milton and his contemporaries, then, the silkworm was one of the most striking examples of Nature's fruitfulness in the New World, and it is surely no accident that Comus singles out as an example of natural abundance the one life-form that the Virginian promoters had emphasized above all others in their catalogs of the colony's potential productivity.

In Milton's masque, however, the theme of nature's abundance has a sinister overtone which is completely absent in Renaissance descriptions of the New World. For its exponent is not an explorer or promoter but a corrupt and sensual tempter who uses it as a justification for shameless overindulgence in the pleasures of the material world. If men and women do not consume more than they need, he argues, the result will be an ecological catastrophe. Nature would be:

> strangl'd with her waste fertility;
> Th'earth cumber'd, and the wing'd air dark't with
>   plumes,
> The herds would over-multitude their Lords,
> The Sea o're fraught would swel, & th'unsought
>   diamonds
> Would so emblaze the forehead of the Deep,
> And so bestudd with Stars, that they below
> Would grow inur'd to light, and com at last
> To gaze upon the Sun with shameless brows.
>
> (lines 728–36)

In *Paradise Lost* itself the wild luxuriance of the garden has equally ominous implications. They are most clearly evident in Adam's speech to Eve in Book 4 describing the tasks that await them the next day. "With first approach of light," he tells her:

> we must be ris'n,
> And at our pleasant labour, to reform
> Yon flourie Arbors, yonder Allies green,
> Our walk at noon, with branches overgrown,
> That mock our scant manuring, and require
> More hands than ours to lop thir wanton growth;
> Those Blossoms also, and those dropping Gumms,
> That lie bestrowne unsightly and unsmooth,
> Ask riddance, if we mean to tread with ease.
>
> (4.624–32)

So central is this passage to Milton's description of Eden that Eve repeats it almost word for word when she proposes in Book 9 that she and Adam should divide their labors.[44] In both cases the implications are inescapable. Without enough "Partakers" (4.731) to keep the burgeoning vitality of nature under control, the "wanton growth" of the garden threatens to overwhelm its gardeners, "for much the work outgrew / The hands dispatch of two Gardning so wide" (9.202–3). The only thing lacking in Virginia, according to Edward Waterhouse, was "store of hands" to harvest its riches.[45] Milton's Eden, too, needs "more hands" to cultivate it—and more mouths to consume its produce. Until they arrive, the kind of anarchy that Comus describes is an ever-present possibility.

The reason for this extremely unusual characteristic of the earthly paradise in *Paradise Lost* is to be found, I believe, in a second and very different image of the New World which had begun to assert itself with increasing emphasis in the writings of Puritan apologists for New England by the time Milton began serious work on *Paradise Lost*, the image of America as a "a desert wilderness replete only with a kind of savage people and overgrown trees." Although Puritan writers rarely described this phenomenon in any great detail—even William Bradford and Edward Johnson provided little more than brief adjectival descriptions of the "remote, rocky, barren, bushy, wild-woody wilderness" which the Pilgrims had encountered—the concept played a crucial role in shaping their definition of the holy community.[46] As Peter Carroll has shown in his classic study of *Puritanism and the Wilderness*, it embodied the Satanic forces which the children of God were required to resist, and eventually to conquer.[47] The "pleasant gardens of Christ" which the Puritans had established in New England were the moral and spiritual antithesis of the "hideous and desolate wilderness" which threatened them on all sides.[48]

The wilderness is also a powerful physical and symbolic presence in *Paradise Lost*, though Milton does not give us very much information about it either. Adam and Eve's garden, he tells us, is surrounded by: "a steep wilderness, whose hairie sides / With thicket overgrown, grottesque and wilde, / Access deni'd" (4.135–37). Consequently, when Satan attempts to ascend "that steep savage Hill" (4.172) he can make no progress because:

> so thick entwin'd,
> As one continu'd brake, the undergrowth
> Of shrubs and tangled bushes had perplext
> All path of Man or Beast.
>
> (4.174–77)

But the wilderness around Eden will not necessarily remain outside the garden. Indeed, as Raphael makes his way into "the blissful field" (5.292) we see him passing through:

> A Wilderness of sweets; for Nature here
> Wantond as in her prime, and plaid at will
> Her Virgin Fancies, pouring forth more sweet,
> Wild above Rule or Art.
>
> (5.294–97)

So just as John Cotton was haunted by the fear that "if the weeds grow so neere the inclosure (or hedge) round about the garden," then they might "easily creep into the Garden, and . . . choak the good herbes," so Adam and Eve are constantly aware of the possibility that their pastoral retreat will be gradually engulfed by the jungle outside it.[49] In *Paradise Lost* no less than in New England, any failure to cultivate the garden of God ran the risk of "turning the pleasant gardens of Christ into a wilderness."[50] Unless Adam and Eve perform their "pleasant labour" with relentless diligence, the "overwoodie" trees which reach "too farr" (5.213) with their "branches overgrown" (4.627), the gums and blossoms which "lie bestrowne, unsightly and unsmooth," will inexorably transform the earthly paradise into a wilderness. Paradoxically, the expansiveness of nature upon which John White and others had based their whole justification of colonialism could have disastrous consequences for the actual colony if it was not rigorously controlled.

Brutal kind (9.565)

Different though they are in virtually every respect, the two colonial sites in *Paradise Lost* have one very important feature in common: for one reason or another they are both exempt from the principal source of conflict in the New World, the tension between the competing interests of the colonists and the natives that erupted in such events as the Virginia massacres and the Pequot war.

In the case of the infernal colony the reason for this phenomenon is very simple: Hell contains no natives. Until Satan and his companions arrive there, the "hollow Deep" (1.314) is completely uninhabited. The closest we get to the kind of violent confrontation that broke out repeatedly in the English settlements during the seventeenth century is the short scene at the end of Book 2 in which Satan encounters, to his surprise, two monstrous figures whom he takes at first to be "Hell-born" (2.687). His instinctive reaction, therefore, is to assert his imperial dominance. Appropriating the frequently reported Indian belief that the European explorers were visitors from Heaven, the Devil demands immediate submission:

> Whence and what art thou, execrable shape,
> That dar'st, though grim and terrible, advance
> Thy miscreated Front athwart my way
> To yonder Gates? through them I mean to pass,
> That be assur'd, without leave askt of thee:
> Retire, or tast thy folly, and learn by proof,
> Hell-born, not to contend with Spirits of Heav'n.
>
> (2.681–87)

We might be listening to Prospero railing at Caliban.

Death, in turn, behaves exactly like a hostile werowance, rejecting the newcomer's claim to superiority and insisting on his own monarchical authority:

> And reck'n'st thou thyself with Spirits of Heav'n,
> Hell-doom'd, and breath'st defiance here and scorn
> Where I reign King, and to enrage thee more,
> Thy King and Lord?
>
> (2.696–99)

But before the two adversaries can come to blows Sin intervenes to reveal that both she and Death are fellow exiles from the celestial kingdom; she herself was an "inhabitant of Heav'n, and heav'nlieborn" (2.860) and her son was conceived long before her expulsion "into this Deep" (2.773). All three members of the Satanic family are immigrants. As a result, the fundamental problem of the whole colonial enterprise is averted by erasing one of the conflicting parties from the colonial landscape. Hell offers, rather, a paradigm of the enduring European myth that the recently discovered territories on the other side of the Atlantic were to all intents and purposes vacant, waiting for some external agency to fill them.

In the garden of Eden the situation is rather more complicated by virtue of the fact that the "New World" is the focus of two opposing colonial powers. When Satan voyages to earth in order to displace the native inhabitants with his own followers, Adam and Eve are obviously the counterparts of the American Indians with whom they are compared shortly after the Fall. In the diabolic version of the imperial narrative, the rivalry between the colonial intruder and the native residents lies at the very heart of the story. But, as we shall see in the next chapter, when God "plants" (1.652) the human pair in the terrestrial paradise with instructions to cultivate it on his behalf, Adam and Eve take on the role of indentured servants obediently performing their "day-labour" (5.232) in Heaven's new outpost. Seen in this latter context, the garden of Eden also appears to lack an indigenous population. Like Hell, it seems to be a colony in which there is no one to be colonized.

In reality, however, Milton's treatment of God's plantation embodies a still more insidious fantasy, for the garden contains a crucial component that has no counterpart in Hell: the animals. Their presence there was mandated, of course, by the text of Genesis 1.28 with its description of Adam and Eve's "dominion over the fish of the sea, and over the fowl of the air, and over every living thing that moveth upon the earth." But in *Paradise Lost* Milton elaborates the animals' role in a way that makes it possible to see them as surrogates for the Indians in colonial America.

To many of the poet's contemporaries the substitution would have seemed only too natural, for very early in the development of English colonial propaganda, the men and women of Virginia and New England were equated with wild animals. "These savages," wrote Robert Gray in 1609, "have . . . only a generall residencie there, as wild beasts have in the forrest, for they range and wander up and downe the Country, without any law or government, being led only by their owne lusts and sensualitie." Indeed, in their godless ignorance and blasphemous idolatry they were even "worse than those beasts which are of most wilde and savage nature." The comparison was subsequently reinforced by Robert Johnson, who informed his readers that Virginia was inhabited "with wild and savage people that live and lie up and downe in troupes like heards of Deare in a Forrest," and by the authors of *Mourt's Relation*, who declared that the Indians of New England, too, "doe but run over the grasse, as doe also the Foxes and wilde beasts."[51]

The immediate goal of these analogies, of course, was to dehumanize the native population and thus to deprive them of any property rights they might otherwise legitimately claim in the territories settled by the English. But the equation had other uses, too. John Underhill, for instance, compared the Pequots to "roaring lions, compassing all corners of the country for a prey," thereby justifying, at least in his own eyes, the slaughter which took place at Mystic Fort, while Robert Cushman remarked that although the Indians around Plymouth Plantation "were wont to be the most cruel and treacherous people in all these parts, even like lions," nevertheless "to us they have been like lambs, so kind, so submissive, and trusty, as a man may truly say, many Christians are not so kind, nor sincere." But whether they were hostile or friendly, wild or tame, the Indians were commonly assumed to be, in John White's phrase, "men transformed into beasts."[52]

Somewhat surprisingly, the beasts in *Paradise Lost* have more in common with submissive and trusty lambs than with cruel and treacherous lions—surprisingly because, as I pointed out in *"Paradise Lost" and the Genesis Tradition*, the most common interpretation of God's commandment to dress the garden and to keep it was based on the assumption that the Creator was referring to the damage which the animals might otherwise inflict upon the plants and flowers growing there. Milton's contemporary, Henry More, for instance, explained that one of Adam's principal duties in Eden was "to keep things handsome and in order in it, and that it should not be any wise spoil'd or misus'd by incursions or careless ramblings of the heedlesse beasts."[53] As we have just seen, however, in *Paradise Lost* it is the vegetation that constitutes the chief threat to the garden's well-being. The animals are entirely benign:

> About them frisking playd
> All Beasts of th'Earth, since wilde, and of all chase
> In Wood or Wilderness, Forrest or Den;
> Sporting the Lion rampd, and in his paw
> Dandl'd the Kid;
>
> (4.340–44)

The only hint of the animals' destructive potential occurs when Satan takes up temporary residence among "the sportful Herd" (4.396):

> A Lion now he stalks with fierie glare,
> Then as a Tyger, who by chance hath spi'd
> In some Purlieu two gentle Fawnes at play,
> Straight couches close, then rising changes oft
> His couchant watch, as one who chose his ground
> Whence rushing he might surest seize them both
> Gript in each paw.
>
> (4.402–8)

But this brief vision of nature red in tooth and claw is clearly a fore-shadowing of the fallen world in which "Beast now with Beast gan war" (10.710). Until Adam and Eve eat the forbidden fruit, the animals behave precisely like the innocent and subservient Indians described by Robert Cushman.

For Milton's readers, the first hint of a connection between the two groups may have been provided by the animals' freedom from the horticultural duties imposed on Adam and Eve. According to John Eliot, for instance, one of the most important differences between the Puritan planters in New England and the native Massachusetts was that "we labour and work in building, planting, clothing our selves, &c. and they doe not."[54] In much the same terms, Adam identifies perpetual leisure as the distinguishing characteristic of the animals in the garden of Eden; ranging freely through the woods and meadows, they "Rove idle unimploid" (4.617) by day and night, unconstrained by the "daily work of body or mind" (4.618) required of their human masters. While the colonists are engaged in their fruitful toil, the natives roam the countryside in purposeless locomotion.

The most suggestive parallels between the animals and the Indians, however, emerge during Adam's description of the events leading up to the birth of Eve in Book 8. In Genesis 1, the basis of Milton's account of the creation in Book 7, the animals are created before man, but in Genesis 2 the sequence is reversed; God creates the animals and brings them to Adam to be named only after He has determined that "It is not good that the man should be alone; I will make him an help meet for him." The implication seems to be that the beasts of the field were created in order to provide Adam with the companionship he needed. Committed as he was to the order of events in Genesis 1, Milton consequently adapted the narrative of Genesis 2 in order to make it conform with the prior creation of the animals. In *Paradise Lost* the still nameless "Creatures that livd, and movd, and walk'd, or flew" (8.264) already exist when Adam springs to life, and the desirability of creating a companion for him does not become an issue until he has given them names. Disengaged from the Creator's perception of man's need for a mate, the naming episode thus takes on a rather different significance in *Paradise Lost*. The animals are brought to Adam to be christened, as it were, not so that he can select a partner but so that they can pay him "fealtie / With low subjection" (8.344–45). The process of naming them has become an expression of personal superiority rather than social preference.

For any of Milton's readers familiar with the discourse of colonialism this reorganized version of Genesis 2 would have had obvious political overtones. For as Jan van der Straet's famous engraving of Amerigo Vespucci's arrival in the New World clearly illustrates, and as Anthony Pagden, Peter Hulme, and Stephen Greenblatt have recently reminded us, naming was the quintessential colonial act, the act that recorded and secured the explorer's property rights over the territory he had just "discovered."[55] So when Christopher Columbus landed on what he believed to be "the Indies," as Anthony Pagden notes," he "then assumed his political authority over them by giving them names."[56] To name something, in short, was to assert political as well as linguistic sovereignty over it, to make it one's own.

The naming of the animals in *Paradise Lost* thus points toward an essentially colonial relationship between Adam and the other creatures who occupy the garden of Eden. Summoned, like feudal servants, to pay "fealtie" (8.344) to their "Lords" (8.339), the animals react in much the same way as the tribal chief Nichotawance, who came to Jamestown to "doe homage and bring Tribute to King Charles."[57] "With low subjection" (8.345), they obediently acknowledge Adam as their master, "cowring low" (8.350) as they pass him.

What is more, the substitution of the animals for the Indians allows Milton to portray this scene of colonial submission without compromising his belief in "fair equalitie" (12.26). So when Adam learns from Michael that soon after the flood Nimrod will claim "Dominion undeserv'd / Over his brethren" (12.27–28) he draws an explicit contrast between his own rightful authority over the animals and Nimrod's "empire tyrannous" (12.32):

> [God] gave us onely over Beast, Fish, Fowl
> Dominion absolute; that right we hold
> By his donation; but Man over men
> He made not Lord; such title to himself
> Reserving, human left from human freee.
> (12.67–71)

Here in Book 8, however, the presence of the animals allows the fantasy of a peaceful and harmonious colonial society in which the colonized unquestioningly accept the authority of the colonists to proceed unchallenged. In God's colony the natives know their place.

The search for "an help meet for Adam" begins in *Paradise Lost* only when this imperial rite of possession is over. In response to Adam's request for a companion, God playfully suggests that he look for a consort among the creatures over whom he has just acquired "dominion." What had only been implicit in the biblical scene now becomes fully explicit: in colonial terms, the settler is being invited to take one of the natives as his wife. Adam's immediate rejection of the offer on the grounds that true "fellowship" (8.389) cannot exist "among unequals" (8.383) reflects in turn the orthodox English view that intermarriage with the Indians was contrary to the best interests of the colony, if not to the law of nature itself. As early as 1609, for example, William Symonds instructed the Virginian colonists that they must "keep to themselves." "They may not marry nor give in marriage to the heathen," he wrote, for "the breaking of this rule may break the neck of all good success of this voyage."[58] Although Symonds does not offer any reason for his prohibition, the explanation is clear: transgressive alliances with the native population would soon blur the distinction between colonist and colonized, thereby undermining the hierarchical relationship upon which the whole colonial enterprise was based. Small wonder that when John Rolfe violated the taboo by marrying Pocahontas he felt compelled to excuse himself in a long letter of apology to the governor pleading that his motive was evangelical rather than carnal.[59]

It is worth noting, in conclusion, that Adam's reasons for rejecting the animals as suitable companions are linguistic as well as political, and that, as such, they have still further colonial overtones. Although the beasts of the field could "reason not contemptibly" (8.374), as God had pointed out, although they even had their own "language" (8.373), they could not "converse" (8.396) with man, and were consequently incapable of providing him with the kind of "rational delight" (8.391) he sought. The emphasis on "conversation" (8.418) in this argument is revealing. For language was not only "the perfect instrument of empire" in Antonio de Nebrija's much-quoted phrase.[60]

It was also the distinguishing characteristic of human beings, a prime indicator of their rationality and consequently of their superiority over lesser species. Almost inevitably, then, those promoters and colonists who regarded the Indians as mere "talking animals"[61] took it for granted that their language, such as it was, could express only the most primitive feelings and concepts. As Stephen Greenblatt has pointed out in a seminal essay, "the view that Indian speech was close to gibberish remained current in intellectual as well as popular circles at least into the seventeenth century," and it clearly underlies Milton's observation that thanks to the legal jargon of his time "our speech is, I know not what, American, I suppose, or not even human!"[62] So when the serpent addresses Eve "with human voice" (9.561) in Book 9, it confronts her with a profound ontological crux:

> What may this mean? Language of Man pronounc't
> By Tongue of Brute, and human sense exprest?
> The first at least of these I thought deni'd
> To Beasts, whom God on their Creation-Day
> Created mute to all articulat sound.
>
> (9.553–57)

As it turns out, indeed, the reptile's apparent ability to engage in rational discourse is the key to the entire temptation. Eve falls in part because she allows herself to be persuaded that a creature "of brutal kind" (9.565) has learned to speak and reason like a human being, because she treats one of the inarticulate natives as if he were her linguistic equal.

3

The Colonists

In all societies there are off-casts; this impure part serves as our
precursors or pioneers. . . . Thus are our first steps trodden, thus
are our first trees felled, in general, by the most vicious of our people; and thus the path is opened for the arrival of a second and
better class, the true American freeholders, the most respectable
set of people in this part of the world: respectable for their indus-
try, their happy independence, the great share of freedom they
possess, [and] the good regulation of their families.
    —Hector St. John de Crèvecœur, *Letters from an American Farmer*

Almost from the moment Columbus and his companions arrived in
the New World in 1492 the figure of the colonist has been fraught
with contradiction. Initially, the Spanish explorers were greeted by the
inhabitants of Hispaniola as visitors from Heaven, and entertained with
all the largesse and reverence that befitted their supposed status. But
Columbus's men behaved so badly on the island that within a relatively
short time they came to be regarded by the native population as devils
rather than gods, and the inhabitants of subsequent Spanish possessions rapidly came to the same conclusion. If Heaven was populated
with Spaniards, declared a Cuban cacique in Las Casas's famous anec-
dote, he would prefer to spend eternity in Hell.[1]

The same radical disjunction is evident in English descriptions of
the men who explored and settled North America. The tone of the
earliest accounts of these intrepid spirits is suggested by the concluding stanza of a poem written by a certain Captain Bingham in
commendation of Sir George Peckham's *true Report*:

> Then launch, ye noble youths, into the main;
> No lurking perils lie amid the way;

Your travail shall return you treble gain,
and make your names renowned another day.
For valiant minds through twenty seas will roam,
And fish for luck, while sluggards lie at home.[2]

In much the same vein Michael Drayton, anxious to drum up volunteers for the new plantation in Virginia, began his ode "To the Virginian Voyage":

> You brave heroic minds
> Worthy your country's name,
> That honor still pursue,
> Go and subdue,
> Whilst loitering hinds
> Lurk here at home for shame.[3]

Whether they were perceived as discoverers, explorers, settlers,[4] or all three rolled into one, those who journeyed to the New World were consistently portrayed in early colonial literature as being more ambitious, more energetic, and more daring than those who stayed behind in the Old. In his heroic refusal to "renounce the quest / Of what may in the sun's path be assayed," Dante's Ulysses might well have been their prototype.[5]

As soon as the initial glamor of the enterprise wore off, however, a very different image began to emerge. For Drayton's "brave heroic minds" turned out in many instances to be the dregs of Renaissance English society. As John Hammond observed in 1656, for the first few decades of its existence Virginia was "a nest of Rogues, whores, desolute and rooking persons." Nor does Hammond appear to have been exaggerating, for over and over again the early administrators of Virginia complained of the laziness, greed, malice, and lawlessness of the immigrants, "ten times more fit to spoyle a Commonwealth then either begin one, or but helpe to maintaine one. For when neither the feare of God, nor the law, nor shame, nor displeasure of their friends could rule them [in England], there is small hope ever to bring one in twentie of them ever to be good [in Virginia]." By the time Sir Francis Bacon published his essay *Of Planta-*

tions in 1625 there was ample evidence to support his arguments against treating the New World as a dumping ground for England's social outcasts.[6]

In *Paradise Lost*, I now want to suggest, these contradictory perceptions generate a whole series of competing images which continually call into question both the character and the motives of the early explorers and settlers. In the final analysis, Milton's extraordinarily complex anatomy of the figure of the colonist permits us to side neither with Bingham nor with Bacon.

Great adventurer (10.440)

During the course of his triumphant speech in Book 10 announcing the conquest of the terrestrial paradise Satan informs his followers: "Long were to tell / What I have don, what sufferd, with what paine / Voyag'd th' unreal, vast, unbounded deep" (469–71). He sounds very much like Amerigo Vespucci reporting to Lorenzo Pietro di Medici on his latest voyage to the New World: "But what we suffered on that vast expanse of sea, what perils of shipwreck, what discomforts of the body we endured, with what anxiety of mind we toiled, this I leave to the judgment of those who out of rich experience have well learned what it is to seek the uncertain and to attempt discoveries even though ignorant."[7] The echo itself is almost certainly accidental, but the general resemblance is not, for of the various roles that Satan plays in *Paradise Lost* none is more richly elaborated than his impersonation of a Renaissance explorer.

To begin with, Milton arranges the early part of the story so that we experience it as a diabolic voyage of discovery. Just as Columbus and his contemporaries heard rumors of the New World long before its existence had been confirmed, so we learn from Satan in Book 1 that "a fame in Heav'n" has spread stories of "new Worlds" (650–51) elsewhere in the universe. In Books 2 and 3 we then accompany him on the perilous "voyage" (2.426, 919) across the "gulf" (2.441) of chaos to "the coast of Earth" (3.739). And at the beginning of Book 4 we finally see the garden of Eden at least partially through the Devil's consciousness.[8]

The motives which impel Satan on his voyage replicate, in turn, virtually all the social and political arguments that were advanced in favor of England's colonial expansion in the late sixteenth and early seventeenth centuries. The first of them emerges in Beelzebub's speech at the end of the infernal debate in Book 2. After mentioning the rumors circulating in Heaven about the creation of the world, he proposes that even though:

> Heav'n be shut,
> And Heav'ns high Arbitrator sit secure
> In his own strength, this place may lye expos'd
> The utmost border of his Kingdom, left
> To their defense who hold it: here perhaps
> Sum advantagious act may be achiev'd
> By sudden onset, either with Hell fire
> To waste his whole Creation, or possess
> All as our own, . . .
>
> (2.358–66)

This bears a startling resemblance to the political rationale for Elizabethan raids on Spanish possessions in the New World offered by writers such as Richard Hakluyt the elder a century before. "But the plantinge of twoo or three stronge fortes upon some god havens (whereof there is greate score) betwene Florida and Cape Briton," he wrote in his *Discourse on Western Planting*, "woulde be a matter in shorte space of greater domage as well to his flete as to his westerne Indies; for wee shoulde not only often tymes indaunger his flete in the returne thereof, but also in fewe yeres put him in hazarde in loosinge some parte of Nova Hispania."[9] Beelzebub's proposal momentarily transforms Satan into a demonic Sir Francis Drake, setting off to singe God's beard. The assault on Eden will be a daring naval raid performed by an infernal buccaneer.

The second motive for undertaking the journey across chaos is disclosed by Satan himself in his parting speech to his followers in Pandemonium. Oppressed by God's vengeance, he tells them, "I abroad / Through all the Coasts of dark destruction seek / Deliverance for all" (2.463–65). In a diabolic parody of the Pilgrims on the *Mayflower* he presents himself as the ultimate separatist, a victim of religious persecution in search of a new home where he and his fellow dissidents can practice their infernal rites in peace—in Heaven, we have already been told by Mammon, the angels were constrained by "Strict laws impos'd" to celebrate God's throne with Laudian ceremoniousness, worshipping their "envied Sovran" with "warbl'd Hymns" and "Forc't Hallelujahs" (2.242–43). Satan's purpose, he tells Sin shortly afterwards, is:

> to set free
> From out this dark and dismal house of pain,
> Both him and thee, and all the heav'nly Host
> Of Spirits . . .
> To search with wandring quest a place foretold
> Should be . . .
> And bring ye to the place where Thou and Death
> Shall dwell at ease.
>
> (2.822–41)

Like the faithful and freeborn Englishmen who, in Milton's words, "have bin constrain'd to forsake their dearest home, their friends, and kindred, whom nothing but the wide Ocean, and the savage deserts of America could hide and shelter from the fury of the Bishops," the Devil claims to be seeking refuge from the oppression of a tyrannical power.[10]

As Satan approaches the garden of Eden, however, a third motive makes its appearance. His underlying purpose, he now confesses, is territorial expansion. By raiding this vulnerable outpost of the heavenly kingdom he hopes to share at least "Divided Empire with Heav'ns King" (4.111). Hence the extraordinary scene in Book 10 when Sin greets her triumphant parent at the foot of the "wondrous Pontifice" (348) which she and her son have contructed across chaos "by wondrous Art / Pontifical" (312–13). "Thine now is all this World," she declares:

> here thou shalt Monarch reign,
> . . . . . . there let him still Victor sway,

As Battel hath adjudg'd, from this new World
Retiring, by his own doom alienated,
And henceforth Monarchie with thee divide
Of all things, parted by th'Empyreal bounds,
His Quadrature, from thy Orbicular World.

(372–81)

Cued by Milton's antipapal puns, we seem to be witnessing a grotesque reenactment of Pope Alexander VI's division of the western world between the Spanish and the Portuguese in 1493, a cosmic *Inter Caetera.*[11]

Several additional motives for Satan's expedition emerge later in the poem, some of them explicitly acknowledged in the literature of colonialism, others visible only beneath the surface of the narratives. Prominent among the latter is what might be called colonial libido. The association of erotic experience with transatlantic discovery had already been established, of course, in such poems as John Donne's elegies "Love's Progress" and "To His Mistress Going to Bed" in which the poet greeted his partner as if she were the Indies:

Oh my America, my new found land,
My kingdom safeliest when with one man mann'd,
My mine of precious stones, my Empiree,
How blest am I in this discovering thee.

(27–30)

She is his America, and he, by implication, is her Columbus. Like most Renaissance analogies, however, this equation was reversible. If making love was like a voyage of discovery, then a voyage of discovery could be like making love. Consequently, as Annette Kolodny, Patricia Parker, and others have noted, the relationship between sexual and territorial conquest soon produced in the art and literature of the period an image of America as a submissive and almost invariably naked young virgin waiting to yield up her charms to an older and more sophisticated lover, Europe.[12] "You swore freely," wrote Richard Hakluyt to Sir Walter Raleigh, "that no terrors, no personal losses or misfortunes, could or ever would tear you from the sweet embrace-ments of your own Virginia, that fairest of nymphs—though to many insufficiently well known—whom our most generous sovereign has given you to be your bride."[13] And in less courtly vein, a sea captain in George Chapman, Ben Jonson, and John Marston's play *Eastward Ho*, exhorted his companions to cross the Atlantic because "Virginia longs till we share the rest of her maidenhead."[14]

The image was most highly developed in the writings of Samuel Purchas, who addressed himself to Virginia as if he were proposing marriage: "Whether shall I warble sweete Carols in prayse of thy lovely Face, thou fairest of Virgins, which from our other Britaine World, hath wonne thee Wooers and Suters . . . to make thee of a ruder Virgin, not a wanton Minion; but an honest and Christian wife?" Only the English, he asserted, were deserving of her favors, for the "savage inhabitants" were "unworthie to embrace with their rustike armes so sweet a bosome." In his *Pilgrimes*, too, he invited his readers to "look upon Virginia; view her lovely lookes (howsoever like a modest Virgin she is now vailed with wild Coverts and shadie Woods, expecting rather ravishment than Mariage from her Native Savages) survay her Heavens, Elements, Situation; her divisions by armes of Bayes and Rivers into so goodly and well proportioned limmes and members; her Virgin portion nothing empaired, nay not yet improved, in Natures best Legacies . . . in all these you shall see, that she is worth the wooing and loves of the best Husband."[15]

Nor was the image confined to Virginia. In the author's prologue to *New English Canaan*, Thomas Morton compared New England to:

> a faire virgin, longing to be sped,
> And meete her lover in a Nuptiall bed,
> Deck'd in rich ornaments to'advaunce her state
> And excellence, being most fortunate,
> When most enjoy'd. . . .

And John Hammond described Maryland as a beautiful young maiden who had been "deflowred by her own Inhabitants, stript, shorne and made deformed." "Yet such a naturall fertility and comeliness doth she retain," he continued, "that she cannot be loved but be pittied."[16] So when the modern American historian, Samuel Eliot

Morison, writes of "those October days in 1492 when the New World gracefully yielded her virginity to the conquering Castilians," he is accurately reflecting the way in which many Renaissance authors themselves pictured the process of colonization.[17] The theme that Vladimir Nabokov was accused of rehearsing in *Lolita*—"old Europe debauching young America"—goes back a long way.

From the concept of America as a willing young virgin it was only a short step to the concept of American women as the predestined mistresses of European men. The female inhabitants of the New World, Vespucci proudly informed his contemporaries, "showed themselves very desirous of copulating with us Christians," and if the travel literature of the next two centuries is to be believed, the Christians were only too happy to oblige. In his stern rejection of the thirty naked Indian maidens who accosted him crying "Love you not me, love you not me," the virtuous Captain John Smith was the exception rather than the rule.[18]

In this context it is hardly surprising that in *Paradise Lost* the demonic colonist's first encounter with an inhabitant of the New World should be portrayed as an act of sexual conquest. When he saw Adam and Eve making love in Book 4 the Devil had turned aside "for envy, yet with jealous leer malign / Ey'd them askance" (503–4). Here in Book 9 the famous "town and country" simile immediately establishes him as a sophisticated London rake ogling an innocent country girl, and during the initial stages of the temptation he approaches his prey as if she were a prospective mistress, courting her with all the hyperbole of a Renaissance love poet. Her looks, he tells her, are a "Heaven" (534), her beauty is "Celestial" (540), and she herself should be "a Goddess among Gods, ador'd and serv'd / By Angels numberless" (547–48). Eating the forbidden fruit has only heightened his appreciation of her beauty:

> I turnd my thoughts, and with capacious mind
> Considerd all things visible in Heav'n,
> Or Earth, or Middle, all things fair and good;
> But all that fair and good in thy Divine
> Semblance, and in thy Beautie's heav'nly Ray
> United I beheld; no Fair to thine

Equivalent or second, which compel'd
Mee thus, though importune perhaps, to come
And gaze, and worship thee of right declar'd
Sovran of Creatures, universal Dame.

(9.603–12)

These lines encapsulate a whole tradition of love poetry, from Sidney's courtly sonnets to Donne's idolatrous songs and Marvell's plaints to his coy mistress. Eve is being seduced sexually as well as morally.[19]

In the second stage of the temptation Satan takes on a rather different colonial role. He presents himself to Eve in much the same way that John Rolfe evidently presented himself to Pocahontas, as a missionary who has been called upon by Providence to convert the ignorant and illuminate the unenlightened. When he first fell in love with the Indian princess, Rolfe revealed in a letter written to Sir Thomas Dale in 1614, he thought that the Devil might be responsible for his desire to link himself "with one whose education hath been rude, her manners barbarous, her generation accursed, and so discrepant in nurture from myself." But then he heard the voice of conscience exhorting him, "Why doest thou not endeavor to make her a Christian?" In view of "her great appearance of love to me, her desire to be taught and instructed in the knowledge of God, her capableness of understanding, her aptness and willingness to receive any good impression," Rolfe was consequently moved to ask himself: "Shall I be so unnatural as not to give bread to the hungry? or uncharitable as not to cover the naked?" The answer was all too obvious. "I will never cease," he promised, "until I have accomplished and brought to perfection so holy a work, in which I will pray daily to God to bless me, to mine and her eternal happiness." He was motivated, he therefore asks the Governor to believe, not by "the unbridled desire of carnal affection" but rather by the Christian impulse to convert "an unbelieving creature" to the true knowledge of God.[20]

Satan likewise claims that his approach to Eve is motivated purely and simply by his "Zeal of Right" (9.676). He has come to liberate her from the lowly state of ignorance in which he finds her. Indeed, his arguments for eating the forbidden fruit promise Eve nothing less than a Satanic equivalent of the Pauline conversion experience. "So ye shall die perhaps by putting off / Human, to put on Gods" (713–14), he tells her, echoing St. Paul's phrases in Colossians 3: "Lie not to one another, seeing that ye have put off the old man with his deeds; and have put on the new man, which is renewed in knowledge after the image of him that created him."[21] It is hardly surprising that as soon as the Devil's evangelical mission has been accomplished, Eve behaves just like a new convert, worshipping the tree as if it were a sacred icon:

> O Sovran, vertuous, precious of all Trees
> In Paradise . . . henceforth my early care,
> Not without Song, each Morning, and due praise
> Shall tend thee. . . .
>
> (9.795–801)

The infernal missionary has turned Eve into an idolater.

In practice, as we saw in Chapter 1, conversion was often merely a pretext for commercial profit, and this motive, too, plays an important role in the colonization of Eden. The crudest exemplars of naked greed are Satan's destructive plenipotentiaries, Sin and Death. The scent "of carnage, prey innummerable" (10.268) draws them across the gulf like "a flock / Of ravenous Fowl . . . lur'd / With the scent of living Carcasses" (10.273–77), and their "Adventrous work" (10.255) is rewarded with a Satanic patent to plunder the "new World" (10.257) which they have just united with the "Infernal Empire" (10.389). In a distorted echo of God's commandments in Genesis 1.28, Satan transforms the infernal pair into another Adam and Eve taking possession of their colonial outpost:

> You two this way, among these numerous Orbs
> All yours, right down to Paradise descend;
> There dwell and Reign in bliss, thence on the Earth
> Dominion exercise and in the Aire,
> Chiefly on Man, sole Lord of all declar'd,
> Him first make sure you thrall, and lastly kill.
>
> (10.397–42)

But Milton makes it clear that Eden's new occupants are predators who come to their "new Kingdom" (10.406) to plunder, not to multiply, to consume rather than to govern. Their "Dominion" is clearly going to be a reign of terror.

At a more sophisticated level their patron is portrayed as one of "the great Merchants of this world" who, in Milton's words, "abuse the people, like poor Indians with beads and glasses."[22] As B. A. Wright has pointed out, the Devil's voyage to the New World has been accompanied throughout by similes drawn from the familiar seventeenth-century world of merchant adventurers seeking the riches of the Indies across "the Trading Flood" (2.640).[23] And in the summary of the Fall which he gives to his fellow angels in Book 10, Satan describes his exploits as a successful business venture which has produced a huge profit:

> Him by fraud I have seduc'd
> From his Creator, and the more to increase
> Your wonder, with an Apple; he thereat
> Offended, worth your laughter, hath giv'n up
> Both his beloved Man and all his World
> To Sin and Death a prey, and so to us,
> Without our hazard, labour, or allarme,
> To range in, and to dwell, and over Man
> To rule, as over all he should have rul'd . . .
> A World who would not purchase with a bruise,
> Or much more grievous pain? Ye have th'account
> Of my performance: What remains, ye Gods,
> But up and enter now into full bliss.
>
> (10.485–503)

The commercial language reduces the fall of man to a shrewd business "purchase." Like the settlers who bought Manhattan Island from the Indians, Satan thinks he has got a bargain; the ignorant natives, he sneers, were willing to sell out for an apple. The "account" he presents is almost all profit.

During the course of the poem, then, Satan rehearses virtually all the major roles in the repertoire of English colonial discourse. By turns buccaneer, pilgrim, empire-builder, lover, missionary, and merchant, he embodies not only the destructive potential of imperial conquest but something of its glamor and energy as well. It may well be no accident that the critical glorification of Milton's Devil took place during the heyday of England's imperial power, while his descent from hero to fool coincided with its subsequent decline.

Heav'nly stranger (5.316)

Satan is not the only figure in the poem who embodies the colonial quest, however. God's emissaries, too, function as agents of imperial authority. Indeed, in some ways Raphael has even more in common with such figures as Columbus and Amerigo Vespucci than his diabolic antagonist does. For the extraordinary scene in which the archangel is greeted by two naked human beings as a "Native of Heaven" (5.361) reenacts an encounter which had been described in countless Renaissance descriptions of the discovers' arrival in the New World. Columbus's account is the prototype:

> The natives of Hispaniola were very firmly convinced that I, with these ships and men, came from the heavens, and in this belief they everywhere received me after they had mastered their fear. At present, those I bring with me are still of the opinion that I come from Heaven . . . They were the first to announce this wherever I went, and the others went running from house to house and to the neighboring towns, with loud cries of 'Come. Come. See the men from Heaven.'[24] (See fig. 2)

Like the ideally submissive and subservient Indians of those early narratives, Adam welcomes his "god-like Guest" (351) with "submiss approach and reverence meek" (359). Unquestioningly he recognizes that he possesses the garden of Eden "by sov'ran gift" (366) from Raphael's divine master. Then he and Eve proceed to entertain "the Heav'nly stranger" (316, 397) in their "Silvan lodge" (377) with all the bounty their world has to offer:

> whatever Earth all-bearing Mother yields
> In India East or West, or middle shoare

FIGURE 2. "The Indians Greeting Columbus" from Theodore de Bry, *America, Pars Quarta* (Frankfurt, 1594). Reproduced by permission of the Huntington Library, San Marino, California.

> . . . . . fruit of all kindes, in coate,
> Rough, or smooth rin'd, or bearded husk, or shell
> She gathers, Tribute large, and on the board
> Heaps with unsparing hand; for drink the Grape
> She crushes, inoffensive moust, and meathes
> From many a berrie, and from sweet kernels prest
> She tempers dulcet creams.
>
> (5.338–47)

Eve's preparations for her "Angel guest" (328) read like a poetic paraphrase of Arthur Barlowe's account of the Virginia colonists' reception by Granganimo's wife on Roanoke:

She brought us into the inner roome, where shee set on the boord
standing along the house, some wheate like furmentie, sodden Veni-
son, and roasted, fish, sodden, boyled, and roasted, Melons rawe and
sodden, rootes of divers kindes, and divers fruites: their drinke is commonly water, but while the grape lasteth they drinke wine, and for
want of caskes to keepe it; all the yere after they drink water, but it is
sodden with Ginger in it, and blacke Sinamon, and sometimes Sas-
saphras, and divers other wholesome, and medicinable hearbes and
trees. We were entertained with all love and kindnesse, and with as
much bountie (after their maner) as they could possibly devise.[25]

All that is missing in the Miltonic account is the slight hint of conde-
scension conveyed by Barlowe's concluding parenthesis. The "new
delights" (5.431) that Raphael is enjoying in the garden of Eden are
comparable, he tells Adam shortly afterwards, with those available in
Heaven.

The archangel's reaction to his hostess's nudity, on the other
hand, differs quite markedly from that of most European colonists to
the unclothed women of the New World. For although Raphael ex-
periences "real hunger" (5.437) at the prospect of his *déjeuner sur
l'herbe*, Milton goes out of his way to emphasize that his sexual appetite remains unstimulated by Eve's naked presence:

> O innocence
> Deserving Paradise! if ever, then,
> Then had the Sons of God excuse to have bin
> Enamour'd at that sight; but in those hearts
> Love unlibidinous reign'd, nor jealousie
> Was understood, the injur'd Lover's Hell.
>   (445–50)

The contrast with the diabolic colonist who had spied on Adam and
Eve the previous day "with jealous leer maligne" (4.503) is all too
clear.

The implicit eroticism of the scene is too powerful to be sup-
pressed for long, however, and it eventually finds an outlet in Milton's deft adaptation in Book 8 of a topic that appears very early in
English colonial literature: the Indians' evident interest in the dis-

covers' reproductive system. According to Thomas Hariot, for instance, the native inhabitants of Virginia, noting that "we had no
women amongst us," concluded that the English "were not borne of
women, and therefore not mortal."[26] Adam, too, is fascinated by his
visitor's sexuality, or lack of it. "Love not the heav'nly Spirits," he asks
after Raphael has rebuked him for over-admiring Eve's physical per-
fections, "and how their Love / Express they, by looks onely, or do
they mix / Irradiance, virtual or immediate touch?" (8.615–17). The
brief account of celestial intercourse which Raphael offers in reply
apparently leads Adam to the same conclusion as the Virginian Indians: the world from which his heavenly guest has voyaged, he believes, is peopled exclusively by "Spirits Masculine" (10.890).

When the meal is over the "Empyreal Minister" (5.460) of the
Almighty proceeds to fulfil his principal function, namely to instruct
Adam and Eve in the indispensable colonial virtues of loyalty and
obedience. In order to do so he delivers, in effect, a free adaptation
of the extraordinary declaration which all Spanish explorers were instructed to read aloud to the local inhabitants wherever they landed
in the New World, the *requerimiento*. This "strange blend of ritual, cyn-
icism, legal fiction, and perverse idealism," as Stephen Greenblatt
calls it, had been composed by the royal jurist, Palacios Rubios, in
1513 and was used by the Spanish *conquistadores* throughout the sixteenth century.[27] After asserting that "our Lord God Eternal created
Heaven and earth and a man and woman from whom we all descend," it went on to assert that God's appointed deputy on earth,
the Pope, "gave these islands and mainland of the ocean and the
contents thereof" to King Ferdinand and his daughter Juana, to
whom the Indians consequently owed their allegiance. "Respecting
your freedom and that of your wives and sons and your rights of possession," the injunction continued, the Spanish would not compel
the Indians to be baptized as Christians "unless you, informed of the
Truth, wish to convert to our Holy Catholic Faith." Should the Indians fail to comply, however, they were assured that the Spanish, "with
the help of God," would use force against them, enslaving "your persons, wives and sons," and disposing of them "as the King sees fit."[28]

Needless to say, Raphael's version of this document is far less
threatening, but it presents Adam and Eve with a remarkably similar

set of propositions. Together with the angels, the first pair learn to begin with, they share a common origin:

> O Adam, one Almightie is, from whom
> All things proceed, and up to him return,
> If not deprav'd from good, created all
> Such to perfection, one first matter all,
> Indu'd with various forms, . . .
>
> (469–73)

Provided that they: "be found obedient, and retain / Unalterably firm his love entire / Whose progenie you are" (501–3), they will continue to enjoy their blissful condition. But God "ordain'd thy will / By nature free" because: "Our voluntarie service he requires, / Not our necessitated, such with him / Finds no acceptance" (526–31). As a result, both angels and men may choose whether to serve God or not:

> in this we stand or fall:
> And some are fall'n, to disobedience fall'n,
> And so from Heav'n to deepest Hell; O fall
> From what high state of bliss into what woe!
>
> (540–43)

The progression of the argument is essentially the same, and the concluding vision of the hellish punishment awaiting the disobedient offers a cosmic equivalent of the threats with which the *requerimiento* concluded.

What distinguishes Raphael's declaration to Adam and Eve from the Spaniards' injunction to the Indians, of course, is simply its validity. In the context of *Paradise Lost* the imperial claims of "the sovran Planter" (4.691) are entirely justified. In place of the Indians' tragic misconception of their future oppressors, the poem consequently offers us an authentic encounter between man and angel, an encounter in which the problematic territorial and political claims of Spain and England have been replaced by the Creator's legitimate authority over his creation. In *Paradise Lost* the anxiety attaching to the discoveries has been at least partially relieved by the simple device of rewriting the scene as if the Indians and the Spanish had both been right. Unlike Columbus and his companions, Adam's visitor really has come from Heaven, as the Indians believed, and the sovereign he represents really does own the land, as the Spanish insisted.

Thanks to Milton's revision of the imperial encounter, Adam and Eve are thus spared the violent aftermath of Columbus's arrival in the New World. Unlike the Indians, they do not experience the horrors of Renaissance warfare at first hand; they learn about such murderous inventions as gunpowder only at second hand from their heavenly instructor. The appalling butchery and violence which characterized the Spanish conquest of America is displaced onto Satan's campaign against his Maker.

As Raphael proceeds to enlighten Adam and Eve about the Devil's activities and the Creator's response to them, he slips imperceptibly into the role that Satan plays so effectively in Book 9, that of a missionary bringing the word of God to the benighted inhabitants of his most distant possessions. He is confronted, as a result, with the same fundamental problem that faced the Christian missionaries in the New World: in John White's words, "how shall a man expresse unto [the Indians] things meerely spirituall, which have no affinity with sense?"[29] How, in this particular instance, is Raphael to communicate the destructive power of Satan and the creative love of God in a way that Adam and Eve will understand. As he puts it himself: "how shall I relate / To human sense th'invisible exploits / Of warring Spirits?" (5.564–66) The answer is not only, as C. A. Patrides has shown, a poetic adaptation of the theological doctrine of accommodation according to which the expositors of God's word tailored their language to the intellectual capacity of their auditors.[30] It is also an extended example of the evangelical technique which John Eliot and his colleagues in New England developed to communicate the doctrines of the Christian Church to the American Indians. In answering the Indians' questions about the Christian religion, Eliot explained, "we endeavoured to speake nothing without clearing of it up by some familiar similitude," using concrete physical images to illustrate spiritual truths.[31] In much the same way, Raphael tells Adam that he will translate the immaterial into the material:

> What surmounts the reach
> Of human sense, I shall delineate so,
> By lik'ning spiritual to corporal forms,
> As may express them best.
>
> (571–74)

Drawing on the limited resources of Adam's experience for his similes, the angel is consequently able to convey to his human audience a vivid image both of the war in Heaven and the creation of the cosmos.[32] The guilt generated by the relative failure of the English missionaries to convert the Indians of Virginia and New England has, it might appear, been dissipated by Raphael's success in the garden. But although Adam has understood the angel's advice, he conspicuously fails to act on it when the moment comes to do so. In the final analysis, Raphael's evangelical efforts come to nothing.

As a result, the rebellious natives receive a second visitor from Heaven, with orders to fulfil the threats that concluded Raphael's *requerimiento* and drive them forth "without remorse" (11.105) from their terrestrial paradise into the wilderness beyond it. Michael's mission thus recapitulates in mythic form not only Spain's campaigns in Mexico and Peru—during his vision of future human history Adam is shown the seats of Montezuma and Atabalipa (11.407–9)—but England's more recent dispossession of the Indians in New England and Virginia. The image of the colonist as a ruthless invader is too powerful to exclude entirely, and although Milton insists that God's motives are entirely benevolent, Adam and Eve's expulsion from the garden of Eden by a force of "flaming Warriours" (11.101) could hardly have failed to summon up in the minds of seventeenth-century English readers disquieting memories of the final act of the colonial drama.

Fellow servant (8.225)

The colonial figures we have considered so far were all, for one reason or another, eager to cross the Atlantic. Whether they were ambitious imperialists, enterprising merchants, persecuted religious minorities, or zealous evangelists, they undertook the voyage to America largely on their own initiative. A significant proportion of the early emigrants to England's colonies, however, had to be actively recruited. Lacking both the ideological motivation for making the journey and the financial means to pay for it, the men and women who formed the principal source of labor in Virginia and Maryland would not have chosen to settle in the New World if the colonial authorities themselves had not made it possible and desirable for them to do so. In 1617, after experimenting with a variety of incentives, the Virginia Company finally devised the system which was to provide England's southern colonies with the bulk of their work force for the rest of the century, the system of indenture.[33]

Essentially, indentured service was a mechanism which permitted potential emigrants to be shipped to America at the expense of a colonial landowner to whom they were subsequently bound as servants for a fixed term of years, usually four or five. In return for their transportation across the Atlantic and their food, lodging, and clothing in the colony, they worked on their masters' property without wages until their term of service expired, at which time they received enough cash, provisions, and land to set up as independent smallholders themselves. In Maryland, for example, John Hammond tells us that the usual allowance for servants at the expiration of their indenture was "a years provision of corne, dubble apparrell, tooles necessary, and land according to the custome of the Countrey."[34]

Clearly, this system was vulnerable to all kinds of abuse. Once labor became a commodity that could be bought and sold for a profit, the temptation to exploit the system became almost irresistible. Dishonest masters maltreated their servants; unscrupulous agents, "spirits" as they were known, having lured innocent young country dwellers into servitude with false promises (or in some cases actually kidnapping them), sold them off to merchants and sea captains as cargo;[35] and the sea captains in turn put entire shiploads of servants up for public auction on the eastern seaboard of America.[36] Not surprisingly, as Abbot E. Smith has pointed out, the system "smacked enough of the eastern slave markets to give an occasional scandal to delicate-minded observers."[37] One such observer was George Gardyner, who noted in 1651 that:

we are upbraided by all other Nations that know that trade for selling our own Countrymen for the Commodities of those places. And I affirm, that I have been told by the Dutch and others, that we English were worse than the Turks, for that they sold strangers onely, and we sold our own Countrymen . . . and it were better for them to serve fourteen years with the Turks, then four in the Plantations with most of the Masters in those places, especially in Virginia, for besides their being back-beaten and belly-beaten, it is three to one if they live out their servitude by reason of the unwholsomenesse of the Countreys.[38]

John Hammond's *Leah and Rachel* appears to have been written for the express purpose of countering the effects of such criticisms. For after warning prospective emigrants against the wiles of "mercinary spirits," Hammond goes on to urge his readers not to let "that brand of selling of servants, be any discouragement to deter any from going, for if a time must be served, it is all one with whom it be served, provided they be people of honest repute, with which the Country is well replenished." Given these precautions, he goes on to observe, "those servants that will be industrious may in their time of service gain a competent estate before their Freedomes, which is usually done by many."[39]

The principal function of an indentured servant, of course, was labor, and this fact alone may perhaps account for the tremendous importance which the virtue of industriousness soon came to assume in English colonial literature.[40] For after a brief flirtation with the fantasy of effortless prosperity embodied in the myth of the Golden Age, the promoters of English settlement in the New World quickly concluded that idleness was the greatest single threat to the success of the entire undertaking.[41] Rejecting what he called "the Fiction of the land of Ease," John Hammond consequently laid all the blame for Virginia's early difficulties on the disinclination of the settlers to engage in productive labor, and the same point was made by many of the historians of New England.[42] "Whereas many do disparage the land," wrote William Wood in 1634:

saying a man cannot live without labor, in that they more disparage and discredit themselves in giving the world occasion to take notice of their dronish disposition that would live off the sweat of another man's brows. Surely they were much deceived, or else ill informed, that ventured thither in hope to live in plenty and idleness, both at a time. And it is as much pity as he that can work and will not should eat, as it is pity that he that would work and cannot should fast. . . . For all in New England must be workers in some kind.[43]

Seen in this general context, Adam's situation in *Paradise Lost* resembles nothing so much as an idealized form of indentured servitude. Placed in an earthly paradise by the "sovran Planter" (4.691), he is destined to serve out a fixed term of "pleasant labour" (4.625), at the end of which, by "long obedience tri'd" (7.159), he may be given the status of an angel and allowed to dwell permanently in the terrestrial or the celestial paradise (5.500). His biblical counterpart, of course, had long been regarded as a paradigm of the colonial settler. "A Colony is therefore denominated, because they should be *Coloni*, the tillers of the earth, and stewards of fertilitie," wrote the authors of *A True Declaration*. "God sels us all things for our labour, when Adam himselfe might not live in paradice without dressing the garden." And Robert Johnson commended "that most wholeome, profitable and pleasant work of planting in which it pleased God himself to set the first man and most excellent creature Adam in his innocencie."[44] In *Paradise Lost*, however, the current of correspondence between the two figures is reversed. The result is a vision of prelapsarian man unlike any other in the history of the Genesis myth.

To begin with, the concept of indentured labor may well be responsible for the quite unprecedented significance that Milton gives to Adam's daily toil in *Paradise Lost*. As I have shown elsewhere, in no other version of the biblical story is the necessity of cultivating the garden so emphatically asserted.[45] Shortly before they retire for the night in Book 4, for example, Adam informs Eve that labor is what distinguishes the human race from the animals. Whereas other creatures "all day long / Rove idle unimploid," he explains, "Man hath his daily work of body or mind / Appointed, which declares his Dignitie" (616–19). As we saw in Chapter 2, Milton's garden of Eden is distinguished from its predecessors by virtue of the fact that it will not remain perfect of its own accord; if the first pair stopped working, the surrounding wilderness would soon engulf them. In *Paradise Lost* as in *Candide,* "il faut cultiver notre jardin."

Adam and Eve's work in *Paradise Lost,* however, is not only physical but mental. They are required to cultivate both the material paradise around them and the moral paradise within them, and Milton renders their unfallen life in such a way that the two forms of labor are intimately related. For just as it was necessary for the first pair to lead the vine to "wed her Elm" (5.216), so Eve's untutored love must be directed toward Adam. Like the plants around her, her feelings do not grow in the right direction spontaneously; they require guidance. And by the same token, Adam's feelings do not automatically stop growing when they reach the limits of moderation; they have to be "lopped" (4.629) in order to prevent them from becoming "overgrown" (4.627).

Initially, these operations are performed by God or his surrogates—the voice in Book 4 which saves Eve from the "Fruitless imbraces"(5.215) of her own reflection, the angel in Book 8 who "prunes" Adam's intellectual and sensual aspirations—but once the limits have been defined it is man who is expected to undertake this moral horticulture. The idea of spontaneous self-discipline, so common in earlier treatments of Milton's theme, is totally foreign to *Paradise Lost* and indeed to all Milton's thinking: "Wherefore did [God] create passions within us, pleasures round about us," he asked, "but that these rightly temper'd are the very ingredients of virtue? . . . This justifies the high providence of God, who though he command us temperance, justice, continence, yet pours out before us even to a profuseness all desirable things, and gives us minds that can wander beyond all limit and satiety."[46] At the very heart of the poem's theodicy lies the concept of moral effort. Even in Eden, Milton insists, the life of virtue was necessarily hot and sweaty.[47]

When Adam and Eve eventually break the terms of their contract, they behave at first like runaway servants—they hide from their master and blame him for their disobedience. Adam, in particular, makes it sound as if he had been kidnapped by a "spirit" and forced to work against his will on God's plantation:

Did I sollicite thee
From darkness to promote me, or here place
In this delicious Garden? As my Will
Concurd not to my being, it were but right
And equal to reduce me to my dust,
Desirous to resigne, and render back
All I receiv'd, unable to perform
Thy terms too hard, by which I was to hold
The good I sought not.

(10.744-52)

In spite of the care with which the system of indentured labor has been purged of its most flagrant abuses—in Milton's definition of the human situation the master is benevolent and just, the servants are well fed and well lodged, the labor is strenuous but not backbreaking—a residue of uneasiness is still detectable in Adam's protest. He may admit that "then should have been refus'd / Those terms whatever, when they were propos'd" (10.756–57), but the lawyerly debating point cannot entirely dispose of the underlying objection. For when Adam was presented with the conditions of his contract, his existence was already a *fait accompli.* Like the convicted criminals who were beginning to be shipped to the New World in ever greater numbers, Eden's original colonist had only two choices: indenture or death.

That fixt mind (1.97)

The purpose of Columbus's second voyage, wrote Hernan Perez de Oliva in 1528, was "to give those strange lands the form of our own," and for the next two and a half centuries or so that is precisely what Europe endeavored to do.[48] With the exception of a few intellectuals such as More and Montaigne, the advocates and practitioners of colonialism assumed almost without question that the principal goal of settling America was to Europeanize it, to turn the New World into a replica of the Old by inscribing it with the languages, the social practices, and the ideologies of their own culture.

In particular, as we have seen, the colonists sought to transform the godless savages of the American wilderness into civilized members of the Christian family, "praying Indians" who wore European clothes, adopted European ways of living, and accepted European religious beliefs. "For lyke as rased or unpaynted tables, are apte to receaue what formes soo euer are fyrst drawne theron by the hande of the paynter," declared Peter Martyr in a famous simile, "euen soo these naked and simple people, doo soone receaue the customes of owre Religion, and by conuersation with owre men, shake off theyr fierce and natiue barbarousnes."[49]

But the process of assimilation could also work in the opposite, anti-colonial direction; much to the dismay of the promoters, the American "other" could, under certain circumstances, incorporate the European invader, either physically through the practice of cannibalism or culturally through admission to Indian society. Whether they were English or Spanish, missionaries or planters, Protestants or Catholics, newcomers to America were all vulnerable to this widely advertised threat to their European identity. According to John Brinsley, for instance, "manifold perils" awaited Christians in the New World, "especially of falling away from God to Sathan, and that themselves, or their posterity should become utterly savage, as they are."[50] So common was the phenomenon in early Virginia that Sir Thomas Dale was forced to impose quite extraordinarily ferocious penalties on those who "did runne away unto the Indyans."[51] In order to protect themselves from falling prey to the attractions of the native way of life, William Symonds suggested, the colonists should scrupulously avoid intermarriage with the indigenous population.[52] But marriage was not the only way in which the danger of "going native" presented itself. The Indian practice of "adopting" their prisoners could also lead to the wrong kind of assimilation, and according to Francis Jennings "it was a constant crying scandal that Europeans who were adopted by Indians frequently preferred to remain with their Indian 'families' when offered an opportunity to return to their genetic kinsmen."[53] For every "praying Indian" who had assumed the ways of the colonists there was at least one "white Indian" who had defected to the indigenous community and thus reversed the entire dynamic of the colonial enterprise.[54]

Travelers who were determined to resist this subversive form of cultural assimilation often took as their motto the famous tag from Horace's *Epistles—coelum non animum mutant qui trans mare currunt,* "those who cross the ocean change their sky but not their mind." While he was on his way home from the perilous environs of Catholic Italy Milton himself copied a version of it into the autograph album of Count Camillo Cerdogni in Geneva.[55] So when Satan declares in Book 1 of *Paradise Lost* that he has "a mind not to be chang'd by Place or Time" (253) he may well be echoing Horace's famous line and the cultural assumptions it embodied.[56] Certainly, of all the characters in *Paradise Lost* he seems to be the most impervious to assimilation by any "other":

> for within him Hell
> He brings, and round about him, nor from Hell
> One step no more than from himself can fly
> By change of place.
>
> (4.20–23)

Like the archetypal empire-builder that he is, the Devil is determined to give the New World the form of his own.

Yet at the same time Satan is the only colonial figure in the poem who even contemplates the possibility of submerging his identity in the native culture:

> League with you I seek,
> And mutual amity so strait, so close,
> That I with you must dwell, or you with me
> Henceforth.
>
> (4.375–78)

For a brief moment the "great adventurer" (10.440) has almost succumbed to the greatest single danger the New World had to pose, the loss of his colonial self. And shortly afterward he comes even closer to emulating the "white Indians" of Virginia and New England. In a scene that has not attracted as much critical attention as it deserves, he is completely transformed by Eve's appearance:

> her Heav'nly forme
> Angelic, but more soft, and Feminine,
> Her graceful Innocence, her every Aire
> Of gesture or lest action overawd
> His Malice and with rapine sweet bereav'd
> His fierceness of the fierce intent it brought:
> That space the Evil one abstracted stood
> From his own evil, and for the time remaind
> Stupidly good, . . .

(9.457–65)

The Devil is hovering on the brink of complete moral submersion in the innocent integrity of his prospective victim. But only for a moment. The "hot Hell that always in him burns" (9.467) quickly restores him to his true diabolic self, intent on stamping on Eve whatever belief he wishes to give her. As we shall see in the next chapter, it is the natives, not the colonists, who yield to the threat of assimilation in *Paradise Lost*.

4

The Colonized

Savagism elucidated human origins and explained contemporary peoples, who, by remaining attached to the simple existence of the primal age, failed to replicate the European mode of life, but it left open the nature of that presocial condition. Savages might be either noble or ignoble, either the guardians of pristine virtue or the agents of violent disorder.

—Bernard W. Sheehan, *Savagism and Civility: Indians and Englishmen in Colonial Virginia*

One of the most fundamental problems posed by the Discovery grew directly out of Milton's biblical source. According to the book of Genesis, Adam and Eve were the original ancestors of the entire human race, yet the New World was populated by men and women who were separated from the Old by a vast ocean, and who could not, it therefore appeared, have been descended from the first pair. As a result, the relationship of the American Indians to the men and women of Europe was deeply problematical. As John Rastell put it in 1520:

> But how the people first began
> In that country, or whence they came
> For clerks it is a question.[1]

The question did not go unanswered for long. In the same year one well-known "clerk," Paracelsus, hypothesized: "No one will easily believe that [the inhabitants of America] are of the posterity of Adam and Eve, for the sons of Adam by no means departed into out-of-the-way islands. It is most probable that they are descended from another Adam. For no one will easily prove that they are allied to us by flesh and blood."[2]

The implications of this theory were momentous. For if indeed the natives of the New World were the descendants of "another Adam," then it was entirely possible that in the newly discovered world across the Atlantic the forbidden fruit had remained untasted—in which case, of course, the Indians were still living in a state of unfallen innocence such as Adam and Eve had once enjoyed in the garden of Eden. According to Bartolomé de las Casas, for instance, the inhabitants of the Lucayo islands off the coast of Cuba were "so blessed among all Indians in gentleness, simplicity, humility and other natural virtues, it seems Adam's sin left them untouched."[3] Even a thoroughgoing sceptic such as John Donne was able to assert in 1598 that the natives of America lived:

> as though man there
> From Paradise so great a distance were,
> As yet the newes could not arrived bee
> Of Adam's tasting the forbidden tree.[4]

The population of the New World, it thus appeared, might well be exempt from the terrible consequences of the Fall.

Speculations of this kind were fueled by reports that the men and women of America wore no clothes and felt no shame. "All of both sexes go about naked," observed Amerigo Vespucci in his pamphlet *The New World*, "and just as they spring from their mothers' wombs so they go unto death."[5] Their physical nakedness, moreover, was only the outward sign of their inward purity, for according to such influential writers as Columbus's biographer, Peter Martyr, the Indians led lives of uncorrupted simplicity and virtue. "But emonge these simple sowles," he wrote, "a fewe clothes serue the naked: weightes and measures are not needefull to such as can not skyll of crafte and deceyte and haue not the use of pestiferous monye, . . . they seeme to lyue in that goulden worlde of the which owlde wryters speake so much: wherin men lyued simplye and innocentlye without enforcement of lawes, without quarellinge Judges and libelles, contente onely to satisfie nature."[6]

As Martyr's allusion to the classical myth of the golden age suggests, he may well have been recalling Ovid's description of the Age of Gold in Book I of the *Metamorphoses*:

> In the beginning was the Golden Age when men of their own accord,
> without the threat of punishment, without laws, maintained good
> faith and did what was right. There were no penalties to be afraid of
> . . . indeed there were no judges, men lived securely without them. . . .
> The peoples of the world, untroubled by any fears, enjoyed a leisurely
> and peaceful existence.[7]

Over and over again one can hear these words being echoed in Renaissance accounts of America. Pierre de Ronsard insisted in his
Complainte contre Fortune that the indigenous population of Nicholas
Durand de Villegagnon's colony in Brazil were "now living in their
golden age," blissfully ignorant of such words as "virtue" and "vice,"
"senate" and "king," free of "that terror of the law which makes us
live in fear."[8] Michel de Montaigne, who had conversed with some
native Brazilians through an interpreter, virtually paraphrased Ovid's
lines in his essay "On Cannibals," and Shakespeare in turn versified
John Florio's translation of Montaigne's tribute to American innocence in *The Tempest*.[9] If these accounts were to be believed, Adam
and Eve were alive and well and living in the terrestrial paradise on
the other side of the Atlantic.

From the very beginning, however, there was another side to the
image of *homo Americanus* as he appeared in the literature of the Discovery. For the difficulty of reconciling the existence of the American
Indians with the doctrine of the universal descent of the human race
from Adam and Eve could be solved, of course, in a second way: by
denying the Indians' humanity. This solution became increasingly
popular after it was first rumored and then confirmed that certain
tribes in the West Indies and South America habitually transgressed
one of the most deep-seated of all human taboos: they practiced cannibalism. In his letter to Luis de Santangel, Columbus stated that he
had heard of a tribe called the Caribes "who are regarded in all the islands as very fierce and who eat human flesh."[10] And Vespucci, whose
view of the Indians was consistently more negative than Columbus's,
claimed to have encountered the phenomenon at first hand: "They
eat one another, the victors the vanquished, and among other kinds
of meat, human flesh is a common article of diet with them. . . . I likewise saw salted human flesh suspended from beams between the

houses, just as with us it is the custom to hang bacon and pork."[11] Nor was this the only respect, Vespucci continued, in which the Indians' manner of living was "barbarous." They urinated wherever and whenever the mood took them, they freely practiced polygamy, sodomy, and incest, and they treated their sick with a callousness that would have been unthinkable in most European countries.

As the existence of such practices revealed, whatever else they were, the natives of America were clearly not Christians. Indeed, according to more than one writer, they were in league with Satan himself. In *Les Singularités de la France Antarctique autrement nomée Amérique* the Franciscan missionary, André Thevet, who had spent two months in the French colony in Brazil, reached the conclusion that the native inhabitants "were irredeemably given over to the Devil," and the association was reinforced by the anonymous Portuguese painter of a mid-sixteenth-century "Inferno" who depicted the ruler of Hell wearing a typical Indian headdress and a tunic made of feathers.[12]

Despite Pope Paul III's declaration in the bull *Sublimis Deus* of 1537 that "the Indians are truly men" and Francisco de Vitoria's elaborate demonstration of their humanity in his great treatise *De Indis* two years later, the belief that the natives of the New World were to all intents and purposes subhuman was still a powerful force when the great public debate on the nature of the Indians took place in Valladolid in 1550 under the auspices of the Emperor Charles V. On the one side, Juan Ginés de Sepúlveda, drawing on the observations of Gonzalo Fernández de Oviedo's *Historia general y natural de las Indias*, reaffirmed John Mair's thesis that the inhabitants of the New World conformed precisely to the Aristotelian definition of a natural slave. Weak in mind and strong in body, they were incapable of understanding the complexities of Christian theology or acquiring the refinements of European civility. The only role they were equipped to play in the economy of the New World was to labor for the Spaniards.[13]

On the other side, Bartolomé de las Casas vehemently insisted on the complete humanity of the so-called savages. In direct opposition to the theory broached by Paracelsus, he argued that "the Indians descend from Adam our father, and this suffices for us to respect the divine principle of charity toward them."[14] But in his efforts to refute

Sepúlveda's and Oviedo's characterizations of the native Americans as a nation of "lazy, idle, melancholy and cowardly, vile and ill-natured liars, with a short memory and no perseverance" Las Casas described the Indians in terms which reduced them to little more than docile children. Here, for instance, is his well-known account of human nature in the New World at the beginning of his *Brevíssima relación*:

> This infinite multitude of people was so created by God, as that they were without fraud, without subtilty or malice, to their natural Governours most faithful and obedient. Toward the Spaniards whom they serve, patient, meek and peaceful, and who laying all contentious and tumultuous thoughts aside, live without any hatred or desire of revenge; the people are most delicate and tender, enjoying such a feeble constitution of body as does not permit them to endure labour, so that the Children of Princes and great persons here, are not more nice and delicate then the Children of the meanest Countrey-man in that place. The Nation is very poor and indigent, possessing little, and by reason that they gape not after temporal goods, neither proud not ambitious. . . .
>
> They are of a very apprehensive and docible wit, and capable of all good learning, and very apt to receive our Religion, which when they have but once tasted, they are carryed on with a very ardent and zealous desire to make a further progress in it.

Indeed, the Indians contributed to their own exploitation, Las Casas wrote, "by being *toto genere* gentle and humble, extremely poor, defenseless, very simple and, above all, people long-suffering and patient," in short the ideal subjects for colonial exploitation.[15]

Both the positive and the negative images of the Indians permeate the colonial discourse of seventeenth-century England. To begin with the former, the benevolence of the native population was an essential element in the promotional literature accompanying the expeditions to Virginia in 1607 and 1609, for as Loren E. Pennington has remarked, "what person in his right mind could be induced to settle among savages who posed a continual threat to his life and property?"[16] In phrases that echoed Arthur Barlowe's influential account of a people "most gentle, loving and faithful, void of all guile and treason, and such as live after the manner of the golden age" Robert Johnson thus assured prospective emigrants that the inhabitants of Virginia were "generally very loving and gentle, and doe entertaine and relieve our people with great kindnesse." As late as 1655, Peter Heylyn was still informing his fellow countrymen that the Virginian Indians were "for the most part well enough disposed, if not roughly handled, hospitable and more civil than the rest of their Neighbours. So tractable and docile in matters of Religion, that liking well the Rites and Ceremonies of the English, at their first settling there, An. 1608, that they would use to say that King James was a good King, and his God a good God."[17]

The same general characteristics were attributed to the Indians of New England in the tracts that appeared in the 1620s and 1630s. According to Richard Eburne, the people of America were "exceeding tractable, very loving and kinde to our Nation above any other: industrious and ingenious to learne of us and practice with us most Arts and Sciences." Thomas Morton, writing in 1637, emphasized the Indians' intelligence, tractability, natural modesty, and temperance. "According to humane reason," he concluded, "guided onely by the light of nature, these people leade the more happy and freer life, being voyde of care, which torments the mindes of so many Christians."[18]

Even in the earliest English accounts of the New World, however, the negative image was equally strong. In the words of George Abbott, the archbishop of Canterbury, the first explorers found "the people naked, uncivill, some of them devourers of mens flesh, ignorant of shipping, without all kind of learning . . . never having heard of any such Religion as in other places of the world is knowne."[19] Still more to the point, the Spaniards' experience was repeated by the English colonists in North America, who encountered, in the words of Robert Gray, "brutish savages, which by reason of their godless ignorance and blasphemous Idolatrie, are worse than those beasts which are of a most wild and savage nature." For many Englishmen, the Virginia massacre of 1622, when three hundred forty-seven settlers were slaughtered by the native inhabitants, furnished conclusive proof that the Indians were barbarous and untrustworthy savages.

Captain John Smith, in particular, argued passionately that the colony must reverse its earlier conciliatory policy and either "beat the Salvages out of the Countrie" altogether or "bring them in that feare and subiection that euery man should follow their businesse securely." In much the same vein, Samuel Purchas declared in a work dedicated to Archbishop Abbott that by violating the natural law "the Barbarians" responsible for the massacre had proved themselves to be "a bad people, having little of Humanitie but shape, ignorant of Civilitie, of Arts, of Religion; more brutish than the beasts they hunt, more wild and unmanly then that unmanned wild Country, which they range rather then inhabite; captivated also to Satans tyranny in foolish pieties, mad impieties, wicked idlenesse, busie and bloudy wickednesse."[20]

Reinforced by such visual images as De Bry's representation of the Indians being persecuted by assorted demons (fig. 3), the association of "the savages" with the Devil persisted in English descriptions both of Virginia and of New England throughout the colonial period, usually as a justification for the work of conversion. Paradoxically, the argument used by Las Casas to uphold the human dignity of the Indians, namely that they could and should be converted, generated in the English colonies a profoundly negative portrayal of the native Americans as "the bondslaves of Sathan"[21] who "have ever sate in hellish darknesse, adoring the Divell himself for their God."[22] It was the manifest duty of Christians "to bring those infidell people from the worship of Divels to the service of God," Robert Johnson advised the Virginia colonists, and his sentiments were echoed repeatedly by such writers as Alexander Whitaker and Patrick Copland.[23]

By far the most powerful and coherent image of the American heathen as the servants of the Devil, however, emerged in the missionary literature produced in New England by John Eliot, Henry Whitfield, Thomas Shepard, and Edward Winslow during the 1640s and 1650s. For in order to justify their activities to their financial sponsors back in London, the New England missionaries consistently portrayed the "poor Indians" in terms that recalled Samuel Purchas's *Pilgrimes* rather than Arthur Barlowe's *First Voyage*.[24] In petitioning Parliament for the establishment of the Society for the Propagation of the Gospel in America, William Castell had urged his fellow coun-

FIGURE 3. "Devils Persecuting the Indians" from Theodore de Bry, *America, Tertia Pars* (Frankfurt, 1592). Reproduced by permission of the Huntington Library, San Marino, California.

trymen to bring salvation to "the immortall soules of innumerable men, who still sit in darkness, and in the shadow of death, continually assaulted and devoured by the Dragon, whose greatest delight is to bring others with himselfe into the same irrecoverable gulfe of perdition," and his vision of the Indians' predicament pervades the tracts produced by those who responded to his call. Trapped in "the snares of the Devill," the native inhabitants of New England may have descended from the first man, but they were only "the dregs and refuse of Adam's lost posterity." As John Eliot explained to a potential convert who had enquired whether the colonists and the natives were related to each other, although "it was true that at first wee had all one father . . . hee had divers children, some bad and some good." Unfortunately for them, the Indians derived from the former; their "forefathers were stubborne and rebellious children, and would not heare the word, did not care to pray nor to teach their children, and hence Indians that now are, do not know God at all." The population of the New World, the apostle to the Indians concluded, had inherited "a grievous and fearefull curse . . . for some great sinnes of their Ancestors."[25] In the eyes of the English missionaries, the inhabitants of America were thus doubly handicapped. In addition to the hereditary guilt of original sin shared by all the descendants of Adam and Eve, they had been further corrupted by a second Fall which, together with their geographical isolation, cut them off completely from the knowledge of God.

The long-standing debate over the status of the Indians thus generated a wide variety of theories concerning the nature of the human species in its original uncivilized condition. These theories furnished Milton with an invaluable set of metaphorical and conceptual tools with which to explore and represent the moral experience not only of Adam and Eve but of their tempter as well.

This new happie Race of Men (3.679)

As the first human occupants of the New World in *Paradise Lost*, Adam and Eve are the most obvious counterparts of the Indians. Shortly after they have eaten the forbidden fruit, indeed, Milton directly compares the fallen pair with the Taino of Hispaniola:

> Such of late
> Columbus found th'American so girt
> With featherd Cincture, naked else and wilde
> Among the Trees on Isles and woodie Shores.
> (9.1115–18)

But long before this simile has made the connection explicit, the poem has invited us to see in Adam and Eve a clear reflection of the first explorers' descriptions of the native Americans. As I pointed out earlier, the scene in Book 5 in which Raphael is welcomed by a naked man and woman as a visitor from Heaven replicates the primal encounter between the inhabitants of the Old World and those of the New. And from that point on, virtually all the correspondences that led the chroniclers of the Discovery to associate the Indians with Adam and Eve are neatly reversed with the result that Milton's description of the first pair living in their prelapsarian paradise constantly evokes the memory of their American counterparts as they appear in the colonial discourse of the sixteenth and seventeenth centuries.

But which American counterparts? As we have just seen, there were at least four quite different images of the Indians to choose from: the naked innocents who "lived after the manner of the golden age," the contemporary exemplars of Aristotle's theory of natural slavery, the obedient children eager for instruction from the Spanish missionaries, and the demonic savages who slaughtered the English settlers at Jamestown. Obviously the second and fourth of these were fundamentally incompatible with Milton's theme, though to judge from his scattered comments on the subject in his prose works, the poet's view of the Indians corresponded rather closely to the opinions of Samuel Purchas and Edward Waterhouse. In the *Second Defense*, for example, he described the inhabitants of the New World as the "dullest of mortals" living in a condition of "barbarism" so vile that they worshipped "malignant demons," and in *Prolusion* 1 he claimed that they offered sacrifices to the sun "with incense and with other ceremonial."[26]

For rather different reasons, the first of the images listed above was not a viable option either, for as we saw in the preceding chapter Milton believed passionately in the dignity and worth of labor in the unfallen as well as in the fallen world. Even if it had not been totally discredited by bitter experience both in Virginia and in New England, the classical fantasy of a golden age of blissful leisure would have had few attractions for him. Only the third possibility, Las Casas's and Vitoria's description of the Indians as submissive and vulnerable children, still at the bottom of the evolutionary ladder, remained open. It was this account of primitive man, I now want to argue, that provided Milton with the overall conceptual framework within which he worked out his unique interpretation of prelapsarian human nature.

As Anthony Pagden has shown in *The Fall of Natural Man*, his magisterial study of the great debate that took place in sixteenth-century Spain over the status of the Indians, the basis of Las Casas's and Vitoria's arguments against the theory of natural slavery was the Thomist notion of "the age of natural law," the period before the Flood when the human race lived in harmonious conformity with the fundamental laws of nature but had not yet acquired, to any significant degree, the arts of civilization or the insights of revealed religion.[27] More specifically, the age of natural law was an age of guilt-free sexuality, communal ownership, social equality, and vegetarian diet, all of which were thought at one time or another to be characteristic features of Indian society. In Montaigne's classic formulation, "those people are wild just as we call wild that fruit produced by nature itself . . . they have been fashioned very little by the human mind and are still very close to their original natural state. The laws of nature still hold sway over them, scarcely corrupted by ours. . . . They are still at the happy point of wanting only what their natural needs require. Anything beyond that is superfluous for them."[28]

These words could also serve as a description of Adam and Eve's unfallen condition in *Paradise Lost*. Most obviously, their nakedness, like that of the Indians, reflects the "simplicitie and spotless innocence" (4.318) of natural man: "Nor those mysterious parts were then conceald, / Then was not guiltie shame: dishonest shame / Of natures works" (4.312–14). Like the garden they inhabit, where the flowers are ruled by "Nature boon" rather than "nice Art" (4.241–42), Milton's Adam and Eve are guided by "the light of nature," as Thomas Morton called it, wholly uncontaminated by the pretentious trappings of European civilization.[29] The concept of private property is as alien to them as it was believed to be to the native Americans. Married love, Milton tells us, is "sole proprietie / In Paradise of all things common else" (4.751–52). They make their home not in a palace but a "sylvan lodge" (5.377) whose "verdant wall" and "roofe / Of thickest covert" (4.692–97) are reminiscent of the Indian "arbors" described by Thomas Hariot, John Smith and others.[30] Their dinner is not a "marshalld Feast / Serv'd up in Hall with Sewers, and Seneshals" (9.37–38) but the kind of vegetarian meal that Columbus and Palacios Rubios attributed to the Indians: "savorie pulp" (4.335) scooped out of the garden's "Nectarine fruits" (4.332) and water from the "brimming stream" (4.336) that irrigates it.[31] And when Adam sets out to greet Raphael he:

> walks forth, without more train
> Accompani'd than with his own complete
> Perfections; in himself was all his state,
> More solemn then the tedious pomp that waits
> On Princes, when thir rich Retinue long
> Of Horses led, and Grooms besmear'd with Gold
> Dazzles the crowd, and sets them all agape.
>
> (5.351–57)

The only area of prelapsarian life that owes anything to "the skill of Artifice" (9.39) is the task of cultivating the garden. As Eve goes off to work with her "Gard'ning Tools as Art yet rude . . . had formd" (9.391–92) she has evidently reached the same stage of technological development as the Indian women in William Wood's *New Englands Prospect* who till the earth "with their clamshell hoes as if it were a garden."[32] The exception, however, is extremely significant, for it indicates that Adam and Eve share what for Las Casas and Vitoria was the most significant single attribute of the American Indians: their capacity to learn. In his great treatise *De Indis* the latter had argued that in the state of nature the inhabitants of the New World were, to all intents and purposes, grown-up children whose rational faculties, though complete, were "still potential rather than actual."[33] That they could become actual was demonstrated by the Indians' ability to manufacture such tools as clamshell hoes. All they required to become fully developed members of the civilized Christian community was prolonged and patient instruction by their Spanish masters. "Since uncultivated soil produces only thistle and thorns but possesses the innate goodness to yield useful fruit if it is cultivated," wrote Las Casas, "so all manner of men, however barbaric or bestial, possess the use of reason and are capable of being taught. Consequently no man and no nation in the world, however barbarian or inhuman, is incapable of bearing the reasonable fruit of excellence, if taught in the manner required for the natural condition of man, especially with the doctrine of the Faith."[34] With the right education, the Indians were capable of becoming Europeans.

English advocates of transatlantic evangelism were even more optimistic about the Indians' capacity for cultural progress. Not only were the inhabitants of the New World "industrious and ingenious to learn of us and practice with us most arts and sciences," wrote Richard Eburne; they were "very ready to leave their old and blinde Idolatries, and to learne of us the right service and worship of the true God."[35] In John Eliot's words some years later, the questions posed by his potential converts revealed that "their soules be in a searching condition after the great points of Religion and Salvation."[36]

Almost from the moment of his creation, Adam's soul, too, is "in a searching condition." His very first sentence is a question—"Thou Sun . . . Tell, if ye saw, how came I thus, how here?" (8.273–77)—and his appetite for instruction is so great that three of the first eight books of the poem are taken up by Raphael's attempt to satisfy his interlocutor's "desire to know" (7.61). As I suggested in Chapter 3, their dialogue replicates, albeit on a vastly expanded scale, the kind of conversation John Eliot claimed to have had with his Indian parishioners in New England. Adam's questions may be far more sophisticated, and Raphael's answers far more elaborate, but the intellectual dynamic is essentially the same. In the state of nature, the human mind has an almost insatiable hunger for knowledge.

One of the first lessons that Adam learns from his divine instructor is that he and Eve are destined to undergo the only fate that even relatively enlightened colonial theorists such as Vitoria and Las Casas were able to imagine for the native Americans: assimilation. For both writers, the whole purpose of the educative mission was to "civilize" the Indians, to turn them into Europeans, and the same is true of the English missionaries in New England. As James Axtell has observed, "conversion was tantamount to a complete transformation of cultural identity. To convert the Indians of America was to replace their native characters with European personae."[37] By the same token, the transformation of the colonized into living facsimiles of the colonizers defines the very essence of Adam and Eve's situation as Raphael describes it to his eager student in Book 5 of *Paradise Lost*. Provided that they accept the authority of their colonial overlord and faithfully follow his instructions, the unfallen pair will eventually assume the form of their heavenly visitor; their bodies, Raphael tells them:

> may at last turn all to Spirit,
> Improv'd by tract of time, and wingd ascend
> Ethereal as wee, or may at choice
> Here or in Heav'nly Paradises dwell;
> If ye be found obedient.
>
> (497–501; see also 7.153–61)

Just as the Indians of Noonanetum in New England adopted such handsome "English apparell" that "you would scarce know them from English people,"[38] so the natives of Eden will one day become indistinguishable from God's colonial emissary as the colony itself is absorbed into the homeland, "One Kingdom, Joy and Union without end" (7.161).

Thanks to the Fall, of course, Adam and Eve never experience the colonial *summum bonum*, at least not the kind that Raphael defines. In their dealings with the "great adventurer" (10.440) from Hell, on the other hand, they yield completely to the assimilative process. As soon as she has eaten the forbidden fruit, for example, Eve begins to think and talk exactly like the Devil. The God whose bounty she had celebrated in Book 5 suddenly becomes "Our great Forbidder, safe with all his Spies / About him" (9.815–16) and the divinely ordained hierarchy of husband and wife she had accepted in Book 4 now seems to her oppressive in light of the characteristically Satanic doctrine that no one who is "inferior" can be "free" (9.825). Adam's transformation is equally dramatic. In order to reassure his wife that her decision will not bring about their destruction, he actually makes up a short speech for the "Adversary" (9.947) that has an authentically diabolic ring to it: "Fickle their State whom God / Most Favors, who can please him long? Mee first / He ruin'd, now Mankind; whom will he next?" (9.948–50). And as he contemplates a future of eternal sinfulness in Book 10 he explicitly associates himself with the cause of his predicament: "To Satan only like both crime and doom" (10.841).

But in fact Adam and Eve's assimilation is only partial. The Fall may prevent them from evolving into spiritual citizens of the heavenly empire but it does not render them wholly demonic. They degenerate, rather, into the kind of beings that Oviedo and Sepúlveda had described in their attempts to apply Aristotle's theory of natural slavery to the American Indians. The principal characteristic of all natural slaves, according to this theory, was their failure to achieve rational mastery over their physical passions, and this, Oviedo and Sepúlveda argued, was the distinguishing feature of the primitive inhabitants of the New World. Like animals, they were completely at the mercy of their bodily appetites, and as a result they were totally incapable of making the kind of spiritual, intellectual, and material progress that Las Casas and Vitoria envisaged for them. As the Spanish jurist Juan de Matienzo put it, the Indians were "participants in reason so as to sense it, but not to possess or follow it. In this they are no different from the animals (although animals do not even sense reason) for they are ruled by their passions."[39] This is precisely the condition into which Adam and Eve precipitate themselves when they eat the forbidden fruit. As Michael explains to Adam shortly before expelling him from the garden of Eden:

> Since thy original lapse, true Libertie
> Is lost, which alwayes with right Reason dwells
> Twinn'd, and from her hath no dividual being:
> Reason in man obscur'd, or not obeyd,
> Immediately inordinate desires
> And upstart Passions catch the Government
> From Reason, and to *servitude* reduce
> Man till then free.
>
> (12.83–90, my italics)

In terms of the protracted debate that was carried on in sixteenth-century Spain concerning the nature of the Indians, Adam and Eve have transformed themselves from potential Europeans into American savages, from nature's children into natural slaves.

In this context it is surely no accident that Milton's explicit association of the first pair with the "wilde" (9.1117) Indians discovered by

Columbus takes place immediately after the Fall. For as his comments in the *Second Defense* and *Prolusion* 1 make clear, Milton himself did not subscribe to the theory that the recently discovered inhabitants of the New World were exempt from the effects of the Fall. The only human beings to have really lived in the condition attributed to the Indians by Vitoria and Las Casas were the first man and woman before they ate the forbidden fruit. So although Adam and Eve mimic the Taino by greeting their visitor from Heaven in a state of naked innocence in Book 5, Milton rewrites Columbus's account of the incident here in Book 9 by clothing "th'American" with a "feath-erd Cincture." The "naked Glorie" (9.1115) of prelapsarian humanity, Milton implies, has been lost on both sides of the Atlantic.

Now that they have fallen, then, Adam and Eve proceed to replicate not an intellectual construct but what Milton probably believed was the actual behavior of the American Indians. Like the uncivilized barbarians who haunt the pages of Oviedo's *Historia*, they worship trees instead of God (9.795–810), they become "intoxicated" with the fruit they have eaten (9.1008–11), they make love wherever and whenever the mood takes them (9.1011–45), they yearn to live "savage, in some glade / Obscur'd, where highest Woods impenetrable / To Starr or Sun-light, spread their umbrage broad" (9.1085–87), they wear "Skins of Beasts" (10.217) to cover up their nakedness, they learn to make fire "by collision of two bodies (10.1072), and they finally abandon their permanent residence for a life of endless "wandring" (12.648). In short, they become savages.[40]

The convergence of biblical and colonial images that seems to me to be taking place with particular intensity at this point of Milton's text has its iconic parallel in a remarkable engraving which Theodore de Bry used as the frontispiece for his great edition of Hariot's *Briefe and true report* in 1590. For there, at the beginning of the book that made Hariot's treatise and John White's watercolors of the Virginian Indians famous all over Europe, is a representation of the temptation and fall of Adam and Eve (fig. 4). In the foreground, two classically posed nude figures are just about to pluck the apple, urged on by the traditional human-headed serpent. In the background, a crudely clothed Adam tills the ground on one side while, on the other, his wife nurses a baby in what appears to be

FIGURE 4. "The Fall of Adam and Eve" from Theodore de Bry, *America, Prima Pars* (Frankfurt, 1590). Reproduced by permission of the Huntington Library, San Marino, California.

a primitive lean-to shelter. In the context of Hariot's narrative and White's paintings, the implication is clear enough, but De Bry makes it explicit in his preface to the reader:

> Although (frendlye Reader) man by his disobedience, weare deprived of those good Gifts where with he was indued in his creation, yet he was not berefte of wit to prouyde for hym selfe, nor discretion to devise things necessarie for his use, except such as appartayne to his soules healthe, as may be gathered by this savage nations, of whome this present worke intreateth.[41]

The condition into which Adam and Eve fell through their disobedience is the condition in which the natives of Virginia, untouched by European civilization, still exist. The "savage nations" of America are an image of unredeemed postlapsarian man, and vice versa.

Just as De Bry's Indians still have sufficient "wit" to provide for themselves, however, so Milton's Adam and Eve still retain their essential human attributes; in their fallen state they may resemble natural slaves, but they have not descended as low as the fourth of the descriptive categories I mentioned earlier. As we shall see in the next section, it is Satan who embodies the demonic aspect of "th' American . . . wilde / Among the Trees."

Alienate from God (5.877)

In the summer of 1608, Captain John Smith and twelve of his men came under attack by a group of Indians from the Hassinunga tribe. During the course of the skirmish the colonists managed to capture one of their attackers, and when the fighting was over they asked their prisoner why he and his companions "came in that manner to betray vs, that came to them in peace, and to seeke their loues; he answered, they heard we were a people come from vnder the world, to take their world from them." In January of the next year Powhatan himself informed Smith that he had heard the colonists' purpose was "to invade my people and possesse my Country." And shortly afterward an Indian orator called Okanindge announced that "we perceiue and well know you intend to destroy vs that are here . . . and to enioy our houses and plant our fields, of whose fruit you shall participate."[42] From the very beginning, it appears, the natives of Virginia correctly perceived the English as an imminent threat to their lives and property.

As we saw in Chapter 3, the intentions which the Chesapeake Indians attributed to the colonists correspond precisely to Satan's motives for bringing about Adam and Eve's expulsion from the garden of Eden in *Paradise Lost*. He too has come "from under the world" to "destroy" its inhabitants and "possess" their country. In the words of his spokesman, Beelzebub, the purpose of the Devil's expedition is "either with Hell fire / To waste his whole Creation, or possess / All as our own" (2.364–66). Characteristically, however, the poem does not allow us to rest in this straightforward equivalence without immediately complicating it with a second and very different homology. For it is not, as we might have expected, Adam, the native occupant of Eden, who voices the fear that a new race of beings has appeared on the scene to take his world from him; it is Satan, the invader himself.

In order to understand this extraordinary reversal, we need to consider for a moment the events that preceded Satan's voyage of discovery. Shortly after the Devil's unsuccessful rebellion, God had declared his intention to replace the fallen angels with the progeny of Adam and Eve:

> But lest his heart exalt him in the harme
> Already done, to have dispeopl'd Heav'n
> My damage fondly deem'd, I can repaire
> That detriment, if such it be to lose
> Self-lost, and in a moment will create
> Another World, out of one man a Race
> Of men innumerable, there to dwell,
> Not here, till by degrees of merit rais'd
> They open to themselves at length the way
> Up hither.
>
> (7.150–56)

Long before Milton began work on his epic, this traditional motive for the creation of the human race[43] had been given a distinctively colonial slant by Samuel Purchas, who began his defence of the English plantation in Virginia by citing two examples of divinely sanctioned territorial conquest, the Jewish occupation of the Holy Land and the Christian occupation of Satan's seat in the heavenly kingdom. Just as "the Israelites entred upon the houses, Cities and possessions of the cursed Canaanites," he argued, "so Christians [will enter] into those Thrones and celestiall Dominions, which those spirituall Thrones and Dominions lost."[44] Now, as we saw in Chapter 1, in English promotional literature the dispossession of the Canaanites was the standard biblical precedent for the forcible settlement of North America. The parallel between that event and the great migration that will take place after the day of judgement turns God's plan to repopulate Heaven with human beings into an essentially colonial strategy. In Purchas's view, Satan and his angels are the Indians, Adam and Eve and their descendants the colonists, who will one day occupy the displaced natives' "houses, Cities, and possessions."

Exiled from their "native seat" (1.634) in Heaven, the Devil and his followers can thus be cast by Milton in the role of the dispossessed Indians eager to avenge themselves on the newcomers who have been "by our exile / Made happie" (10.484–85). Far from being the destructive invader who evidently haunted the minds of the Chesapeake Indians, Satan consequently presents himself in Book 9 as a fellow victim of colonial aggression, and it is he rather than Adam who voices the fear that a new race of beings has arrived to "possess my country":

> hee to be aveng'd,
> And to repair his numbers thus impair'd, . . .
> Determin'd to advance into our room
> A Creature form'd of Earth, and him endow,
> Exalted from so base original,
> With Heav'nly spoils, our spoils.
>
> (9.143–51)

This is the first time in the poem that Satan defines his mission as a preemptive strike against a potential rival. Earlier in the story, when he was playing the part of the heroic *conquistador*, the creation of the

human race was totally unrelated to the rebel angels' expulsion from
Heaven. In Book I the Devil mentions a rumour that God would create a new race: "whom his choice regard / Should *favor equal* to the
Sons of Heaven" (1.653–54, my italics). In Book 2 Beelzebub goes
one stage further, claiming that "prophetic fame in Heav'n" had pre-
dicted:

> some new Race call'd Man, about this time
> To be created like to us, though less
> In power and excellence, but *favour'd more*
> Of him who rules above."
>
> (2.346–51, my italics)

In neither case, however, does God's decision have any direct connection with the war in Heaven and its aftermath. Not until Satan
meets Sin and Death at the gates of Hell is the creation of the human
race represented as the direct result of the devils' expulsion, and
then only tentatively. God has placed "a race of upstart Creatures" in
the "Pourlieues of Heav'n," Satan tells his daughter, "to supply / *Perhaps* our vacant room" (2.833–35, my italics). But as the Luciferan
warrior of Isaiah gives way in Book 4 to the Satanic tempter of Genesis, the Devil's transformation is signaled by a drastic shift in his perception of cosmic history and of his place in it. "O Hell!" he cries
when he first sees Adam and Eve: "what do mine eyes with grief be-
hold, / Into our room of bliss thus high advanc't / Creatures of
other mould" (4.358–60). The colonizing aggressor becomes a colonized victim and the innocent Indians he had planned to subjugate
are transformed into usurping colonists who must at all costs be prevented from occupying his "room."[45] The tempter's goal in Milton's
epic is fundamentally the same as Powhatan's in Virginia.

So too are the strategies he employs. According to John Smith, in
their campaign to regain control over their lands the Indians rarely
confronted the colonists directly, preferring to make use of "Strat-
egems, trecheries, or surprisals."[46] In doing so they conformed precisely to the prevailing image of the native American in English
colonial discourse, for as Karen Kupperman has observed, "of all the
accusations made against the Indian, the most universal and perhaps

the most serious was that he was treacherous."[47] In William Morrell's words:

> Those well seen Natives in grave Natures Hests,
> All close designes conceale in their deep brests:
>
> . . .
>
> Their well advised talke evenly conveyes
> Their acts to their intents, and nere displayes
> Their secret projects, by high words or light,
> Till they conclude their end by fraud or might.[48]

The most obvious example of Indian duplicity, of course, was Opechancanough's assault on the Jamestown colony in 1622. The "devilish murder" of the settlers, Smith explains, was accomplished not so much by force of arms as by "the treachery of those people." Feigning friendship for the colonists, the native "hellhounds" took advantage of the trusting English whom "they found so carelessly secure, that they were not prouided to defend themselues against any enemy, being so dispersed as they were."[49]

In much the same way, Satan, having failed to achieve his ends by open warfare, decides "To work in close design, by fraud or guile" rather than by "force" (1.646–47) in his campaign against the "Eternal Empire" (7.96). Skulking in the backwoods and undergrowth, he stalks his prey like an Indian hunter, who, according to John Smith:

> useth the skinne of a Deere slit on the one side, and so put on his arme, through the neck, so that his hand comes to the head, which is stuffed, and the hornes, head, eyes, eares, and every part as artificially counterfeited as they can devise. Thus shrowding his body in the skinne, by stalking, he approacheth the Deere, creeping on the ground from one tree to another. If the Deere chance to find fault, or stand at gaze, he turneth the head with his hand to his best advantage to seeme like a Deere, also gazing and licking himselfe. So watching his best advantage to approach, having shot him, he chaseth him by his bloud and straine till he get him."[50]

Disguising himself first as a lion, then as a tiger, then as a toad, and finally, of course, as a serpent, the Devil makes his assault when

Adam and Eve are so "carelessly secure" that they, too, are "dispersed."[51] And while Satan's speeches of persuasion during the temptation itself were largely dictated by the text of Genesis, it would be hard to improve on Christopher Levett's warning against Indian cunning as a description of the Devil's non-biblical effort to ingratiate himself with his potential victim before they even arrive at the forbidden tree. "They will quickly find any man's disposition," Levett wrote, "and flatter and humour him strangely if they hope to get anything of him."[52] In the context of English colonial discourse, the proverbial cunning and subtlety of the serpent takes on a distinctly contemporary overtone.

The resemblances between Satan and the Indians, moreover, extend to his followers and progeny as well. One of the most popular theories concerning the identity of the men and women of the New World was the notion first proposed by José d'Acosta that they were Tartars who had made their way to the North American continent by means of an ice bridge across the Bering straits. "Whence these Indians came here to inhabit is not certaine," wrote John Wilson in 1647, but "his reasons are most probable who thinke they are Tartars passing out of Asia into America by the straits of Anian, who being spilt by some revenging hand of God upon this continent like water upon the ground are spread as farre as these Atlanticke shores."[53] Milton's similes suggest that the fallen angels, too, are closely related to the Tartars. As he approaches Eden, Satan looks like "a vulture on Imaus bred, / Whose snowie ridge the roving Tartar bounds"[54] (3.431–32) and when he returns to Hell after seducing Adam and Eve he finds the outskirts of his kingdom deserted "As when the Tartar from his Russian Foe / By Astracan over the Snowie Plaines / Retires" (10.431–33).

Now for Milton, as for most of his contemporaries, the Tartars were the very epitome of barbarism, the nation that had produced the ferocious Jingis Khan and Tamburlaine, the nation which Richard Hakluyt had described as "rather Monsters then men, thirsting and drinking bloud, tearing and devouring the flesh of Dogges and Man."[55] If Satan and his followers are comparable to these savage ancestors of the American Indians, then they too might be expected to behave like bestial predators, governed not by their reason but by their bodily appetites. And so indeed they do. When Sin and Death have crossed the "Bridge / Of length prodigious" (10.301–2) that joins earth to Hell, they greedily anticipate the prospect of "drinking bloud" and "tearing and devouring the flesh" of animals and men. In reply to her son's demand for "ravin" to "stuff this Maw" (10.599–601) Sin urges him to glut himself on the inhabitants of Eden:

> Thou therefore on these Herbs, and Fruits, and Flours
> Feed first, on each Beast next, and Fish, and Fowl,
> . . . devour unspar'd
> Till I in Man residing through the Race,
> His thoughts, his looks, words, actions all infect,
> And season him thy last and sweetest prey.
>
> (10.603–9)

In *Paradise Lost* as in most Renaissance histories of America, the New World was invaded soon after its creation by a race of cannibalistic monsters.

Satan himself is not represented in quite such bloodthirsty terms, but he is no less susceptible than his wife and child to the forces of unreason. While he was delivering his first soliloquy in Book 4:

> each passion dimm'd his face,
> Thrice chang, d with pale, ire, envie, and despair,
> Which marr'd his borrow'd visage.
>
> (4.114–16)

And the same "distempers foule" (4.118) continue to afflict him throughout his stay in the garden of Eden. Arrested by Zephon, he is "overcome with rage" (4.857), challenged by Gabriel he "wax[es] more in rage" (4.969), and confronted by the beauties of the new world he can only pour his "bursting passion" (9.98) into an expression of spite and envy. Despite his repeated assertions of personal liberty, Satan's behavior in the garden of Eden makes it clear that he is totally at the mercy of his bestial passions.

Which brings me to the second of the two points I mentioned earlier: the Devil's relationship to his immediate environment. One of the most puzzling features of the Indians' life, as the early explorers and settlers first perceived it, was their apparent inability to take advantage of America's extraordinary natural bounty. In William Cronon's words, "how could the land be so rich and its people so poor?"[56] Thomas Morton replied that the problem lay in the eye of the beholder. If English travelers were surprised that "the natives of the land lived so poorly, in so rich a Country" it was only because they judged what they saw by the corrupt standards of the Old World and consequently failed to realize that the Indians "are supplied with all manner of needfull things."[57] The more common solution to the riddle, however, was to argue that the natives' savage condition prevented them from exploiting the region's natural advantages. James Rosier, for example, reported that he and his companions had come upon:

> a River, which the All-creating God, with his most liberall hand, hath made above report notable with his foresaid blessings, bordered with a land, whose pleasant fertility bewraieth it selfe to be the garden of nature, wherin she only intended to delight hir selfe, having hitherto obscured it to any, except to a purblind generation, whose understanding it hath pleased God so to darken, as they can neither discerne, use, or rightly esteeme the unvaluable riches in middest whereof they live sensually content with the barke and outward rinds.[58]

The barbarism of America's inhabitants had blinded them to the potential wealth of their native land.

In *Paradise Lost*, Satan is equally alienated from the "Terrestrial Heav'n" (9.103) he sees around him. What prevents him from taking any "delight" in it, however, is not his failure to "discerne" or "rightly esteem" its "riches"—he is only too well aware of the beauty and fertility of God's handiwork—but his inability to take pleasure in any manifestation of divine goodness:

> With what delight could I have walkt thee round,
> If I could joy in aught, sweet interchange
> Of Hill and Vallie, Rivers, Woods and Plaines,
> Now Land, now Sea, and Shores with Forest crown'd,
> Rocks, Dens, and Caves; but I in none of these
> Find place or refuge; and the more I see

Pleasures about me, so much more I feel
Torment within me, as from the hateful siege
Of contraries; all good to me becomes
Bane. . . .

                    (9.114–23)

In the case of the Devil, the radical disjunction between the "garden of Nature" and the "purblind" sensibility that observes it is moral rather than intellectual. The primitive ignorance of the American savage, unaware of the "unvaluable riches" of his native environment, has given way to the terrible spiritual perversity of those who are "alienate from God" (5.877).

5

The Narrator

> I have beene carefull to report nothing of New-England but what
> I have partly seene with mine owne Eyes, and partly heard and en-
> quired from the Mouthes of verie honest and religious persons,
> who by living in the Countrey a good space of time have had ex-
> perience and knowledge of the state thereof, and whose testi-
> monies I doe beleeve as my selfe.
>   —Francis Higginson, *New-Englands Plantation*

If *Paradise Lost* is as deeply imprinted with the thematics of colonialism as I have suggested in the preceding chapters, it would be
surprising if the poem's narrator did not also speak in the characteristic accents of European colonial literature.[1] For Milton is engaged
in essentially the same project as writers like John Frampton (*Joyfull
newes oute of the newe founde worlde*), Alexander Whitaker (*Good Newes
From Virginia*), Edward Winslow (*Good News from New-England*), John
Underhill (*Newes from America*), and John Clarke (*Ill Newes from New-
England*). He is bringing back "news" from a world his readers have
never seen. Just as Jean de Léry claims that he is going to speak "of
things that it is very probable that no one before has ever seen, much
less written about," Milton announces, in plain defiance of literary
history, that his song will pursue "Things unattempted yet in Prose or
Rime" (1.16), things which until now have remained "invisible to
mortal sight" (3.55).[2]

With the notable exception of Anthony Pagden's comprehensive
study, *European Encounters with the New World*, recent discussions of the
way in which America was represented in the literature of Europe
have focused mainly upon the linguistic aspects of the subject.[3] My
emphasis here will be rather different, for like Pagden I am more interested in the various cognitive and narrative strategies deployed by

the chroniclers of the Discovery and its aftermath. In this concluding chapter I will argue that Milton's great "organ voice" is not a single euphonious instrument but a chorus of individual and sometimes discordant voices which echo the complex acoustics of Renaissance colonial discourse.

Hesperian Fables true (4.250)

The first task facing any seventeenth-century writer who attempted to describe England's American colonies in print was to overcome a significant degree of skepticism in the mind of the contemporary reading public. As a genre, of course, travelers' tales had always been notoriously unreliable—in the words of a popular Renaissance proverb, travelers could "lie by authority because none can control them"[4]—but in the case of the New World there was a second factor at work. For in their attempts to persuade their monarch and their fellow countrymen to look favorably on the colonial enterprise, the early advocates of the Virginian plantation in particular had often crossed the line separating fact from fiction. As David Cressy has remarked, early reports of transatlantic voyages, "often written to gain funding for future expeditions, presented America as a land of plenty and of immeasurable promise. The stony reality was often obscured in these first flickerings of the American dream."[5]

Arthur Barlowe's account of the 1584 expedition to Roanoke is a classic case in point. In phrases which eventually found their way into Michael Drayton's ode "To the Virginian Voyage," Barlowe assured his enthusiastic patron that Virginia was a land "of incredible abundance." The soil was "the most plentiful, sweet, fruitful and wholesome of all the world," which produced "all things in abundance, as in the first creation, without toile or labor." And as to the native Americans, "a more kind and loving people" could not be found on the face of the earth.[6] But when a small group of would-be colonists under the command of Sir Richard Grenville attempted to establish a settlement in Virginia in 1585, it soon discovered that Roanoke island was no garden of Eden. Food was hard to grow in any significant quantity, and the local inhabitants showed every sign of being suspicious if not actively hostile. After running short of the former and alienating the latter, the settlers sailed back to England with Sir Francis Drake in July of 1586 leaving behind them a handful of men who were never heard from again. The expedition of 1587, which culminated in the famous lost colony, was no less disastrous, and even when a permanent settlement was finally established in Jamestown in 1607 the Utopian vision still stubbornly refused to come true. The land which Drayton hailed in his ode as "earth's only paradise" was in reality a harsh and savage wilderness. Far from producing harvests "without your toil," as he naively imagined, it demanded intense and skillful cultivation. By the first decades of the seventeenth century the optimistic fantasies of the early promoters had vanished in the mists of the Atlantic.

As a result, succeeding generations of colonial writers felt compelled to defend themselves against the charge that they were producing nothing but "Utopian, and legendarie fables."[7] Christopher Levett thus assured readers of his *Voyage into New England* that:

> I will not do therein as some have done to my knowledge, speak more than is true; I will not tell you that you may smell the corn fields before you see the land, neither must men think that corn doth grow naturally (or on trees), nor will the deer come when they are called or stand still and look on a man until he shoot . . . nor the fish leap into the kettle, nor on the dry land, neither are they so plentiful that you may dip them up in baskets, nor take cod in nets to make a voyage, which is no truer than that the fowls will present themselves to you with spits through them.[8]

And in rather similar terms John Hammond declared that although his description of Virginia would portray "the Country to be wholesome, healthy and fruitfull," he would not go so far as to claim that the colony was "such a lubberland as the Fiction of the land of Ease is reported to be, nor such a Utopian as Sr Thomas Moore hath related to be found out." Unlike other writers on Virginia who had "rendred their Books rediculous and themselves infamous lyars," he was determined to avoid extolling "the places as if they were rather Paradices than earthly habitations; but truly let ye know, what they are, and how the people there live."[9]

One obvious device for convincing the reader of your trustworthiness was to insist at the outset that your report was "true," and in fact no adjective occurs more frequently in the titles and subtitles of English descriptions of America, from George Peckham's *True Report of the late discoveries* and Thomas Hariot's *Brief and true report of the new found land of Virginia* to Ralph Hamor's *True Discourse of the Present Estate of Virginia* and Phillip Vincent's *True Relation of the late Battell fought in New-England.*

At a rather more sophisticated level, the writers of the seventeenth century made frequent use of two traditional narrative strategies in order to dispel their readers' often well-founded suspicions. The first, which goes all the way back to Herodotus and Tacitus, was to emphasize that their observations were based on personal experience. According to Thomas Chaloner's introduction to *The English-American*, for instance, the works of Hakluyt, Purchas, and Ramusio were merely "reck'nings of anothers score" whereas Gage's narrative offered:

> the fruits of self-experience:
> Wherein our Author useth not the sence
> Of those at home, who doe their judgments leave,
> And after wandring farr with vast expence,
> See many things, which they doe ne'r perceive. . . .
> He speaks not of a City or a Street,
> But where himself hath often gone the round.[10]

In his preface to *Newes from Virginia. The lost Flocke Triumphant*, Richard Rich insisted that he was no mercenary author hired by the Virginia Company to advertise its activities: "No, I disclaime it, I have knowne the Voyage, past the danger, seene that honorable work of Virginia, & I thanke God am arrivd here to tell thee what I have seene, don, & past: . . . I am a Soldier, blunt and plaine, and so is the phrase of my newes: and I protest it is true."[11] And in similar terms John Smith declared in the dedicatory epistle to his *Generall Historie of Virginia* that "I am no compiler by hearsay, but have been a real actor."[12]

When attention shifted to New England in the wake of the Pilgrims' expedition in 1620, it was evidently still necessary to persuade readers to "doubt nothing of the truth thereof." The authors of the very earliest account of the Plymouth colony consequently felt compelled to point out that it was written "by the severall Actors themselves, after their plaine and rude manner." Thomas Morton announced that his only purpose in writing *New English Canaan* was to communicate "the knowlege, which I have gained and collected together, by mine owne observation, in the time of my many yeares residence in those parts." And William Wood promised readers of *New Englands Prospect* that all his observations were based on "my personal and experimental knowledge."[13] In all these cases, as Pagden remarks in his analysis of the autoptic imagination, "it is the 'I' who has seen what no other being has seen, who alone is capable of giving credibility to the text."[14]

The second, less common, strategy was to locate the author at one remove from the events themselves while insisting that his information derived from an unimpeachable authority who had witnessed or participated in them personally. Thus William Crashaw, after relating the miraculous survival of Sir Thomas Gates and Sir George Somers when their ship was driven onto the coast of Bermuda in 1609, offers the following grounds for accepting his report at face value: "All this to be true, I know well, and if any man aske how I know it, for their satisfaction I answere; I have it from the faithful relation of that religious, valourous and prudent Gentleman, Sir Thomas Gates, then and yet our Liesetenant generall, who being himselfe in his owne person a doer of much, a sufferer of more, and an eye-witnes of the whole, hath since related this and much more unto mee, face to face: and all that know him, know him for such a man, as well deserves to be beleeved."[15] The narrative itself may be secondhand, but it derives directly from an unimpeachable firsthand source. Milton himself employed this strategy in the one discovery narrative he ever produced in prose, *Moscovia: Or, Relations of Moscovia, As far as hath been discover'd by English Voyages.* His work, he announced on the title page, was "gather'd from the Writings of several Eye-witnesses," and in order to substantiate his claim, he provided on the final page a list of the authors "from whence these Relations have been taken; being all either Eye-witnesses, or immediate Relaters from such as were."[16] As in the case of the first-person narratives I discussed above, the "authority of the eyewitness," as Stephen Greenblatt and Anthony Pagden call it, is still the foundation upon which the text's claim to truthfulness ultimately rests.[17]

Neither of these strategies is without its potential drawbacks, however. The first, like all first-person reporting, runs the risk of making the author himself rather than the places he visited the principal object of the reader's attention, with the result that the narrative can all too easily turn into a species of personal memoir. John Smith's fear that he would "be taxed for writing so much of myself," for example, turned out to be well founded; the *Generall Historie*, according to one of its recent editors, is the "self-centred," "egocentric" work of a "braggart" in which "the 'history' is really autobiography."[18] The same charge could also be brought, perhaps, against Thomas Gage whose "new survey of the West-India's" is simultaneously the story of "his miraculous and wonderful Conversion, and Calling from those remote Parts to his Native Country."[19] In such works, as Wayne Franklin has noted, "the question no longer concerns what the new lands are; it centers instead on who the voyager is, on how his experience has altered his essential nature."[20]

In fact, Smith and Gage are rather unusual in the amount of attention they devote to themselves. Most of the writers I mention in this chapter were able to avoid making themselves the heroes of their stories by the simple expedient of describing what they saw rather than what they did. Despite their insistence that they were "actors" in the colonial drama, Christopher Levett, William Wood, Francis Higginson, Richard Rich, and John Hammond play virtually no role in their own narratives other than that of observer. We look through them, not at them.

But this solution created in turn a second problem, for the experience of seeing the New World through the lens of another sensibility inevitably raises the possibility that the lens itself may not be entirely neutral. Ironically, therefore, the author's claim to be reporting "nothing . . . but what I have . . . seene with mine owne Eyes" can have exactly the opposite effect from the one he intended. Far from trusting the narrative because it comes to us at first hand, we cannot help wondering if the facts have been distorted, whether intentionally or not, by the sensibility of the individual who originally witnessed them.[21] Was John Smith really rescued from death by Pocahontas, or was he unwittingly participating in an Indian adoption ceremony? Were the inhabitants of Virginia and New England really nomads, or were they misidentified as such so that the colonists could appropriate their land with a clear conscience?[22] In short, did the actor-narrator merely see what he wanted to see?

And the same problem arises in narratives which follow the second strategy. For although a secondhand report like Crashaw's tends to remove the narrator from our line of vision and so to create the illusion that what we are seeing is indeed a relatively objective representation of reality, as soon as we remember that the story is based upon information the author has acquired "from the Mouthes of verie honest and religious persons, who by living in the Countrey a good space of time have had experience and knowledge of the state thereof" we are brought face to face with the same basic question: were the perceptions of those "honest and religious persons" really as accurate as the author would have us believe? To what extent were their "experience and knowledge" shaped by the assumptions and expectations they brought with them across the Atlantic? How reliable, in short, is the "primal act of witnessing" upon which, according to Stephen Greenblatt, "the entire discourse of travel is constructed"?[23]

In *Paradise Lost* Milton capitalizes brilliantly upon both these potential difficulties by exemplifying them in the firsthand report delivered in Book 10 by the only character in the poem who has experienced the complete colonial cycle of exploration, discovery, conquest, and return. For the Devil's account of his exploits in the New World not only provides a model of the kind of egotistical and self-glorifying narrative which several scholars have accused John Smith of writing; it also engages in precisely the kind of conscious and unconscious distortion to which any eyewitness description may be liable. To begin with, from the moment he arrives back in Hell Satan has carefully been setting the stage for his triumphant reappearance in Pandemonium. First he slips into the council chamber in disguise; then, so that no one will notice him ascending his throne, he becomes invisible; finally, when he has paused to take stock of his audience, he bursts upon them in a dazzling explosion of light. It is pure showmanship, calculated to focus all eyes on him, but it works.

He then proceeds to deliver a brilliant impersonation of the "great adventurer" newly returned "from the search / Of Forrein Worlds" (10.440–41) that his followers have been expecting. In phrases redolent of European colonial literature he informs them that thanks to his "adventure hard" they "now possess, / As Lords, a spacious World" (10.466–68). Like Sir Ferdinando Gorges and Lord Baltimore, the devils are acquiring feudal authority over territory they have yet to see, "a Fabrick wonderful / Of absolute perfection" (10.482–83). But the real center of attention in the speech is not so much the empire that Satan has conquered as the heroism and cleverness of its conquerer:

> Long were to tell
> What I have don, what sufferd, with what paine
> Voyag'd th'unreal, vast, unbounded deep
> Of horrible confusion. . . .
>
>   (10.469–72)

Here is the self-glorifying narrator with a vengeance: "I / Toild out my uncouth passage . . . I found / The new created World . . . I have seduc'd . . . Man I deceav'd . . . I am to bruise his heel" (10.474–98). The true purpose of this relation is not so much to convey information as it is to inspire admiration.

The fundamental principle underlying Satan's speech was succinctly expressed by John Smith in the preface to his *Generall Historie.* "That which hath been endured and passed through with hardship and danger," he wrote, "is thereby sweetened to the actor when he becometh the relator."[24] Satan is clearly enjoying himself to the full, and in the last part of his speech in particular he plays quite blatantly to the gallery, milking his audience for every gasp of astonishment— "the more to increase / Your wonder" (10.486–87)—and every snigger of amusement—"worth your laughter" (10.488)—that he can squeeze out of them. The Devil is not only the star of his "performance" (10.502); he is its director.

In order to present himself in such heroic terms, Satan must also be a rather skilful editor, for not all his perils were as great as he would like his audience to believe. He has to exaggerate, for instance, the hazards he encountered on his way to Eden—night and chaos did not, in fact, oppose his journey "with clamorous uproare" (10.479)—and leave out altogether his humiliating arrest by Ithuriel and Zephon when he got there. The fallen angels, who last saw their "mighty Chief" (10.455) at his most impressive as he set off on his lonely voyage of exploration, might not be aware of the gap between the rhetoric and the reality, but the reader who remembers Book 2 and Book 4 can hardly fail to be aware of the calculated distortions in Satan's narrative.

What is more, his speech contains at least one example of unconscious misrepresentation. The ignorant natives, the Devil sneers, were willing to sell out for an apple that belonged to their Creator; the only purchase price he himself must pay for the "World" he thereby acquired is a "bruise" on the head (10.500). What Satan is referring to, of course, is Christ's promise to the serpent that "[Eve's] Seed shall bruse thy head, thou bruise his heel" (10.181), but as Milton's gloss on the phrase in lines 182–90 enables us to realize, the tempter has completely misinterpreted the meaning of the curse.[25] For in reality Christ's sentence on the serpent was a *protevangelium*, the original prophecy of Christ's victory over Satan at the Crucifixion. The "account" (10.501) that the Devil presents to his followers is thus based on a terrible miscalculation. As we might expect, the father of lies is the epitome of the unreliable narrator.

By comparison with Satan's firsthand report of his voyage of discovery and conquest, Milton's own narrative in *Paradise Lost* is relatively impersonal. It begins, at least, as a secondhand account. In the prologue to Book 1 the poet claims, like Crashaw, to be recording "the faithful relation" of "an eye-witnes of the whole" that has "since related this . . . unto mee." His source, we are told, is the Holy Spirit, who "from the first / Wast present" (1.19–20) and who consequently can "Instruct" (1.19) him in every detail of the story. "Say first," Milton asks:

> what cause
> Mov'd our Grand Parents in that happy state
> Favour'd of Heav'n so highly, to fall off
> From thir Creator, and transgress his Will

For one restraint, Lords of the World besides?
Who first seduc'd them to that foul revolt?
(1.27–33)

Strictly speaking, the rest of the epic from 1.34 onward is an answer to that question, delivered by the poet's divine informant. In literature as in life the author of *Paradise Lost* is playing the role of secretary.

As the story progresses, however, Milton gradually shifts to a version of the first strategy. He himself, we learn in the prologue to Book 3, has voyaged with Satan to the shores of Hell and back again:

Thee I re-visit now with bolder wing,
Escap't the Stygian pool, though long detain'd
In that obscure sojourn, while in my flight
Through utter and through middle darkness borne
With other notes than to th'Orphean lyre
I sung of Chaos and Eternal Night,
Taught by the heav'nly Muse to venture down
The dark descent, and up to reascend,
Though hard and rare: thee I revisit safe. . . .
(3.13–21)

And from this point on, Milton writes as if he has been physically present in Hell, Heaven, and Eden. In the prologue to Book 7 he tells us that he has been "an earthly guest" in the Heaven of heavens, where he has "drawn Empyreal Aire" (7.14). Back on earth in his "Native Element" (7.16) he is "with dangers compasst round" (7.27), threatened, like so many explorers, with dismemberment by "barbarous" (7.32) savages. We are being offered not a second- but a first-hand account of Satan's colonial mission. The poet still questions his divine informant—"Say Goddess, what ensu'd . . . ?" (7.40) but the sentence is so prolonged, and its syntax so complicated, that by the time we reach the end of it we have forgotten that it is an enquiry. The distinction between question and answer has all but disappeared.

In the prologue to Book 9, Milton is consequently able to assume full responsibility for his poem: "I now must change / Those notes to tragic" (9.5–6). His "Celestial Patroness" (9.21) is still acknowledged but only in the third person. For the first time the preface is addressed neither to the muse nor to the Holy Spirit but to the reader, assuring him that "fabl'd Knights" and "Battels feign'd" (9.30–31) will have no role in this narrative. And no longer does the prologue lead up to a request to the divine muse for further information. The story resumes on its own, without the customary act of interrogation: "The Sun was sunk, and after him the Star . . ." (9.48).

This extraordinary shift in the poem's narrative strategy, as remarkable in its way as the sudden change from first-person monologue to third-person narration at the end of *Lycidas*, leaves Milton in a rather curious position in relation to the story he is telling. As a narrator like Smith who participates at first hand in the world his characters inhabit, he is himself an eyewitness of their actions. Yet as a narrator like Crashaw who is recording at second hand a story he has heard from someone else, he is unable to intervene in the events he is describing. As Satan is about to come within sight of Eden at the beginning of Book 4, for example, the poet behaves like a benevolent Las Casas, desperately seeking to ward off the Spanish invasion:

> O for that warning voice, which he who saw
> Th'Apocalyps, heard cry in Heaven aloud,
> . . . . . . that now,
> While time was, our first-Parents had bin warnd
> The coming of thir secret foe, and scap'd
> Haply so scap'd his mortal snare; for now
> Satan, now first inflam'd with rage, came down. . . .
>
> (4.1–9)

The recurrent "now"s (lines 5, 8, 9, 23, 27, 30) combined with the predominantly present tense of the verbs in lines 15–23. ('Begins,' 'boiles,' 'recoiles,' 'distract,' 'stirr,' 'brings,' 'can,' 'wakes') place the narrator directly at the scene, but there is nothing he can do to avert the tragedy he foresees. However much he would like to influence the events that are taking place in front of his eyes, he is powerless to do more than observe them. Even when he addresses the first pair directly as they retire to their bower later in the same book, his words are audible only to the reader:

> Sleep on
> Blest pair; and O yet happiest if ye seek
> No happier state, and know to know no more.
>
> (4.773–75)

Once again his warning goes unheard as he hovers helplessly around the margins of the scene. All he can do is watch, record, and predict.

His ability to perform the last of these functions is a direct result of the hindsight Milton enjoys as a secondhand narrator who has heard the entire story before he starts retelling it. So when Eve leaves Adam in order to work alone in Book 9 not only can he address her as if he were himself physically present on the scene; wise after the event, he can foretell with absolute certainty the future consequences of her decision:

> O much deceav'd, much failing, hapless Eve,
> Of thy presum'd return! event perverse!
> Thou never from that houre in Paradise
> Foundst either sweet repast, or strong repose.
>
> (9.404–7)

The voice that speaks these lines belongs to someone who is both a firsthand witness reporting what he is seeing "with [his] owne Eyes" and a secondhand commentator recording what he has "heard and enquired from the Mouthes of verie honest and religious persons." The narrator of *Paradise Lost* has "a double point of view" not only because he is simultaneously a fallen human being and a divinely inspired bard, as Anne D. Ferry has argued,[26] but because he is situated both inside the poem and outside it. By fusing together the two principal strategies of Renaissance colonial discourse Milton has created the ideal mediator, a figure who can participate at one and the same time in the world of his characters and in the world of his readers.

Adventrous song (1.13)

The reason that credibility is such a central issue in colonial narrative derives from the unique character of the information which that narrative seeks to convey. For the phenomenon that Columbus and his successors sought to describe was in many ways completely alien from the experience of their readers. Just how strange it appeared to be may be measured by considering for a moment the implications of one of the earliest and most popular names they gave it: not the new country, the new lands, or the new territories, but the new *world*, and this is true not only of England but of Italy, Spain, and France as well. As Jean de Léry put it in the preface to his *History of a Voyage*, "in this new land of America . . . everything to be seen—the way of life of its inhabitants, the form of the animals, what the earth produces—is so unlike what we have in Europe, Asia, and Africa that it may very well be called a 'New World' with respect to us."[27] What Europe believed it had found, in short, was not just a hitherto unknown land mass but another sphere, quite literally another globe, *orbis alter* as the geographers of the time called it. The discovery of America was tantamount to the discovery of another planet.

By using this extraordinary term to describe the new continent across the Atlantic, the writers of the fifteenth and sixteenth centuries were expressing the profound sense of disjunction which they felt between Europe and America. The New World was so totally unlike the Old that it really did seem inconceivable that the two could be connected in any way. For virtually everything that Europe first learned about America was completely alien to its own history and experience. Not only did the New World contain innumerable fruits and vegetables which were unknown in the Old, mammals and reptiles which had never been seen before, and men and women whose very humanity seemed open to question; it had developed economic, political, social, and religious systems which were in many respects antithetical to those in operation in Europe. From Columbus's letter to Santangel and Vespucci's *Mundus Novus* to John Hammond's *Leah and Rachel* and Sir Ferdinando Gorges's *America Painted to the Life*, the basic function of the colonial narrator was to bridge the colossal gulf between these two realities, to serve as an intermediary between Europe and America.

To a greater or lesser extent, of course, all narrators are go-betweens, mediating between the world of the reader on the one hand and the world of the story on the other. The two worlds may be separated by history, geography, ontology, or a mixture of all three, but whether the gap is between now and then, here and there, or fact and fiction, the narrator's primary task is to span it. What distinguishes travel literature from other forms of narrative is the predominance of geographical over historical or ontological considerations; the world the narrator describes coexists with ours and is as real as ours. The only gap between it and us is spatial. In the case of Renaissance writings about America, however, the reader is separated from that other world by more than the Atlantic ocean; the gap to be bridged is historical as well as geographical.

In order to understand why this should be so we need to return briefly to Las Casas. In one of the most telling passages in the *History of the Indies* the great defender of the Indians had reminded his contemporaries that their own ancestors once lived in conditions not far removed from those of the "barbarous" Americans. "Many nations," he wrote, "today smoothly organized and Christianized, lived like animals, without houses and without cities, before their conversion to the Faith."[28] Like many of Las Casas' ideas, this humbling allusion to Europe's primitive past was subsequently incorporated into English colonial discourse. De Bry's illustrated edition of Hariot's *Briefe and true report of the new found land of Virginia*, for example, contained an appendix showing some pictures of the Picts "which in the olde tyme dyd habite one part of the great Bretainne." The reason for including these engravings, the editor explained, was "to showe how that the Inhabitants of the great Bretannie have bin in times past as savage as those of Virginia."[29]

The lesson was not lost on Hariot's successors, who never tired of reminding their readers that the British had been in much the same condition as the American Indians when they were colonized by the Roman army and converted by the Roman church. "How much good we shall performe to those that be good, and how little injury to any," wrote Robert Johnson in 1609, "will appeare, by comparing our present happinesse with our former ancient miseries, wherein wee had continued brutish, poore and naked Britanes to this day if *Julius Caesar* with his Romane Legions (or some other) had not laide the ground to make us tame and civil."[30] William Castell, on the other hand, emphasized the role of Christianity, pointing out that "what those blind and spirituyall distressed Americans are, we were, and so had continued had not Apostollicall men afforded greater charity unto us . . . by long journeying, and not without great hazard of their lives then (as yet) hath beene shewed by us unto them." And Richard Eburne advised his contemporaries "to consider that time was, the old Britons, the ancient Inhabitants of this land, were as rude and barbarous as some of those in forraigne parts and with whome we have to doe: And therefore considering, *Qua sumus Origine nati,* (for wee are also their off-spring) wee ought not to despise even such poore and barbarous people, but pitty them, and hope, that as wee are become now, by God's unspeakable mercy to us-ward, to a farre better condition, so in time may they."[31]

As a result, the New World had historical as well as geographical significance for the men and women of Renaissance Europe: it confronted them with a living embodiment of their own primitive origins. To visit it in person, then, was to enter a different time zone, to travel back to the long-lost childhood of the human race. Still more to the point, to read an account of it was to rediscover one's own primitive past, to re-enter the garden of Eden.[32] As Mikhail Bakhtin would have said, the New World was a chronotope.

Given the dimensions of the spatial and temporal chasm separating America from Europe, then, where does the colonial narrator stand in relation to the two radically different worlds between which he is expected to mediate? The answer to this question depends on which of the two strategies discussed in the foregoing section he adopts. If he chooses the first and produces the kind of eyewitness report in which "the discoverer relays his account of the strange world he has entered to an audience which remained at home," he will almost inevitably position himself closer to the New World than to the Old.[33] He will write, as it were, from a transatlantic perspective, privy to an experience beyond his readers' wildest dreams. It may well be, indeed, that his sensibility has been enlarged, perhaps even transformed, by his discoveries, for as William Crashaw observed those who visit the New World "doe often become new men."[34] In any case, estranged from his audience by the unique knowledge he has gained in America, the author of a first-hand report is no longer quite one of us.

As a result, he may very well bring that knowledge to bear on European society in ways that are profoundly unsettling to his readers.

Specifically, he may look back at his native land through the eyes of his newly acquired American compatriots. According to Roger Williams, for example:

> When Indians heare the horrid filths,
> Of Irish, English men,
> The horrid Oaths and Murthers late,
> Thus say these Indians then:
> We weare no Cloaths, have many Gods,
> And yet our sinnes are lesse:
> You are Barbarians, Pagans wild,
> Your Land's the Wildernesse.[35]

The uncivilized inhabitants of the New World, Williams obviously believes, were in many respects superior to their civilized counterparts in the Old. Even the barbarous cannibals, some other writers suggested, had something to teach their European critics. At the conclusion of his account of the "man-eating savages" of Brazil, Jean de Léry thus concludes:

> Nevertheless, so that those who read these horrible things, practiced daily among these barbarous nations of the land of Brazil, may also think more carefully about the things that go on every day over here, among us: In the first place, if you consider in all candor what our big usurers do, sucking blood and marrow, and eating everyone alive . . . you will say that they are even more cruel than the savages I speak of. . . . Furthermore, if it comes to the brutal action of really chewing and devouring human flesh, have we not found people in these regions over here, even among those who bear the name of Christian, . . . who, not content with having cruelly put to death their enemies, have been unable to slake their bloodthirst except by eating their livers and their hearts? . . . So let us henceforth no longer abhor so very greatly the cruelty of the anthropophagous—that is, man eating—savages. For since there are some here in our midst even worse and more detestable than those who, as we have seen, attack only enemy nations, while the ones over here have plunged into the blood of their kinsmen, neighbors, and compatriots, one need not go beyond one's own country, nor as far as America, to see such monstrous and prodigious things.[36]

For de Léry, as for so many other visitors to the New World, life "over there" offered a critical standpoint from which the flaws of society "over here" could be identified and judged with special clarity.

This is precisely Milton's position in *Paradise Lost.* Just as the savages of America seemed to Williams and de Léry to be superior in certain respects to the inhabitants of Renaissance Europe, so, we are told in Book 2, the followers of Satan excel the men and women who are reading about them:

> O shame to men! Devil with Devil damn'd
> Firm concord holds, men onely disagree
> Of Creatures rational, though under hope
> Of heavenly Grace: and God proclaiming peace,
> Yet live in hatred, enmity, and strife
> Among themselves, and levie cruel warres,
> Wasting the Earth, each other to destroy:
> As if (which might induce us to accord)
> Man had not hellish foes anow besides,
> That day and night for his destruction waite.
>
> (2.496–505)

In one respect, at least, the diabolical "Indians" are more civilized than the bellicose race whose forebears they are plotting to destroy. Still more to the point, almost everything the narrator encounters in the garden of Eden is a standing reproach to human values and behavior in the world of his readers. When he first describes Adam and Eve, for instance, he is struck by the contrast between their sexual innocence and the shame and hypocrisy of his own culture:

> Nor those mysterious parts were then conceald,
> Then was not guiltie shame; dishonest shame
> Of natures works, honor dishonorable,
> Sin-bred how have ye troubl'd all mankind
> With shews instead, meer shews of seeming pure,
> And banisht from mans life his happiest life,
> Simplicitie and spotless innocence.
>
> (4.312–19)

When the first pair retire to their "blissful Bower" (4.690) for the night, he breaks off to deliver a long lecture on the difference between their genuine passion and the sterile eroticism of seventeenth-century London:

> Here Love his golden shafts imploies, here lights
> His constant Lamp, and waves his purple wings,
> Reigns here and revels; not in the bought smile
> Of Harlots, loveless, joyless, unindeard,
> Casual fruition, nor in Court Amours,
> Mixt Dance, or wanton Mask, or Midnight Ball,
> Or Serenate, which the starv'd Lover sings
> To his proud fair, best quitted with disdain.
>
> (4.763–70)

And as Adam walks forth to greet his angel guest in Book 5, he again interrupts the story to distinguish the naked dignity of the first man from:

> the tedious pomp that waits
> On Princes, when thir rich Retinue long
> Of Horses led, and Grooms besmeard with Gold
> Dazzles the crowd, and sets them all agape.
>
> (5.354–57)

Like Raphael Hythloday in Sir Thomas More's American fable, Milton speaks to us in the superior tones of someone who has seen a better world.

For such a narrator, as all these passages reveal, the principal characteristic of that world is its *difference*. Over and over again he is astonished by the radical otherness of the terrestrial paradise and its occupants. And as in so many accounts of America, the result is the emotion which Stephen Greenblatt has defined as "the instinctive recognition of difference," namely wonder.[37] "At the heart of the discovery narrative," Wayne Franklin has written, "stands the ravished observer, fixed in awe, scanning the New World scene, noting its colors and shapes, recording its plenitude and its sensual riches."[38] These words accurately describe Milton's response to the lost paradise of which he hopes to tell, "if Art could tell" (4.236), his readers. He moves through the poem like a European explorer in the New World, continually startled by its novelty, astonished by its abundance, and moved by its innocence. The sense of wonder he brings with him as a fallen man in an unfallen world is the historical correlative of John Brereton's reaction to the unspoiled landscape of New England. "We stood a while," he wrote, "like men ravished at the beautie and delicacie of this sweet soile."[39]

But how is this feeling, and the experience which inspired it, to be communicated to a reader who is trapped in the perceptual categories of the Old World? What words, what images will do justice to the incredible novelty of the phenomenon the narrator has undertaken to describe? Jean de Léry states the problem very clearly at the beginning of his *History of a Voyage*. How, he asks, can his readers be made to understand "what can only be seen two thousand leagues from where they live: things never known (much less written about) by the Ancients: things so marvelous that experience itself can scarcely engrave them upon the understanding even of those who have in fact seen them?"[40] What possible representational device can bridge the vast epistemological gulf between the colonial narrator, who has seen this world, and the reader, who has never even imagined its existence?

One solution is already implicit in the binary terminology that was used from the very beginning to distinguish America from Europe. Just as we know good by evil, as Milton argued in *Areopagitica*, so perhaps we can know the New World by the Old. If the relationship between the two realities is fundamentally an antithetical one, if, as Pedro de Quiroga observed, everything in America "is the reverse of what it is in Castile,"[41] then in order to create a mental construct of that mysterious Other beyond the horizon we have only to imagine the opposite of our own condition. If Europe is corrupt, overpopulated, and undernourished, then America is innocent, empty, and superabundantly fertile. In essence, this is precisely the technique at work in the passages from *Paradise Lost* quoted above. The unfallen world is an exact antitype of the fallen one, so if postlapsarian man is shameful, promiscuous, and ostentatious, then prelapsarian Adam is innocent, monogamous, and unadorned.

An alternative solution invites the reader not to invert the familiar world around him but to transcend it by using it as a standard of comparison for a place where nature is *more* fertile, the landscape is *more* beautiful, the men and women are *more* virtuous, and human society is *more* just than those they are familiar with. According to Thomas Hariot, for example, he and his companions found the soil of Virginia:

> to be fatter, the trees greater and to grow thinner, the ground more firme and deeper mould, more and larger champions, finer grasse and as good as ever we saw any in England; in some place rockie and farre more high and hilly ground, more plentie of their fruites, more abundance of beastes, the more inhabited with people, and of greater pollicie and larger dominions, with greater townes and houses.[42]

The New World is not so much a negative image of the Old as an enlargement of it.

Milton's version of this solution is characteristically literary. Throughout his description of Eden he invokes the most distant and highly idealized world in his reader's imaginative repertoire, the legendary world of classical mythology, and then goes on to claim that the people and places he is describing exceeded even that. So "that faire field / Of Enna" cannot compare with "this Paradise / Of Eden" (4.268–75), which is "more delicious" (9.439) than the gardens of Adonis or Alcinous; Pan and Silvanus never slept "in shadier Bower" than Adam and Eve (4.705); Eve is "more lovely" (4.714) than Pandora, "more lovely fair" (5.380) than the goddesses who competed for Paris's apple on mount Ida; the serpent is more beautiful than "those that in Illyria chang'd / Hermione and Cadmus, or the God / In Epidaurus" (9.505–7); and the entire story is "more Heroic" (9.14) than the epic deeds of Achilles or of Turnus. Very often these comparisons have distinctly sinister implications,[43] but their primary purpose is to provide a springboard for the imaginative leap into the unknown which Milton requires his readers to perform.

On the other hand, a narrator who adopts the second strategy, as Milton does in the early books of the poem, is still one of us; he has experienced America not directly but at one remove. He writes from a European perspective, as it were, sharing his readers' reaction to the marvels he has learned about from his informants. Whereas the eyewitness narrator typically lays all the emphasis on the differences between the Old World and the New, the secondhand reporter is consequently more likely to call our attention to the points of resemblance between them. The result, more often than not, is a vision of America as a transatlantic replica of Europe, a parallel world in which the history of civilization is being played out for the second time. A characteristic passage from Peter Martyr's biography of Columbus may illustrate the kind of effect I have in mind:

> By the waye, there appeared from the Northe a great Ilande . . . cauled Madanina . . . inhabited only with women: To whom the Canibales haue accesse at certen tymes of the yeare, as in owlde tyme the Thracians had to the Amazones in the Ilande of Lesbos. The men children, they sende to theyr fathers. But the women theye kepe with them selues. They haue greate and stronge caues or dennes in the ground, to the which they flye for safegarde if any men resorte unto them at any other tyme then is appoynted.[44]

The ancient Mediterranean island has been rediscovered in the Caribbean, the Amazons have been reincarnated in its female occupants, the New World has proved to be a distant mirror of the Old.

In *Paradise Lost* the situation is complicated by the disobedience of Adam and Eve, which erects between the pre- and postlapsarian worlds a barrier that is utterly impervious to resemblance. Before the Fall the moral *status quo* is the exact opposite of the moral *status quo* after it, so Milton cannot assert likeness without blurring the distinction between innocence and sinfulness. Instead of creating the kind of broad-ranging historical correspondences we find in *De Orbe Novo*, therefore, he largely restricts his homologies to the one character who shares the reader's fallenness: Satan. It is no accident that the overwhelming majority of the epic similes in *Paradise Lost* are applied to the Devil and his followers, for until Adam and Eve eat the apple the fallen angels are the only characters in the poem whose nature and experience have any real parallels in the postlapsarian world.

During his brief residence in the garden of Eden the tempter is compared to a wide variety of animate and inanimate beings: a merchant *en route* to the spice islands (4.159–65), a wolf plundering the sheepfold (4.183–87), a burglar breaking into a rich man's home (4.188–91), a heap of gunpowder ignited by a spark (4.814–18), a plowman watching the wind blow through a cornfield (4.980–85), a city rake out in the countryside eyeing the milkmaids (9.445–54), and an *ignis fatuus* leading travelers astray in the darkness (9.634–42). But diverse as they are, these similes all have the same basic function: they create a point of entry by means of which the fallen reader can gain imaginative access to the unfallen world.

For Milton, the Devil himself seems to have served a similar purpose. Almost from the beginning of the poem Satan has played Columbus to Milton's Peter Martyr (or Villegagnon to Milton's Jean de Léry), so by the time we reach Book 4 it seems only natural that the poet should enter the garden with the Devil and see it, at least partly, through his eyes. There are times, indeed, when it is not entirely clear whose perception is controlling the scene. For instance, we are told that Adam and Eve "seemd Lords of all, / And worthie seemd . . . though both / Not equal, as thir sex not equal seemd" (4.290–96). But seemed to whom? If this is how they seemed to Satan, then it is possible, as Michael Wilding has argued in an ingenious paper, that the inequality of man and woman is a diabolic misperception, that Adam's "Absolute rule" is merely a reflection of the Devil's own preference for tyranny.[45] If, on the other hand, this is how they seemed to the narrator, and by implication to the Holy Spirit whose words he is repeating, then the hierarchical relationship is real, not imagined, and Eve's subordination to her husband is part of the divine scheme.

Such moments of perceptual ambiguity are rare, however. More often, the narrator's response to the unfallen world is clearly distinguished from the Devil's both by its form and by its content. Whereas Milton's sentiments, as we have seen, are communicated by means of direct speech addressed either to the characters or to the reader, Satan's are expressed principally in his numerous soliloquies—three in Book 4 and another two in Book 9—which constitute a kind of diabolic counter-narrative punctuating the text with insistently self-referential passages of autobiography. And whereas Milton is constantly struck by the difference between the world he is exploring and the world he left behind him, the Devil finds only resemblance. When he first arrives within sight of Eden, the sun reminds him immediately of the "bright eminence" (4.44) he has lost, and that memory of his former glory shapes his subsequent response to everything he sees in "this new World" (4.34). Just as America presented itself to Peter Martyr as another Europe, so the garden of Eden appears to Satan to be a reflection of his lost home, a "Heav'n on Earth" (4.208), which he tells his followers later in the poem is "to our native Heaven / Little inferiour" (10.467–68). "O Earth how like to Heaven" he exclaims when he reenters Eden at the beginning of Book 9. And although he recognizes that its occupants are "Not spirits," nevertheless they too seem to him to be "Little inferior" to the "heav'nly Spirits" (4.361–62) whose companionship he once enjoyed in paradise.

Despite the impenetrable barrier between the fallen and the unfallen worlds, then, Milton is able to incorporate the secondhand narrator's perception of resemblance into Satan's firsthand encounter with the terrestrial paradise, while at the same time embodying the typical perspective of the eyewitness narrator in his own repeated assertions of difference. Once again the two most common narrative strategies in colonial discourse have coalesced to produce a multidimensional representation of "this new World" (4.34) which far exceeds all previous treatments of the subject both in immediacy and in complexity. Milton's song is "adventrous" in more senses than one.

Eternal Providence (1.25)

Whether they were frustrated empire-builders like John Smith or religious idealists like Edward Johnson, virtually all the men who provided seventeenth-century England with its information about the New World had an axe to grind. With very rare exceptions, the tracts they produced were not intended to be objective descriptions of life on the other side of the Atlantic; invariably they had political, economic, or religious designs on the reader.[46] Some were written to induce him to invest either his purse or his person[47] in the colonial enterprise, others to explain why Virginia had so far failed to produce any return on his investment, still others to enlist his sympathies on one side or the other in the political and religious controversies that erupted in Massachusetts during the 1630s and 1640s and in Maryland in the mid 1650s. This was a body of literature designed to persuade.

Most frequently, as I pointed out in Chapter 1, it was designed to persuade the reader that in spite of numerous setbacks and disappointments the "most wholesome, profitable, pleasant work of planting" was making steady progress both in Virginia and in New England.[48] Over and over again, if we are to believe the tracts and sermons of the time, the colonists had snatched victory from the jaws of defeat. And they were able to do so, these reports all agreed, because the English settlements were predestined to succeed by divine Providence itself, which intervened repeatedly to ensure that the chosen people continued to prosper in the New World.

The providential theme in Puritan narratives of New England is too well known to be rehearsed again here,[49] but it is worth noting that the same theme was no less prominent in English accounts of the colonization of Virginia. It made its first appearance in *An account of the particularities of the imployments of the English men left in Virginia . . . under the charge of Master Ralph Lane* published by Richard Hakluyt in *The Principal Navigations*. The role of Providence in this account of the Roanoke colony is somewhat problematical, however, for it seems to be responsible for many of the afflictions which the settlers had to endure as in the case of the sudden storm which carried away their provisions and their boats. This incident, the narrator confesses, "must ever make me to thinke the hand of God onely (for some good purpose to my selfe yet unknowen) to have bene in the matter." Indeed, the conditions brought about "by the hand of God, as it pleased him to try us" finally became so unbearable that the colonists concluded that "the very hand of God as it seemed stretched out to take us from thence." For its own mysterious reasons, "eternall providence" evidently wanted Raleigh's colony to fail.[50]

On a more positive note, Robert Johnson argued that the "manifold difficulties, crosses and disasters" experienced by the Virginia colony were "appointed by the highest providence as an exercise of patience and other vertues, and to make more wise thereby the managers thereof." According to Alexander Whitaker, indeed, the ultimate success of the venture was the direct result of the privations it had been forced to endure:

> As a spreading herbe, whose top hath bin often cropped off, renewes her growth, and spreads her selfe more gloriously, then before, so this Plantation, which the divell hath so often troden downe, is by the miraculous blessing of God revived, and daily groweth to more happy and more hopefull successe. I have shut up many things in few words, and have alleadged this onely to prove unto us that the finger of God hath been the onely true worker heere; that God first shewed us the place, God first called us hither, and here God by his special providence hath maintained us.

Even such catastrophic events as the Indian massacres of 1622 and 1644 were interpreted providentially. The entire colony would have been wiped out, claimed the author of a *Perfect Description* "if God had not abated the Courages of the Savages in that moment of time."[51] Somewhat surprisingly, perhaps, the most emphatic exponent of providential involvement in the colony's affairs was none other than the hard-bitten and self-reliant John Smith. "God, the guider of all good actions," he wrote, drove the first settlers "by His providence to their desired Port beyond all their expectations." When they were starving, "God, the patron of all good indeavors, in that desperate extremitie so changed the hearts of the Salvages that they brought such plenty of their fruits and provision as no man wanted." When Smith was captured by Powhatan, "almightie God (by his divine providence) had mollified the hearts of those sterne Barbarians with compassion." When Powhatan on another occasion plotted against him, "the eternall all-seeing God did preuent him and by strange meanes." And when the colonists were ready to abandon the colony in despair, God brought Lord De La Warr to persuade them to stay. "Neuer had any people more iust cause, to cast themselues at the very foot-stoole of God, and to reuerence his mercie than this distressed Colonie" Smith concludes:

> For if God had not sent Sir Thomas Gates from the Bermudas within fourr daies they had almost beene famished; if God had not directed the heart of that noble Knight to saue the fort from fiering at their shipping, . . . they had been destitute of a present harbour and succour; if they had abandoned the Fort any longer time, and had not so soone returned, questionlesse the Indians would have destroied the Fort. . . . If they had set saile sooner and had launched into the vast Ocean, who would haue promised they should haue incountered the Fleet of the Lord la Ware . . . ? If the Lord la Ware had not brought with him a yeere's prouision, what comfort would these poore soules have receiued to haue beene relanded to a second distruction? This was the arme of the Lord of Hosts, who would haue his people passe the red Sea and Wildernesse, and then to possess the land of Canaan.[52]

Milton was rather less heavy-handed in his commentary than most of the writers I have quoted, but his fundamental purpose was precisely the same: to "assert Eternal Providence / And justify the ways of God to men" (1.24–26). Just as "God himselfe is the founder and favourer of this Plantation" according to William Crashaw's introduction to *Good Newes From Virginia,* so in *Paradise Lost* He is the "sovran Planter" (4.691) of the garden of Eden.[53] Just as God led the colonists into the territories left empty by the epidemics which had decimated the Indian population, so in *Paradise Lost* He ordains:

> in stead
> Of Spirits malign a better Race to bring
> Into thir vacant room, . . .
>
> (7.188–90)

And just as God continually revived the plantation which the Devil had afflicted, so in *Paradise Lost* He repairs the fall of Satan by creating the universe and the fall of Adam by appointing the Son as his redeemer. The principle implicit in Whitaker's image of a plant which grows more vigorously the more it is pruned controls the entire poem. In the words of the angels who celebrate God's victory over the Devil at the end of the Creation: "his evil / Thou usest, and from thence creat'st more good" (7.615–16).

As these examples may already suggest, the providential theme in *Paradise Lost* is usually expounded not by the narrator but by the characters themselves, often by the angels, who serve as a kind of choric commentator on all God's actions, and on at least one occasion by Adam himself, who offers the definitive statement on the subject in Book 12:

> O goodness infinite, goodness immense!
> That all this good of evil shall produce,
> And evil turn to good; more wonderful
> Than that which by creation first brought forth
> Light out of darkness! full of doubt I stand
> Whether I should repent me now of sin
> By mee done and occasiond, or rejoyce
> Much more, that much more good thereof shall spring,
> To God more glory, more good will to Men
> From God, and over wrauth grace shall abound.
>
> (12.469–78)

But whoever is delivering the message, the point is always the same: despite the catastrophes that have occurred in God's plantation, divine Providence will inevitably repair them. In his determination to explain not only how the entire human enterprise has gone so disastrously astray but also how it can still be redeemed, Milton is the garden of Eden's John Smith.

The only occasion on which the narrator intervenes in his own person to assert God's providential oversight coincides, appropriately enough, with the poem's deepest metaphysical crisis, the moment when it appears that Satan's plan to reverse the moral dynamics of the universe and "out of good still to find means of evil" (1.165) has succeeded. As news of the Fall arrives in Heaven Milton asks:

> For what can scape the Eye
> Of God All-seeing, or deceave his Heart
> Omniscient, who in all things wise and just,

> Hinder'd not Satan to attempt the minde
> Of Man, with strength entire, and free will arm'd,
> Complete to have discover'd and repulst
> Whatever wiles of Foe or seeming Friend.
>
> (10.5–11)

Here, if anywhere, is the heart of the poet's "great Argument" (1.24), and it is scarcely surprising that he feels compelled to make it in his own person. For condensed in these seven lines are the three chief components of Milton's attempt to justify the ways of God to men: divine omniscience, divine permissiveness, and human freedom. The sentence begins as a purely rhetorical question designed to answer a question no one has asked: how could God know the Fall had taken place as soon as it had happened? But the answer (God knows everything) generates a second unspoken question: if God was aware of the Devil's impending assault on Eden yet did nothing to prevent it, can He really be omnipotent? The answer to that question (the Devil entered the garden of Eden with God's permission) generates, in turn, still another unspoken question: if God allowed the Devil to tempt Adam, can Adam be held responsible for the Fall? And the answer to that question, (thanks to his free will, Adam was perfectly capable of resisting temptation) brings the sentence to a close. What is remarkable about this defence of God's conduct, it seems to me, is the fact that the answers are given before the questions can even be asked. The qualifying clauses—"who in all things wise and just," and "with strength entire and free will armed,"—appear to be purely descriptive, but in fact they are responses to potential objections. Any challenge to Milton's providential thesis has been, quite literally, silenced before it can be uttered. Back in the fallen world, the narrator who seemed to be so powerless in the garden of Eden has suddenly become authoritarian.

Now that Adam and Eve have sinned, moreover, Milton's entire attitude toward them has changed too. In Books 4–9, as we have seen, he could only marvel at their unfallen majesty. Here in Book 10, however, he speaks from a position of moral superiority:

For still they knew, and ought to have still remember'd
The high Injunction not to taste that Fruit,
Whoever tempted; which they not obeying,
Incurr'd, what could they less, the penaltie,
And manifold in sin, deserv'd to fall.

(10.12–16)

This is a narrative voice so different from the one we heard in the earlier books of the poem that we can scarcely recognize it. Before the Fall it was occasionally stern, but it did not lack respect or compassion. Now it is harsh and querulous, scolding the guilty pair for their forgetfulness and bullying the reader with strident rhetorical questions. As one of the descendants that Adam expects to curse him, Milton may well be angry with his ancestor for losing the colonial paradise he would otherwise have inherited, but the tones we hear at the beginning of Book 10 transcend merely human indignation. As he contemplates the apparent victory of the "infernal Empire" (10.389) the poet has begun to sound like the "sovran Planter" himself.

Conclusion

The greatest event since the creation of the world (excluding the incarnation and death of He who created it) is the discovery of the Indies.

—Francisco López de Gómara, *Prima Parte de la Historia General de las Indias*

From the analysis contained in the previous four chapters it would appear that *Paradise Lost* contains not one but two colonial narratives: first, an anti-colonial text, based on the Spanish conquest of the West Indies, Mexico, and Peru, according to which a corrupt and power-hungry adventurer discovers the New World, enslaves its inhabitants, and takes possession of their land; second, a pro-colonial text, based on the English attempts to settle Virginia and New England, which relates how a sly and treacherous Indian deceives a pair of honest and industrious planters and is subsequently punished by their vengeful sponsor.

The radical bifurcation between these two very different versions of the colonial enterprise reflects with extraordinary clarity the essentially binary character of English colonial ideology as it had existed for most of Milton's lifetime. For throughout the seventeenth century, English empire-building in North America developed in conscious opposition to what its promoters regarded as a morally reprehensible form of the very same activity, Spanish empire-building in the Caribbean and South America. From Raleigh's report of the discovery of Guiana with its relentless emphasis on the deceitfulness and violence of the *conquistadores* to Cromwell's *Declaration Against Spain* with its ringing denunciations of the wrongs and injustices committed by the *encomenderos*, English colonial discourse continually insisted on the contrast between Spanish greed and English generosity,

141

Spanish cruelty and English benevolence, Spanish treachery and English honesty. With the outbreak of war with Spain in 1655 and the revival of the black legend that accompanied it, the contrast between the histories of the two rival empires was sharpened still further, and it would have been surprising indeed if an imperial epic written by an Englishman in the late 1650s and early 1660s did not present a profoundly polarized view of Europe's territorial expansion. The competing narratives in *Paradise Lost* were the natural product of the particular historical moment in which the poem had its origins.

We might well conclude, therefore, that the poem as a whole conforms to Stephen Greenblatt's theoretical model of Renaissance political discourse: a "subversive" critique of diabolic exploration and conquest is "contained" by a larger history of divine imperialism in which England's hegemony over its transatlantic possessions is emphatically endorsed.[1] But in fact the situation is rather more complex than this straightforward antithesis might suggest, for each of the narratives I have just described has its own counter-narrative within Milton's epic. The anti-colonial Spanish text that dominates the first four books of *Paradise Lost* gives way in Book 5 to a comprehensive idealization of the same story in which Raphael, a true visitor from Heaven, correctly informs the inhabitants of the New World that both their lives and their property belong to a distant overlord, and Michael, another angelic emissary, justly expels them from their plantation when they fail to obey the terms of the divine *requerimiento*. And in much the same way, the pro-colonial English text that begins in Book 4 is undercut by the profoundly negative representation of England's plantations that informs Books 1 and 2 where the outcasts of Heaven display all the characteristic vices that might be expected to develop in the kind of penal settlement called for by proponents of a purgative colonial strategy. The negative Spanish text is thus contested not only by an English text but by a positive version of itself. And the positive English text is contested not only by a Spanish text but by a negative version of itself. *Paradise Lost* contains, in short, almost every conceivable permutation of the colonial experience available in the seventeenth century.

The immediate effect of these dichotomies is to destabilize the colonial identities of the poem's central characters and the colonial significance of their actions. The same figures, and occasionally the same events, simultaneously encode diametrically opposing interpretations of the imperial enterprise. In some episodes, for instance, Satan behaves like the Spanish *conquistadores* of the fifteenth and sixteenth centuries, or the English pilgrims and missionaries of the seventeenth; in others, he presents himself as one of the colonists' victims, the dispossesed inhabitants of the New World. In some episodes, Adam and Eve resemble the English settlers laboring in indentured servitude on a royal plantation; in others, they have more in common with the American Indians living in their terrestrial paradise. The only figures who remain constant throughout the colonial drama are God, the "sovran Planter" himself, and his angelic emissaries.

How, then, are we to interpret the drama as a whole? Where in the continually shifting narrative patterns and historical identities that inform the poem can we find firm critical ground to stand on? What is Milton's own position on such issues as the proper way to treat the native population, the desirability of establishing permanent settlements in America, the appropriate relationship between the colony and the state that founded it, the justice of the imperial enterprise itself? Most important of all, perhaps, why did Milton conceptualize the biblical narrative in colonial terms to begin with? And how do the colonial images and tropes that I have tried to identify affect his literal portrayal of man's first disobedience?

Unfortunately, Milton has left us no definitive statement concerning his attitude toward the colonization of the New World, but if we may extrapolate from his comments on two closely related ventures it may be possible to construct a reasonably plausible, albeit hypothetical, model of his opinions on the subject. The ventures I am referring to, of course, are the discovery of Russia, which Milton described in his *Brief History of Moscovia*, and the subjugation of Ireland, which he defended in his *Observations upon the Articles of Peace*. The exploration of Russia by the English, he wrote in the first of these works:

> might have seem'd an enterprise almost heroick; if any higher end than the excessive love of Gain and Traffick, had animated the de-

sign. Nevertheless that in regard that many things not unprofitable to the knowledge of Nature, and other Observations are hereby come to light, as good events ofttimes arise from evil occasions, it will not be the worst labour to relate briefly the beginning, and prosecution of this adventurous Voiage.[2]

In view of this comment on "the discovery of Russia by the northern Ocean" it seems likely that Milton had equally mixed feelings about the discovery of America by the western Ocean. For although "the excessive love of Gain and Traffick" had unquestionably played a large part both in the Spanish conquest of the West Indies, Mexico, and Peru and in the Virginia Company's activities around Chesapeake Bay, there was no denying that "higher ends" had inspired English expeditions to New England and elsewhere. The establishment of Plymouth plantation, in particular, was widely regarded in Puritan circles as "an enterprise almost heroick," and by the mid seventeenth century it was generally recognized that "the knowledge of Nature" had been completely transformed by the results of "adventurous Voiages" made by the Spanish, French, and Portuguese as well as by the English.

In *Paradise Lost*, of course, the only true explorer is Satan—Raphael's journey to earth is not so much a voyage of discovery as a diplomatic mission to a predetermined destination. When he encounters Uriel in Book 3 the Devil pretends that the purpose of his flight is to enlarge his own "knowledge of Nature." "Unspeakable desire to see, and know / All these his wondrous works," he tells the archangel, "Hath brought me from the Choirs of Cherubim / Alone thus wand'ring" (3.662–67). But Milton makes it amply clear that in reality his solitary quest is motived by "the excessive love of gain" that had drawn so many Spanish and English explorers to the New World. The enterprise which seems almost heroic to Satan's followers in Hell has none of the redeeming features that enabled Milton to give his qualified approval to the discovery of Russia by the English.

As regards the colonization of Ireland, with which the settlement of America was so frequently compared, Milton's views seem to have been less complicated.[3] Long before he became a member of Cromwell's government he described the Irish as "a barbarous crew of rebels" whom England had every right to "quell" and "subdue,"[4] and when he became Secretary for Foreign Tongues he vigorously supported his country's violent suppression of any attempt to resist colonization in a pamphlet that Thomas Corns has recently described as "a preemptive justification for that Cromwellian ruthlessness manifest in the storming of Drogheda . . . and of Wexford."[5] The "abhorred" "inhumane" "bloudy" "Irish Barbarians," Milton argued in his *Observations upon the Articles of Peace,* were "justly made our vassalls." Thanks to the "barbarous Massacre" of 1641, which had prompted his outburst in *The Reason of Church Government,* as well as "the long prescription of many hundred yeares," the English were "fixt and seated in that soile with as good a right as the meerest Natives." The latter, however, had proved to be "indocible and averse from all Civility and amendment," preferring their own "absurd and savage Customes before the most convincing evidence of reason and demonstration: a testimony of their true Barbarisme and obdurate wilfulnesse."[6] The only language such people could understand was force, and when Cromwell applied it at Drogheda, Wexford, Kilkenny, and Clonmel, Milton had nothing but praise for the man who "broke the power of the Irish."[7]

Even when we make due allowance for the fact that Milton was "writing on instruction from the Council of State," as Corns points out, the vehemence of his prose suggests that he shared his employers' evident enthusiasm for colonial expansion.[8] He would have had little sympathy, one suspects, for the Indians of Virginia after the massacre of 1622 or for the Indians of New England when they proved to be as "indocible and averse from all Civility" as the Irish. Like Spenser before him, Milton appears to have had no qualms at all about his country's treatment of those natives who were foolish enough to resist English imperialism.

It seems to me unlikely, therefore, that *Paradise Lost* could ever have been intended as "an indictment of European expansion and colonialism that includes [Milton's] own countrymen and contemporaries" as David Quint has recently argued.[9] The mere fact that Satan is characterized as a merchant adventurer intent on cheating the inhabitants of the New World out of their God-given possessions does not necessarily lead to the conclusion that all mercantile exploration is the work of the Devil, first because Satan is depicted elsewhere in the poem as a resentful victim of divine colonialism and second because his voyage to earth is counterbalanced by Raphael's legitimate mission to inform Adam and Eve that they owe allegiance to the "sovran Planter." If Milton had wanted to subvert the Catholic tradition of heroic discovery and conquest, or the Protestant tradition of religious liberation and conversion, why did he cast Adam and Eve in the role of the colonists and Satan in the role of the dispossessed Indians? What is more, any attempt to read *Paradise Lost* as a comprehensive critique of imperialism, whether English or Spanish, must find a way round the overwhelming objection that the poem's most powerful and successful imperialist is God. It is God who, in accordance with the purgative version of England's colonial policy, expels Satan and his angels to the penal colony he has prepared for them in Hell. It is God who "plants" Adam and Eve in the terrestrial paradise he has created for them in the New World.

On the other hand, Milton's text seems equally resistant to the pro-imperial reading that might be suggested by his views on the English conquest of Ireland. For as we saw in Chapter 2, in the first of the poem's colonial sites it is the colonists, not the natives, who are portrayed as rebellious barbarians, "indocible and averse from all Civility and amendment." And so far as the second of the poem's colonial sites is concerned, a work that was written to celebrate English colonial achievements either in Ireland or in America would hardly be likely to depict the Devil himself as the "great adventurer" in search of "Foreign Worlds" or prelapsarian Adam and Eve as the native innocents he corrupts. The interpretation of *Paradise Lost* as "an epic of the imperial victors" is ultimately no more persuasive than those readings which find in it "an epic of the defeated."[10]

The truth of the matter, I suspect, is that Milton's views on the subject of colonization in general, and of the colonization of the New World in particular, were as deeply divided as those expressed in the colonial discourse of seventeenth-century England. If the colonizing power was Spain, then colonization was unquestionably a diabolic act of oppression and exploitation. But if the colonizing power was England, the situation was deeply ambiguous. A colony like Virginia, which sided with Charles I in the Civil War and served as a refuge for exiled royalists when it was over, was clearly a blight on the face of the earth, whereas a colony like New England, which served as a refuge for the "faithfull and freeborn Englishmen" who rejected the authority of the Laudian church, was equally clearly a shining example to the rest of Europe.[11] In and of itself, colonialism was neither good nor bad. Everything depended on the identity of the colonizer, the nature of the colonized, and the purpose of the colony. And so it is in *Paradise Lost.* Imperial expansion, the poem implies, is morally neutral. When it is practiced by the virtuous, it is entirely admirable. When it is practiced by the wicked, it is one of the greatest evils that the human race can endure.

In the final analysis, then, I do not believe that *Paradise Lost* was written in order to advance either a pro-colonial or an anti-colonial agenda. The colonial elements I have identified in Milton's text are there for an entirely different purpose: to perform for the reader an operation similar to that which Raphael performs for Adam and Eve. Confronted with the problem of describing "what surmounts the reach / Of human sense" (5.571–72) to a human audience, the archangel resorts to simile, "lik'ning spiritual to corporal forms, / As may express them best" (5.573–74). In much the same way Milton bridges the temporal and moral gap between Genesis and seventeenth-century England by "likening" biblical to modern forms. And what form could "express" the cosmic power struggle between God and Satan over the fate of the human race more powerfully than the ongoing contest between Spain and England for control of the New World. So just as Raphael measures "things in Heaven by things on earth" (6.893) so Milton measures things in the distant past by things in the immediate present. Europe's colonial adventures offer, as it were, a continuous simile, a rich cultural stockpile of ideas and images, by means of which the ancient rivalry between good and evil can be related directly to the political experience of the poet's contemporaries.

The result is a version of the Genesis narrative that is characterized by all the complexities and ambiguities of Renaissance colonial discourse. For by bringing four competing colonial narratives to bear on the biblical text, Milton is able to represent the central characters and events of the story from a variety of different ideological perspectives.

The duplicitous Algonquians and rebellious outcasts of the English narratives coalesce with the adventurous explorers and ruthless predators of the Spanish narratives in the person of Satan, thus producing a tempter who combines the glamor and destructiveness of the colonizers with the treachery and cunning of the colonized. The good-natured Indians of the Spanish narratives blend with the hard-working settlers of the English narrative in the persons of Adam and Eve, thus producing a portrayal of prelapsarian life that combines the innocence and educability of the colonized with the industriousness and piety of the colonizers. And finally the Spanish narratives of conquest and the English narratives of plantation converge in a description of the Fall that allows us to view Eve as both victim and criminal at the same time. As an innocent and trusting native, she is easy prey to the sophisticated colonist who seduces her with all the rhetoric of European love poetry in the non-biblical prologue to the temptation. As a pious settler, she should have been able to resist the persuasions of the treacherous Indian who subsequently persuades her to ignore the orders of her rightful colonial master. In the discursive context of the Spanish narratives her disobedience is perfectly excusable; she was simply "deceav'd" (9.404) by a superior intelligence. In the discursive context of the English narrative, on the other hand, her disobedience is thoroughly reprehensible; she allowed a bestial savage to subvert her faith in the commands of the "sovran Planter."

Over the past sixty years or so this bifocal vision of the biblical story has given rise to a prolonged and intense debate among Miltonists over such topics as the nature of Milton's God, the role of Satan, the status of prelapsarian Adam and Eve, and the moral character of the Fall itself. The barely submerged pattern of colonial images and themes that this book has attempted to disclose suggests that the poem's ambiguities are at least partly rooted in the geopolitical experience of seventeenth-century England. Seen from this point of view, Milton's imperial epic articulates not only the doctrines of a theological tradition reaching back to the book of Genesis but also the lived history of a culture that was still attempting to come to terms with the challenge of another New World.

Notes

Introduction

1. *Paradise Lost: Books IX–X* (Cambridge: Cambridge University Press, 1973), p. 47.

2. Honour's book, *New Golden Land* (New York: Random House, 1975), was based on the bicentennial exhibit of European representations of America which the author prepared for the National Gallery in Washington and the Cleveland Museum of Art. Chiappelli's two-volume collection, *First Images of America: The Impact of the New World on the Old* (Berkeley: University of California Press, 1976), grew out of a bicentennial conference held at UCLA.

3. Wayne Franklin, *Discoverers, Explorers, Settlers* (Chicago: University of Chicago Press, 1979); Tzvetan Todorov, *The Conquest of America: The Question of the Other*, tr. Richard Howard (New York: Harper and Row, 1984); Peter Hulme, *Colonial Encounters: Europe and the Native Caribbean, 1492–1797* (London: Methuen, 1986); Stephen J. Greenblatt, *Marvelous Possessions: The Wonder of the New World* (Chicago: University of Chicago Press, 1991); Eric Cheyfitz, *The Poetics of Imperialism* (Oxford: Clarendon Press, 1991); Jeffrey Knapp, *An Empire Nowhere: England, America, and Literature from Utopia to the Tempest* (Berkeley: University of California Press, 1992), p. 7; J. H. Elliott, *The Old World and the New, 1492–1650* (Cambridge: Cambridge University Press, 1970); Anthony Pagden, *European Encounters with the New World* (New Haven: Yale University Press, 1993).

4. In a footnote Greenblatt observes that "Milton is, at least by implication, a brilliant reader of the discourse of discovery" (*Marvelous Possessions*, p. 156), but he does not develop the point at any length. To the best of my knowledge, the only scholars who have explored the links between *Paradise Lost* and the colonization of the New World in any detail are Jackie DiSalvo and William C. Spengemann. In her paper " 'In narrow circuit

149

strait'n'd by a Foe,' " delivered at the first International Milton symposium in 1981 and subsequently printed in *Ringing the Bell Backward: The Proceedings of the First International Milton Symposium,* ed. Ronald G. Shafer (Indiana, Penn.: Indiana University of Pennsylvania Press, 1982), DiSalvo argues that both Satan and postlapsarian Adam bear the imprint of Puritan attitudes toward the American Indians. Spengemann's chapter on "*Paradise Lost:* Milton's American Poem" in *A New World of Words: Redefining Early American Literature* (New Haven: Yale University Press, 1994) unfortunately appeared too late for me to make use of it. Drawing in part on DiSalvo's paper, he makes the complementary point that Satan "bears all the traits that readers of Hakluyt and Purchas had come to associate with New World voyagers" (p. 107).

5. By the first decade of the seventeenth century virtually all the major French and Spanish narratives of the discovery and conquest of the New World were available in English. The first three "decades" of Peter Martyr's biography of Columbus and Gonzalo Fernándes de Oviedo's *Historia general y natural de las Indias* were translated into English by Richard Eden in 1555. André Thevet's *Les Singularités de la France Antarctique* appeared in translation in 1568. In 1577 John Frampton published an English version of Nicolás Monardes's treatise on American herbs and plants under the title *Joyfull newes out of the newe founde worlde.* Francisco López de Gómara's history of the conquest of Mexico was rendered into English by Thomas Nicholas as *The pleasant historie of the conquest of the Weast India* in 1578. Bartolomé de las Casas's *Brevíssima relación de la destrucción de las Indias* was translated into English by M. M. S. under the title *The Spanish Colonie* in 1583, abridged in Samual Purchas's *Purchas His Pilgrimes* in 1625, and retranslated by Milton's nephew John Phillips as *The Tears of the Indians* in 1656. And José de Acosta's *Historia natural y moral de las Indias* was translated into English by Edward Grimeston in 1604 under the title *The naturall and morall historie of the East and West Indies.* For a detailed survey of these works see John Parker, *Books to Build an Empire* (Amsterdam: N. Israel, 1965); and Colin Steele, *English Interpreters of the Iberian North West from Purchas to Stevens* (Oxford: Dolphin, 1975), chaps. 1–2.

Since my principal concern has been with those texts which could have made an impact, directly or indirectly, on Milton's literary imagination, I have focused almost exclusively on works that were in print during his lifetime. As a result, I have made little or no use of several well-known works that were not printed until after his death, notably William Bradford's *Of Plymouth Plantation,* William Strachey's *Historie of Travaile in Virginia Britannia,* and John Winthrop's *Journal.*

6. *The North Atlantic World in the Seventeenth Century* (Minneapolis: University of Minnesota Press, 1974), p. 325.

7. See, for instance, 1.114, 117; 7.73, 96; 10.380, 389.

8. Marx, *The Machine in the Garden: Technology and the Pastoral Ideal in America* (New York: Oxford University Press, 1964), chap. 2; Hulme, *Colonial Encounters*, p. 108.

9. Greenblatt, *Renaissance Self-Fashioning* (Chicago: University of Chicago Press, 1980), p. 174.

10. David Quint, *Epic and Empire* (Princeton: Princeton University Press, 1993), p. 368.

11. Robert T. Fallon, *Captain or Colonel: The Soldier in Milton's Life and Art* (Columbia: University of Missouri Press, 1984), chap. 4.

12. The term comes from Hulme's *Colonial Encounters*, pp. 93–94.

13. See *"Paradise Lost" and the Classical Epic* (London: Routledge and Kegan Paul, 1979) and *John Milton and the Transformation of Ancient Epic* (London: Croom Helm, 1986).

Chapter 1. The Colonial Idea

1. I follow W. R. Parker (*Milton: A Biography* [Oxford: Clarendon Press, 1968], 2: 1064–65) in assuming that Milton began work on the epic version of *Paradise Lost* in 1658 or thereabouts.

2. *CW* 13.517. See Walter A. Maltby, *The Black Legend in England: The Development of Anti-Spanish Sentiment, 1558–1660* (Durham, N.C.: Duke University Press, 1971).

3. John Phillips, *The Tears of the Indians* (London, 1656).

4. Colin Steele, *English Interpreters of the Iberian North West from Purchas to Stevens* (Oxford: Dolphin, 1975), p. 66.

5. Milton may have known Davenant personally, for according to one of his early biographers he intervened on Davenant's behalf when the latter was imprisoned after his abortive voyage to Maryland in 1650. See Parker, *Milton*, 1: 419.

6. When Milton began work on *Paradise Lost* in the 1650s, as Robert A. Fallon has recently reminded us ("Milton's Epics and the Spanish War: Towards a Poetics of Experience," *MS* 15 (1981): 3–28), he was still a loyal member of Cromwell's government with access to meetings of the Council of State where such matters as the war with Spain were under discussion.

7. Davies, *The North Atlantic World*, p. 63.

8. Parker, *Milton*, 2: 698; 2: 53.

9. *The Reformed Virginian Silk Worme* (London, 1655).

10. *Milton*, 1: 410, 2: 1008.

11. William Crashaw, Preface to Alexander Whitaker's *Good Newes from Virginia* (London, 1613), sig. A2r.

12. William Symonds, *Virginia, A Sermon Preached at White-Chappel* (London, 1609); Robert Gray, *A Good Speed to Virginia* (London, 1609); Robert Johnson, *Nova Britannia* (London, 1609); Daniel Price, *Sauls Prohibition Staide* (London, 1609); George Benson, *A Sermon Preached at Paules Cross* (London, 1609); Robert Tynley, *Two Learned Sermons* (London, 1609); William Crashaw, *A Sermon Preached in London* (London 1610); Council for Virginia, *A True And Sincere declaration of the purpose and end of the Plantation begun in Virginia* (London, 1610), and *A True Declaration of the estate of the Colonie in Virginia* (London, 1610); R. Rich, *Newes from Virginia. The lost Flocke Triumphant* (London, 1610); [William Strachey], *For the Colony in Virginea Britannia* (London, 1612); Captain John Smith, *A Map of Virginia* (London, 1612); Robert Johnson, *The New Life of Virginea* (London, 1612); Alexander Whitaker, *Good Newes From Virginia* (London, 1613); Ralph Hamor, *A True Discourse of the Present Estate of Virginia* (London, 1615); Virginia Company, *A Declaration of the State of the Colonie and Affaires of Virginia* (London, 1620); Patrick Copland, *Virginia's God be Thanked* (London, 1622); John Donne, *A Sermon Upon The VIII Verse Of The I Chapter Of The Acts Of The Apostles* (London, 1622); Edward Waterhouse, *A Declaration of the State of the Colony and Affaires in Virginia* (London, 1622); Captain John Smith, *The Generall Historie of Virginia, New England, and the Summer Isles* (London, 1624).

13. [William Bradford, Robert Cushman, Edward Winslow, et al.], *A Relation or Iournall of the beginning and proceedings of the English Plantation Setled at Plimoth in New England (Mourt's Relation)* (London, 1622); Council for New England, *A Briefe Relation of the Discovery and Plantation of New England* (London, 1622); Edward Winslow, *Good News from New-England* (London, 1624); [William Morrell], *New England or a Briefe Ennaration* (London, 1625); Christopher Levett, *A Voyage into New England* (London, 1628); Francis Higginson, *New-Englands Plantation, or A Short and True Description* (London, 1630); John White, *The Planters Plea* (London, 1630); William Wood, *New Englands Prospect* (London, 1634).

William Hooke, *New Englands Teares for Old Englands Feares* (London, 1641); Thomas Lechford, *Plain Dealing: or, Newes from New-England* (London, 1642); Samuel Gorton, *Simplicities Defence* (London, 1646); Edward Winslow, *Hypocrisie Unmasked* (London, 1646); Nathaniel Ward, *The Simple Cobler of Aggawam in America* (London, 1647); John Childe, *New England's Jonas Cast up at London* (London, 1647); Edward Winslow, *New Englands Salamander* (London, 1647).

[John Wilson], *The Day-Breaking if not the Sun-Rising of the Gospel with the Indians in New-England* (London, 1647); Thomas Shepard, *The Cleare Sunshine of the Gospell Breaking forth Upon the Indians in New-England* (London, 1648); Edward Winslow, *The Glorious Progress of the Gospel Amongst the Indians in New-England* (London, 1649); Henry Whitfield, *The Light appearing more and more towards the perfect Day* (London, 1651); Henry Whitfield et al., *Strength Out Of Weaknesse; Or a Glorious Manifestation of the further Progresse of the Gospel among the Indians in New-England* (London, 1652); John Eliot and Thomas Mayhew, *Tears of Repentance* (London, 1653); John Eliot, *A Late and Further Manifestation of the Progress of the Gospel amongst the Indians in New-England* (London, 1655); Anon., *The Banners of Grace and Love Displayed in the Further Conversion of the Indians in New England* (London, 1657); John Eliot et al., *A further Accompt of the Progresse of the Gospel amongst the Indians in New-England* (London 1659).

14. *Lord Baltimore's Case* (London, 1653); *Virginia and Maryland* (London, 1655); Roger Heamans, *An Additional Brief Narrative of a Late Bloody Design Against the Protestants in . . . Maryland* (London, 1655); John Hammond, *Hammond versus Heamans* (London, 1655); Leonard Strong, *Babylon's Fall in Maryland* (London, 1655); John Langford, *A Just and Cleere Refutation* (London, 1655); John Hammond, *Leah and Rachel, or the Two Fruitful Sisters Virginia and Maryland* (London, 1656).

15. *A True Declaration*, pp. 3, 16.

16. P. 4.

17. Sig. A2r. As Howard Mumford Jones has remarked in "The Colonial Impulse," *PAPS* 90 (1946): 131, n. 2, the frequent attribution of these criticisms to the playwrights and actors of the period—William Crashaw's *Sermon Preached in London* is particularly vehement on the subject—does not appear to be borne out by the facts. See Robert R. Cawley, *The Voyagers and Elizabethan Drama* (Boston: D. C. Heath, 1938).

18. Council for Virginia, *A Declaration*, p. 3.

19. *Leah and Rachel*, pp. 20, 7.

20. *A Briefe Relation*, sig. Br.

21. P. 20.

22. Printed in Samuel E. Morison, *Builders of the Bay Colony* (Boston: Houghton Mifflin, 1930), pp. 344–46.

23. *Leah and Rachel*, p. 22.

24. P. 200.

25. *The Planters Plea*, p. 37.

26. *Magnalia Christi Americana*, 3.4, quoted in Harry S. Stout, "The Morphology of Remigration: New England University Men and Their Return to England, 1640–1660," *JAS* 10 (1976): 170.

27. See Stout, "Morphology of Remigration."

28. *Coming Over: Migration and Communication between England and New England in the Seventeenth Century* (Cambridge: Cambridge University Press, 1987), pp. vii, 28. Angus Calder uses the same phrase to describe New England in *Revolutionary Empire: The Rise of the English-Speaking Empires from the Fifteenth Century to the 1780's* (London: E. P. Dutton, 1981), p. 237.

29. *Generall Historie*, pp. 41, 82. Over and over again the promoters of New England and Virginia draw their readers' attention to the extraordinary wealth that Spain had garnered from its activities in the New World: "Their Territories enlarged," wrote Robert Johnson, "their Navigations encreased, their subiects enricht, and their superfluitie of coyne over-spreading all parts of the world, procures their Crowne to flourish, and highly commendeth the wisedome of Spaine" (*Nova Britannia*, p. 10). And on the same point Richard Eburne remarked that the king of Spain had become "Lord, not onely of Territories, almost innumerable, but also of Treasures and riches in them inestimable." (*A Plaine Pathway to Plantations* [London, 1624], p. 8).

30. Sig. C3v.

31. See Richard Hakluyt, *The Principal Navigations . . . of the English Nation* (London, 1598; repr. London: J. M. Dent, 1907), 6: 58. Unless otherwise stated, all subsequent citations are from volume 6 of this edition.

32. *Advertisements for the unexperienced Planters of New-England* (London, 1631), p. 171. I quote from the text in John Lankford, *Captain John Smith's America* (New York: Harper and Row, 1967). Smith may have been thinking of men like Sir Francis Bacon, who declared in his essay *Of Plantations* (London, 1625) that he only approved of colonies "where people are not displanted to the end to plant in others. For else it is rather an extirpation than a plantation" (Sidney Warhaft, *Francis Bacon: A Selection of His Works* [Toronto: Macmillan, 1965], p. 134). Perhaps the best known defender of Indian property rights, however, was Roger Williams who directly challenged the "sinfull opinion" that Christian rulers had a divine right to the lands of the heathen.

33. See, for instance, Edward Haye, *A report of the voyage . . . by Sir Humfrey Gilbert*, in Hakluyt, *Principal Navigations*, p. 2.

34. Sig. A2r. In the previous century Francisco de Vitoria had argued along similar lines that the title of first discovery "gives no support to a seizure of the aborigines any more than if it had been they who discovered us" (quoted in Greenblatt, *Marvelous Possessions*, p. 61).

35. *A Plaine Pathway*, p. 96.

36. *Purchas His Pilgrimes* (London, 1625), p. 1810.

37. *Advertisements*, pp. 15–16.

38. *A Briefe Narration of the Originall Undertakings of the Advancement of Plantations Into the parts of America* (London, 1658), p. 62. I quote from the text in *Collections of the Maine Historical Society* (Portland: The Society, 1847), vol. 2. "The Land affords void ground enough to receive more people then this State can spare," confirmed John White, "which comes to passe by the desolation hapning through a three yeers Plague, about twelve or sixteene yeers past, which swept away most of the Inhabitants all

along the Sea coast, and in some places utterly consumed man, woman &
childe, so that there is no person left to lay claime to the soyle which they
possessed" (*The Planters Plea*, p. 14). See also Higginson, *New-Englands
Plantation*, p. 12; Thomas Morton, *New English Canaan* (London, 1632),
pp. 13, 18–19.

39. *Virginia*, p. 15. The comparison of the native population to deer
subseqently became something of a cliché in seventeenth-century discussions of the subject.

40. *A Good Speed*, sig. C3v. In fact, as Francis Jennings emphasizes in *The
Invasion of America* (Chapel Hill: University of North Carolina Press, 1975),
p. 80, the Indians of Virginia, at least, were sedentary and agricultural.

41. *Generall Considerations*, quoted in Gary B. Nash, *Red, White, and Black*
(Englewood, N.J.: Prentice-Hall, 1974), p. 80.

42. Haye, *A report* in Hakluyt, *Principal Navigations*, p. 6. Cf. Henry VII's
commission to John Cabot to "conquer, occupy, and possess" the lands of
"heathens and infidels" (quoted in Jennings, *The Invasion of America*, p. 5).
The formula goes back to Alexander VI's *Inter caetera* in which the mon-
archs of Spain and Portugal were given sovereignty over all the newly discovered lands of the Atlantic "which had not already been occupied by
some other Christian prince" (quoted in Anthony Pagden, *The Fall of Natural Man* [Cambridge: Cambridge University Press, 1982], p. 29). The Virginia colonists were authorized to establish a colony in those parts of
America "which are not actually possessed of any Christian Prince or People" (quoted in William H. Goetzmann, ed., *The Colonial Horizon: America in
the Sixteenth and Seventeenth Centuries* [Reading, Mass.: Addison Wesley,
1969], p. 97).

43. *A Good Speed*, sig. B1v.

44. Ibid., sig. C4r. In much the same vein, after enquiring "how we can
warrant a supplantation of those Indians, or an invasion into their right
and possessions," Robert Johnson offered the following answer: "As for
supplanting the savages, we have no such intent: Our intrusion into their
possessions shall tend to their great good, and in no way to their hurt, un-
lesse as unbridled beastes, they procure it to themselves: Wee purpose to
proclaime and make it knowne to them all, by some publike interpretation
that our comming thither is to plant our selves in their countrie: yet not to
supplant and roote them out" (pp. 12–13). Just how this could be accomplished without displacing the Indians he did not, however, deign to explain.

In order to make the Indians' complicity in their own dispossession
rather more plausible, subsequent defenders of colonization offered a variety of reasons for the natives' supposed willingness to share their land
with the newcomers. The local tribes, some writers declared, would wel-

come the English either because they needed allies in their wars with other tribes in the area or because they needed a firm hand to maintain order among themselves. Thus the President and Council for New England assured their readers that the settlement of the New World would be advanced "without effusion of Christian bloud, or question of wrong to the present Inhabitants. For that they themselves both desire it, & we intend not to take ought, but what they [that] are there, are willing wee should bee seized of, both for the defence of them against their Enemies, and their preservation in peace among themselves" (*A Briefe Relation*, sig. E3r). And Eburne insisted that "when seeking to gaine a Country already somewhat peopled and reasonably inhabited, as is Guiana, we doe upon faire conditions, as by proferring them defence against their enemies, supply of their wants . . . to winne them to enter league with us, to agree that we shall dwell among them, and have Lands and other Commoditie of them to our content" (*A Plaine Pathway*, p. 96).

45. *Advertisements*, p. 172.

46. *A Declaration*, pp. 22–23.

47. *Purchas His Pilgrimes*, p. 1813.

48. *Religion and Empire* (Chapel Hill: University of North Carolina Press, 1943), p. 145.

49. *A True Relation of the Late Battell Fought in New England* (London, 1637); *Newes from America* (London, 1638).

50. *Wonder-Working Providence*, ed. J. Franklin Jameson (New York: Barnes and Noble, 1910), p. 48.

51. Greenblatt, "Invisible Bullets," *Glyph* 8 (1981): 50; Hariot, *A briefe and true report of the new found land of Virginia*, in Hakluyt, *Principal Navigations*, p. 192.

52. Hakluyt, *Principal Navigations*, pp. 53–54.

53. *A Good Speed*, sig. B2v.

54. *Nova Britannia*, p. 15.

55. Ibid., p. 10.

56. P. 34, my italics. See also *The New Life*, pp. 8–9.

57. *New English Canaan*, p. 64.

58. *The Planters Plea*, pp. 22–23. Notwithstanding these cautions, elsewhere in the work White freely invoked the biblical parallel to illustrate the planters' experience; see pp. 3–4, 12. If pressed to its logical conclusion the biblical parallel clearly implied that England was the equivalent of Egypt, the corrupt society from which the Israelites escaped. As a result one might have expected the promoters of New England to endorse the correspondence between the Canaanites and the Indians and the promoters of Virginia to reject it. In fact, as I have shown, the reverse happened.

59. *Mourt's Relation*, p. 66.

60. *A Plaine Pathway*, p. 23.

61. Quoted in Lee E. Huddleston, *Origins of the American Indian* (Austin: University of Texas Press, 1967), p. 113. Jean de Léry believed, likewise, that the Tupinamba of Brazil were descendants of Ham (Pagden, *European Encounters*, p. 43). For a detailed account of the connection between the Indians and the Canaanites see Alfred A. Cave, "Canaanites in a Promised Land," *AIQ* 12 (1988): 277–97.

62. *The Planters Plea*, p. 30. As late as 1640 the planters of Connecticut sent a letter to Massachusetts "wherein they declared their dislike of such as would have the Indians rooted out, as being the cursed race of Ham" (quoted in Karen O. Kupperman, *Settling with the Indians* [Totowa, N.J.: Rowman and Littlefield, 1980], p. 184).

63. *Purchas His Pilgrimes*, p. 1683. On Virginia's evangelical aspirations see Perry Miller, *Errand into the Wilderness* (Cambridge: Harvard University Press, 1964), chap. 4.

64. P. 6. See also p. 12.

65. P. 29.

66. P. 95.

67. Hakluyt, *Principal Navigations*, p. 4.

68. *The Planters Plea*, p. 7

69. *New Englands First Fruits*, pp. 18–19.

70. *A Plaine Pathway*, p. 4.

71. *The Planters Plea*, p. 47. In their own defence the English promoters went out of their way to contrast the benevolence of English missionaries with the cruelty of the Spanish. "The Spaniard boasteth much of what hee hath already done in this kind, but their owne Authors report their unchristian behaviour, especially their monstrous cruelties to be such, as they caused the Infidels to detest the name of Christ" observed William Castell in his petition to the high court of parliament in 1641 (*A Petition of W.C. . . . for the Propagation of the Gospel in America* [London, 1641], p. 5). And in their preface the authors of *Strength Out Of Weaknesse* drew a plaintive contrast between the Spanish and Portuguese, who "have onely sought their owne advantage to possesse their Land, Transport their gold, and that with so much covetousnesse and cruelty, that they have made the name of Christianitie and of Christ an abomination," and the English, who sought to save the souls of the natives. Robert Johnson stipulated that the inhabitants of the English colonies should be converted "not by stormes of raging cruelties (as West India was converted) with rapiers point and Musket shot, murdering so many millions of naked Indians, as their stories doe relate, but by faire and loving meanes suiting to our English natures" (*Nova Britannia*, p. 14).

72. *A Petition*, p. 5.

73. Lechford, *Plain Dealing; New Englands First Fruits*, title page.

74. See K. G. Davies, *The North Atlantic World*, pp. 278 ff.; Samuel E. Morison, *Builders of the Bay Colony*, p. 299; and Alden T. Vaughan, *New England Frontier: Puritans and Indians, 1620–75* (Boston: Little, Brown, 1965), pp. 254–55.

75. *New Englands First Fruits*, p. 1. Cf. *Day-Breaking*, p. 83.

76. William Castell, *A Petition*, p. 5. For a detailed discussion of the entire subject see Louis B. Wright, *Religion and Empire*.

77. Haye, in Hakluyt, *Principal Navigations*, p. 3; Peckham, in Hakluyt, p. 49. Robert Johnson, *Nova Britannia*, pp. 12–13. John Smith quoted in Nash, *Red, White, and Black*, p. 47.

78. Copland, *Virginia's God be Thanked*, p. 24. Francis Bacon, *Of Plantations*, p. 134. Joseph Caryl, *A Late and Further Manifestation*, sig. A4r. Caryl may have been remembering Milton's reference to the "spiritual factory" of America in the preface to the second book of *The Reason of Church Government* (*CW* 3. 1. 230).

Chapter 2. The Colony

1. *A Plaine Pathway*, p. 9.

2. *Nova Britannia*, p. 19. See also *The New Life*, p. 8, where colonization is described as transplantation.

3. *Gods Promise to His Plantations* (London, 1630) in *Old South Leaflets*, vol. 3, no. 53, p. 8. Cf. Symonds, *Virginia*, p. 19; and William Strachey, *The Historie of Travaile Into Virginia Britannia*, p. 17. It is tempting to see a connection between this analogy and the famous passage at the end of Book 1 in which Milton likens the devils to a swarm of bees (1.768–75), but, as Davis P. Harding and others have amply demonstrated, Milton's bee simile derives from Homer and Virgil.

4. *Virginia's God be Thanked*, p. 30. Cf. the comparison between the Indians and the English in *Mourt's Relation*: "to us they cannot come, our land is full: to them we may goe, their land is emptie" (p. 68).

5. *Discourse on Western Planting*, p. 8. See also Eburne, *A Plaine Pathway*, p. 4.

6. *A Plaine Pathway*, ep. ded., sig. A2v. These three purposes of colonization were virtually axiomatic in early promotional literature both for New England and for Virginia. *Mourt's Relation*, for example, states that plantations exist "for the furtherance of the kingdome of Christ, the inlarging of the bounds of our Soueraigne Lord King Iames, and the good and profit of those, who either by purse, or person, or both, are agents in the same" (To the Reader, sig. B1v) and Gray states in *A Good Speed to Vir-*

ginia that colonies are established "for the aduancement of Gods glorie, the renowne of his Maiestie, and the good of your Countrie" (Ep. ded., A3v).

7. Note to 2.836 in *Paradise Lost: Books I–II* (Cambridge: Cambridge University Press, 1972).

8. *Discourse on Western Planting*, p. 37. K. G. Davies notes that after the battle of Dunbar in 1650 the Commonwealth government shipped 150 rebellious Scots to Boston, where they were sold into indentured servitude (*The North Atlantic World*, p. 92).

9. See Donne's *Sermon:* "And truly if the whole country were but such a Bridewell, to force idle persons to work, it had a good use" (p. 8).

10. *Purchas His Pilgrimes*, pp. 1816–18.

11. *The Planters Plea*, p. 19.

12. Crashaw, *A Sermon*, sig. E4v.

13. John B. Broadbent, *Some Graver Subject* (London: Chatto and Windus, 1960), p. 83. Cf. Michael Lieb's discussion of this simile in *The Dialectics of Creation* (Amherst: University of Massachusetts Press, 1970), p. 30. Lieb discovers the same "intestinal" image in Milton's account of the Devil's passage back up to earth through chaos.

14. White, *The Planters Plea*, pp. 20, 28; Winslow, *Good News from New-England*, ep. ded., p. 515; *True Report*, p. 140. Cf. Peter Hulme's discussion of the 1609 Virginia expedition in *Colonial Encounters*, pp. 103–4.

15. *Purchas His Pilgrimes*, p. 1815.

16. *The Planters Plea*, pp. 33, 44; Nathaniel Ward, *The Simple Cobler*, p. 6.

17. Bacon, *On Plantations*, p. 134; Copland, *Virginia's God be Thanked*, p. 24; *True and Sincere Declaration*, Sig. B3v.

18. Smith, *Generall Historie*, p. 53, 92; Whitaker, *Good Newes from Virginia*, p. 39; Bland, *The Discovery of New Brittaine* (London, 1651), p. 13.

19. *Purchas His Pilgrimes*, pp. 1814–15. Cf. Ovid's *Metamorphoses* 138–42: "They explored [earth's] very bowels, and dug out the wealth which it had hidden away, close to the Stygian shades; and this was a further incitement to wickedness. By this time iron had been discovered, to the hurt of mankind, and gold, more hurtful still than iron." Purchas's phrase "precious perils" may be a reminiscence of Chaucer's translation of Boethius's description of gold nuggets as "precious periles" in the *Consolation of Philosophy* 2, meter 5, or of Giles Fletcher's *Christ's Victory* 2. 54 which uses the same words in connection with gold mining. Milton's "precious bane" may be related to all or any of these occurrences, though by the mid seventeenth century Chaucer's phrase was probably something of a cliché. On Renaissance attitudes to gold and gold mining see Bernard Sheehan, *Savagism and Civility: Indians and Englishmen in Colonial Virginia* (Cambridge:

Cambridge University Press, 1980), pp. 16–18; and Greenblatt, *Marvelous Possessions*, p. 64.

20. *The Planters Plea*, p. 14.

21. See Cressy, *Coming Over*, pp. 134–38; Carl Bridenbaugh, *Vexed and Troubled Englishmen* (New York: Oxford University Press, 1968), p. 468. More regulations followed in 1638 provoked by the "frequent resort to New England of divers persons ill-affected to the religion established in the Church of England, and to the good and peaceable government of this state" (quoted in Cressy, p. 139).

22. *A Briefe Narration*, p. 51. Nor was this doubt confined to the Stuart monarchy. Even as Gorges was writing, nine years after Charles's execution, New England was contesting the right of the Commonwealth government to regulate its affairs. H. Mumford Jones notes that Maryland, too, "was plagued by intrigue and rebellion from its beginnings" (*O Strange New World* [New York: The Viking Press, 1964], p. 143).

23. After the Civil War, Virginia, which was governed by the royalist Sir William Berkeley, as well as Barbados, Antigua, and Bermuda, strenuously resisted the authority of Cromwell's government. See J. P. Greene, *Great Britain and the American Colonies, 1606–1763* (Columbia: University of South Carolina Press, 1970), pp. 43–50.

24. *The Planters Plea*, pp. 2, 4, 6.

25. I. S. MacLaren has argued that the scenery in 2. 587–605 was suggested by the journals of English explorers of the Arctic subcontinent ("Arctic Exploration and Milton's 'Frozen Continent'," *NQ* 31 [1984]: 325–26). In *A New World of Words*, Spengemann notes that the fallen angels "comport themselves . . . like the companions of John Smith on the Chesapeake, digging mines and exploring the rivers that feed their newfound lake" (p. 107).

26. Crashaw, *A Sermon*, sig. Elv. Cf. Donne's sermon to the Virginia Company: "You shall have made this island . . . a bridge, a gallery to the new" (p. 241).

27. *"Paradise Lost" and Its Critics* (Cambridge: Cambridge University Press, 1947), p. 94.

28. *The Planters Plea*, p. l.

29. See, for instance: John Armstrong, *The Paradise Myth* (London: Oxford University Press, 1969); Terry Comito, *The Idea of the Garden in the Renaissance* (New Brunswick, N.J.: Rutgers University Press, 1978); Joseph Duncan, *Milton's Earthly Paradise* (Minneapolis: University of Minnesota Press, 1972); A. B. Giamatti, *The Earthly Paradise and the Renaissance Epic* (Princeton: Princeton University Press, 1966); John D. Hunt, "Milton and the Making of the English Landscape Garden," *MS* 15 (1981): 81–105; and John R. Knott, *Milton's Pastoral Vision* (Chicago: University of Chicago Press, 1971).

30. Columbus quoted in Greenblatt, *Marvelous Possessions*, p. 180.

31. Higginson, *A True Relation of the Last Voyage to New-England*, pp. 230–34; Morton, *New English Canaan*, pp. 41–42; and Edward Johnson, *Wonder-Working Providence*, p. 22.

32. Bullock, *Virginia Impartially Examined*, p. 3; and Williams, *Virgo triumphans, or Virginia in General* (London, 1650), pp. 19, 50.

33. Locke, *Two Treatises of Government* (London, 1690), 2. 5. 49.

34. Arthur Barlowe, *The first voyage made to the coasts of America* in Hakluyt, *Principal Navigations*, p. 122.

35. See, for instance: Brereton, *A Briefe and true Relation*, p. 37; Higginson, *New-Englands Plantation*, p. 7; and Morton, *New English Canaan*, p. 44.

36. Milton is clearly using "large" in the same sense it has in "largesse."

37. In similar terms Samuel Purchas describes how Nature "hath wantonized" in Virginia (*Purchas His Pilgrimes*, p. 1818).

38. *"Paradise Lost" and the Genesis Tradition* (Oxford: Clarendon Press, 1968), p. 249.

39. *The Journal*, tr. Lionel C. Jane (London, 1968), p. 192; Hammond, *Leah and Rachel*, pp. 12–13.

40. *Purchas His Pilgrimes*, p. 1819. Cf. Barlowe, *The first voyage* in Hakluyt, *Principal Navigations*, p. 122; Robert Johnson, *Nova Britannia*, pp. 11–12; Symonds, *Virginia*, p. 24; James Rosier, *A True Relation*, p. 137; Brereton, *A Briefe and true Relation*, pp. 36–40; and Winslow, *Good News from New England*, p. 7.

41. *Changes in the Land* (New York: Hill and Wang, 1983), p. 22.

42. Hakluyt, *Principal Navigations*, pp. 168–69; Hamor, *A True Discourse*, p. 35; and Waterhouse, *A Declaration*, p. 4; see also p. 10.

43. Robert Johnson, *Nova Britannia*, p. 16. Purchas also informed his readers that "the Soyle [of Virginia] is no lesse naturally happy in Mulberie Trees of the best kind and some Silke-wormes also" (*Purchas His Pilgrimes*, p. 1819). It is worth noting in addition that in 1655 Milton's close friend Samuel Hartlib published a little tract entitled *The Reformed Virginian Silk Worme . . . For the feeding of Silk-worms in the Woods, on the Mulberry-Tree leaves in Virginia*, while a year later John Hammond argued that silk would soon displace tobacco as Virginia's principal export (*Leah and Rachel*, p. 17).

44. The lines in question read as follows. I have italicized words and phrases common to both speeches:

> Adam, well may we *labour* still to dress
> This Garden, still to tend Plant, Herb and Flour,
> Our *pleasant task* enjoyn'd, but till *more hands*
> Aid us, the work under our *labour* grows
> Luxurious by restraint; what we by day

> *Lop overgrown,* or prune, or prop, or bind,
> One night or two with *wanton growth* derides
> Tending to wilde.
>
> (9.205–12)

45. *A Declaration,* p. 10

46. *A Briefe Narration,* pp. 57–58; Edward Johnson, *Wonder-Working Providence,* p. 210.

47. *Puritanism and the Wilderness: The Intellectual Significance of the New England Frontier, 1629–1700* (New York: Columbia University Press, 1969).

48. *A Brief Exposition,* p. 166; William Bradford, *Of Plymouth Plantation,* p. 62.

49. Cotton, *The Bloody Tenent* (London, 1647), p. 151.

50. *A Brief Exposition,* p. 166. Jackie DiSalvo first called attention to the parallel, " 'In narrow circuit'," pp. 23–24.

51. Gray, *A Good Speed,* sig. B1v, C3v; Johnson, *Nova Britannia,* p. 11. (cf. Symonds, *Virginia,* p. 15); and *Mourt's Relation,* p. 68.

52. Underhill, *Newes from America,* p. 15; Cushman, *A Sermon Preached in Plimmoth* (London, 1622), p. xiii; and White, *The Planters Plea,* p. 22. Las Casas also equated the inhabitants of Hispaniola with "Lambes so meeke" that they provided easy prey for the predatory *conquistadores* from Spain (*Purchas His Pilgrimes,* p. 1569). In his *Declaration,* Waterhouse described the Virginian Indians as "this Viperous brood" (p. 17) in order to rationalize their extermination. Even the English mastiffs, he observed later in the same work, took "these naked, tanned, deformed Sauages, for no other then wild beasts" (p. 24) and thus legitimate prey of the hunt.

53. *Conjectura Cabbalistica* (London, 1653), p. 13. See *"Paradise Lost" and the Genesis Tradition,* p. 259.

54. Shepard, *The Cleare Sunshine,* p. 50.

55. Greenblatt, for instance, remarks that "the founding action of Christian imperialism is a christening" (*Marvelous Possessions,* p. 83). In the pen and ink original of Stradanus' famous engraving of the discovery, Vespucci is actually speaking the word "America."

56. Pagden, *European Encounters,* p. 35.

57. *A Perfect Description of Virginia* (London, 1649), title page. The voluntary submission of the Indians to the authority of the English crown is a recurring theme in English colonial discourse. See Peter Heylyn, *Cosmographie* (London, 1652), p. 1026; Gorton, *Simplicities Defence,* pp. 90–92; Hamor, *A True Discourse,* pp. 11–13; and Bradford et al., *Mourt's Relation,* pp. 58, 61, 68.

58. *Virginia,* p. 35.

59. See Ralph Hamor, *A True Discourse,* pp. 61–64.

60. See, for instance: Lewis Hanke, *Aristotle and the American Indians: A Study in Race Prejudice in the Modern World* (London: Hollis and Carter, 1959), p. 8; Greenblatt, "Learning to Curse" in Chiappelli, *First Images of America*, vol. 2:562; Hulme, *Colonial Encounters*, p. 1; Pagden, *European Encounters*, p. 118; and Pagden, *Spanish Imperialism and the Political Imagination* (New Haven: Yale University Press, 1990), p. 58. In his translation of the phrase Pagden omits the word "perfect."

61. The phrase is Gil Gregorio's, quoted in Pagden, *The Fall of Natural Man*, p. 48.

62. "Learning to Curse," p. 564; *Prolusion* vii in *CW* 12. 277.

Chapter 3. The Colonists

1. *Brevíssima relación de la destrucción de las Indias*, tr. John Phillips, *The Tears of the Indians* (London, 1656), p. 23. All subsequent quotations are from this translation.

2. Quoted in Louis B. Wright, *The Elizabethans' America* (Cambridge: Harvard University Press, 1965), p. 96.

3. Quoted ibid., p. 160.

4. The distinction forms the basis of Franklin's study, *Discovers, Explorers, Settlers*.

5. "Inferno" 26.115–16. I quote from Laurence Binyon's translation of the *Divine Comedy* in Paolo Milano, ed., *The Portable Dante* (New York: Viking Press, 1947). In *Jerusalem Delivered* 15. 25–32, Tasso compares Columbus with Dante's Ulysses.

6. Hammond, *Leah and Rachel*, p. 7; Smith, *Generall Historie*, p. 94; and Bacon, *Of Plantations*, p. 134. Cf. White's comment in *The Planters Plea* that "men nourished up in idlenesse, unconstant, and affecting novelties, unwilling, stubborne, enclined to faction, covetous, luxurious, prodigall, and generally men habituated to any grosse evill, are no fit members of a Colony" (p. 20).

7. *Mundus Novus*, p. 2. I quote from the translation by George T. Northrup in *The New World* (Princeton: Princeton University Press, 1916).

8. Ann D. Ferry objects to the frequently repeated observation that we see Eden only through the Devil's eyes. See *Milton's Epic Voice* (Cambridge: Harvard University Press, 1963), pp. 51–52.

9. *Discourse on Western Planting*, chap. 5.

10. *Of Reformation* (*CW* 3. 1. 50).

11. As might be expected, English Protestants heaped scorn on the papal bull, but at least one writer proposed a horizontal counterpart: "The countreys lying North of Florida, God hath reserved the same to be re-

duced unto Christian civility by the English nation. For not long after that Christopher Columbus had discovered the Islands and continent of the West Indies for Spaine, John and Sebastian Cabot made discovery also of the rest from Florida Northwards to the behoofe of England . . . as if God had prescribed limits unto the Spanish nation which they might not exceed." (Haye, *A report* in Hakluyt, *Principal Navigations*, p. 3).

12. See: Annette Kolodny, *The Lay of the Land* (Chapel Hill: University of North Carolina Press, 1975), chap. 1; Patricia Parker, *Literary Fat Ladies: Rhetoric, Gender, Property* (London: Methuen, 1987), pp. 140–42. Cf. the famous engraving of Vespucci landing in America by Johannes Stradanus (Jan van der Straet) reproduced in Honour, *New Golden Land*, p. 88.

13. Quoted in A. L. Rowse, *The Elizabethans and America* (London: Macmillan, 1959), p. 52.

14. Act 3, scene 3, line 15.

15. *Purchas His Pilgrimage*, p. 754; *Purchas His Pilgrimes*, p. 1818. Peter Heylyn, on the other hand, attributed this concept of the New World to the kings of Spain "who used to say that they esteemed America as their Wife, in whose love they could not brook a Competitor, without foul dishonour" (*Cosmographie*, p. 1017).

16. *New English Canaan*, p. 10; Hammond, *Leah and Rachel*, p. 21.

17. Samuel E. Morison, *Christopher Columbus, Mariner* (Boston: Little, Brown, 1942), p. 308.

18. Vespucci, *Mundus Novus*, p. 7; Smith, *Generall Historie*, p. 67.

19. See William Kerrigan and Gordon Braden, "Milton's Coy Eve: *Paradise Lost* and Renaissance Love Poetry," *ELH* 53 (1986): 27–51.

20. Quoted in Hamor, *A True Discourse*, pp. 61–64.

21. See also Ephesians 5. 24.

22. *The Reason of Church Government* (*CW* 3. 1. 230).

23. *Milton's "Paradise Lost"* (London: Methuen, 1962), chap. 5.

24. *The Journal of Christopher Columbus*, p. 196. In addition to Columbus, both Amerigo Vespucci and Sir Francis Drake reported the same phenomenon.

25. Hakluyt, *Principal Navigations*, p. 128.

26. *A briefe and true report*, p. 192.

27. Greenblatt, *Marvelous Possessions*, p. 98; Todorov, *The Conquest of America*, chap. 6; and Hanke, *Aristotle and the American Indians*, chap. 2.

28. *History of the Indies*, tr. Andrée Collard (New York: Harper and Row, 1971), pp. 192–93.

29. *The Planters Plea*, p. 29.

30. C. A. Patrides, *"Paradise Lost* and the Theory of Accommodation" in W. B. Hunter et al., eds., *Bright Essence: Studies in Milton's Theology* (Salt Lake City: University of Utah Press, 1971).

31. *Day-Breaking*, p. 38.

32. Ann B. Ferry discusses this point in detail in *Milton's Epic Voice*, chap. 3.

33. For the following account I have relied principally on Abbott E. Smith, *Colonists in Bondage: White Servitude and Convict Labor in America, 1607–1776* (Chapel Hill: University of North Carolina Press, 1965), chap. 1, and Bridenbaugh, *Vexed and Troubled Englishmen*, chap. 11. It has been estimated that by 1666 as many as three quarters of all immigrants to Virginia were indentured servants.

34. *Leah and Rachel*, p. 44. By 1635 the practice had become so common that blank contracts of indenture were printed for the use of prospective emigrants. Here is one for use in Maryland: "This Indenture made the blank day of blank in the blank yeere of our Soveraigne Lord King Charles, etc. betweene blank of the one party, and blank on the other part, Witnesseth, that the said blank doth hereby covenant promise, and grant, to and with the said blank his Executors and Assignes, to serve him from the day of the date hereof, untill his first and next arrival in Maryland; and after for and during the tearme of blank yeers, in such service and imployment, as the said blank or his assignes shall there imploy him, according to the custome of the Countrey in the like kind. In consideration whereof, the said blank doth promise and grant, to and with the said blank to pay for his passing, and to find him with Meat, Drinke, Apparell and Lodging, with other necessaries during the said terme; and at the end of the said terme, to give him one whole yeers provision of Corne, and fifty acres of Land, according to the order of the countrey. In witnesse whereof, the said blank hath herunto put his hand and seale, the day and yeere above written." *A Relation of Maryland* (London, 1635), p. 7.

35. At least one English sea captain refused a cargo of servants for Virginia because "servants were sold here up and down like horses" (quoted in Nash, *Red, White, and Black*, p. 54).

36. At one such auction each servant fetched between 250 and 600 lbs. of tobacco (=£6.15).

37. *Colonists in Bondage*, p. 8.

38. *A Description of the New World* (London, 1651), pp. 8–9. Pocahontas's husband John Rolfe observed in 1619 that "buying and selling of men and boys . . . was held in England a thing most intolerable" (quoted in Nash, *Red, White, and Black*, p. 54).

39. *Leah and Rachel*, pp. 10–14.

40. See, for instance, Kolodny, *The Lay of the Land*, chap. 1.

41. In his account of the first voyage to Virginia, Barlowe had assured his readers that the fruits of the earth could be harvested "without your labour." In subsequent versions of this text, however, the phrase was omitted. See below, Chap. 4.

42. *Leah and Rachel,* p. 10.

43. *New Englands Prospect,* p. 68.

44. *A True Declaration,* p. 15; Johnson, *Nova Britannia,* pp. 16–17.

45. *"Paradise Lost" and the Genesis Tradition,* chap. 10.

46. *Areopagitica* (*CW* 4.319–20).

47. I have argued elsewhere that Eve's fall is the result of a form of intellectual carelessness. See my article, "Mortals' Chiefest Enemy," *MS* 20 (1984): 111–26.

48. Perez de Oliva quoted in Elliott, *The Old World and the New,* p. 15.

49. *The Decades of the Newe World,* decade 3, book 9, tr. Richard Eden in Edward Arber, ed., *The First Three English Books on America* (Birmingham: Turnbull and Spears, 1885), p. 117. Cf. Pedro Vaz Caminha's assertion that "it is certain that this people is good and of pure simplicity, and there can easily be stamped upon them whatever belief we wish to give them" (quoted in Honour, *New Golden Land,* p. 55).

50. Quoted in Sheehan, *Savagism and Civility,* p. 48. According to De Léry, a group of Norman interpreters who had lived with the Tupinamba for eight or nine years "accommodated themselves to the savages and lived the lives of atheists. They not only polluted themselves with all manner of lascivious and base behaviour among the women and girls by whom one of them had a boy . . . but some of them, surpassing the savages in inhumanity, even boasted in my hearing of having killed and eaten prisoners" (*History of a Voyage,* p. 227).

51. See Jones, *O Strange New World,* p. 172. Hulme observes that in the early years of the Virginian colony there was "a persistent flow of Englishmen voluntarily leaving the harsh conditions of Jamestown for the Algonquian towns in the surrounding area where, at least before 1622, they were rapidly and unproblematically assimilated" (*Colonial Encounters,* p. 143).

52. See Cave, "Canaanites in a Promised Land," p. 283.

53. *The Invasion of America,* chap. 9. See, for instance, Bernal Diaz's story of Gonzalo Guerrero, who, after living with the Indians for eight years, refused to be ransomed by the Spanish (quoted in Greenblatt, *Marvelous Possessions,* pp. 138–39).

54. See James Axtell, "The White Indians of Colonial America," *WMQ* 33 (1975): 55–88.

55. "I change my sky but not my spirit when I cross the sea" (*CW* 18.271).

56. Samuel Purchas applied the idea to the early settlers in Virginia: "*Coelum non animum mutant qui trans mare currunt.* A prodigious Prodigall here, is not easily metamorphosed in a Virginia passage to a thrifty planter" (*Purchas His Pilgrimes,* p. 1816).

Chapter 4. The Colonized

1. *Interlude of the Four Elements* in W. C. Hazlitt, ed., *A Select Collection of Old English Plays*, 4th ed. (London: Reeves and Turner, 1874), p. 31.

2. Quoted in Honour, *New Golden Land*, p. 58. Andrea Cesalpino, Isaac de la Peyrere, Girolamo Cardano, and Giordano Bruno also hypothesized that the American Indians descended from another Adam or were created spontaneously from the earth. See Pagden, *The Fall of Natural Man*, pp. 22–23, and *European Encounters*, p. 11.

3. *History of the Indies*, p. 155.

4. "To the Countess of Huntington," lines 5–8.

5. *Mundus Novus*, p. 5.

6. *De Orbe Novo*, p. 8.

7. *Metamorphoses*, 1.89–100, tr. Mary M. Innes, *The Metamorphoses of Ovid* (London: Penguin, 1955).

8. Lines 358–79.

9. Act 2, scene 1, lines 137–62. Cf. "On Cannibals," p. 110.

10. *The Journal*, p. 200.

11. *Mundus Novus*, p. 6.

12. Thevet is quoted in Honour, *New Golden Land*, p. 55, and the painting is reproduced as plate 11.

13. *In secundum librum sententiarum* (Paris, 1519). For a detailed account of the debate see Pagden, *Fall of Natural Man*, and Hanke, *Aristotle and the American Indians*.

14. *History of the Indies*, p. 66. The general acceptance of this view is reflected in the infamous *requerimiento*, the declaration that was read to the Indians wherever the Spaniards landed: "In the name of King Ferdinand and Juana, his daughter, Queen of Castile and Leon, etc., conquerors of barbarian nations, we notify you as best we can that our Lord God Eternal created Heaven and earth and a man and a woman from whom we all descend for all times and all over the world" (Las Casas, *History of the Indies*, p. 192).

15. *History of the Indies*, p. 274; *Brevíssima relación*, pp. 2–3; *History of the Indies*, p. 7.

16. "The Amerindian in English Promotional Literature, 1575–1625" in Kenneth R. Andrews, ed., *The Westward Enterprise* (Liverpool: Liverpool University Press, 1978), p. 187.

17. *The First voyage*, in Hakluyt, *Principal Navigations*, p. 274; Johnson, *Nova Britannia*, p. 11; and Heylyn, *Cosmographie*, p. 1026.

18. Eburne, *Plaine Pathway to Plantations*, p. 28; Morton, *New English Canaan*, p. 40.

19. *A briefe description of the whole world* (London, 1599), pp. 240–41. This work was still being reprinted as late as 1656.

20. Gray, *Good Speed to Virginia*, sig. B1v; Smith, *Generall Historie*, pp. 147, 152; Purchas, *Purchas His Pilgrimes*, pp. 1013, 1814. See also Robert Johnson's *Nova Britannia*, p. 7.

21. *The Planters Plea*, p. 22. See also: Eliot's reference to the Indians as "poor captivated men (bondslaves to sin and Satan)" in *Tears of Repentance*, p. 202; Haye's description of the "poore infidels captived by the devill, tyrannizing in most wonderfull and dreadfull maner over their bodies and soules" in *A report of the voyage* in Hakluyt, *Principal Navigations*, p. 3; and Robert Tynley's allusion to "those sillie, brutish, and ignorant soules, now fast bound with the chaines of error and ignorance, under the bondage and slavery of the Divell" in *Two Learned Sermons*, sig. K2r.

22. *New Englands First Fruits*, p. 1. Cf.: Hamor, *A True Discourse*, p. 48; Whitaker, *Good Newes*, p. 24; and Gray, *A Good Speed*, p. 62.

23. *Nova Britannia*, p. 18. See also p. 22. Whitaker asks his readers to "let the miserable condition of these naked slaves of the divell move you to compassion toward them" (*Good Newes*, pp. 23–24). Copland also attempts to enlist the reader's pity for the Indians of Virginia who "groane under the burden of the bondage of Satan" (*Virginia's God be Thanked*, p. 28).

24. This phrase is applied to the Indians with monotonous regularity. See: *Clear Sunshine*, p. 34; *Glorious Progress*, p. 79; *Light Appearing*, pp. 104, 107, 119, 121–22, 131; *Strength out of Weakness*, pp. 153, 163, 185; *Tears of Repentance*, pp. 199, 201, 215; *Late and Further Manifestation*, pp. 266, 284, 286; *Further Accompt*, p. 1; and *Banners of Grace*, ep. ded., sigs. A2v, A3r, B2r.

25. *A Petition*, p. 4; *Strength out of Weakness*, sig. B1r (cf. *Banners of Grace*, sig. B1r, *The Planters Plea*, p. 16); *Light Appearing*, p. 102 (cf. *Day-Breaking*, p. 14); and *Day-Breaking*, pp. 10–14. Eliot's language here is somewhat vague, but it seems more than likely that he had in mind the theory I discussed in Chapter 1, namely that the Indians were the direct descendants of Ham, the inheritors of God's curse on Canaan.

26. *CW* 8.7–9; *CW* 12.139.

27. *Summa*, 1a, 2ae, q. 103, arts. 1–4.

28. "On Cannibals," pp. 267–68.

29. Morton, *New English Canaan*, p. 40.

30. For example, see *Briefe and True Report*, p. 186; *Generall Historie*, p. 7; Vincent, *True Relation*, p. 34.

31. See Pagden, *Fall of Natural Man*, pp. 30, 52. Morton claimed that the Indians' "naturall drinke is of the Christall fountaine" (*New English Canaan*, p. 40).

32. P. 113.

33. Pagden, *Fall of Natural Man*, p. 104.

34. *History of the Indies*, p. 6.

35. *Pathway to Plantations*, p. 28. Cf.: Hariot, p. 190; *Clear Sunshine*, p. 45; *Day-Breaking*, pp. 3–4; and *Light Appearing*, p. 146.

36. *Glorious Progress*, p. 86.

37. *The European and the Indian: Essays in the Ethnohistory of Colonial North America* (New York: Oxford University Press, 1981), p. 42.

38. *Clear Sunshine*, p. 45.

39. See Pagden, *Fall of Natural Man*, pp. 42–47.

40. William Cronon quotes Daniel Gookin's observation that "the Indians' clothing in former times was of the same matter as Adam's was" (*Changes in the Land*, p. 102). For descriptions of the Indian way of making fire see: Cawley, *The Voyagers and Elizabethan Drama*, p. 366; and Brereton, *A Briefe and true Relation*, p. 44. Cf. DiSalvo, " 'In narrow circuit'," pp. 26–27 for a similar account of Adam and Eve after the fall. Her claim that they degenerate "from civilized rationality to barbarian sensuality" (p. 27) seems to me, however, to misrepresent their prelapsarian condition.

41. "To the gentle Reader."

42. *Generall Historie*, pp. 63, 75, 84.

43. For earlier versions of the motive see *"Paradise Lost" and the Genesis Tradition*, pp. 134–35, 157–58, 199, 207.

44. *Purchas His Pilgrimes*, p. 1810.

45. Cf. Edward Johnson's phraseology in *Wonder-Working Providence:* "and in [the Indians'] roome . . . this poore Church of Christ . . . increased" (p. 48).

46. *Generall Historie*, p. 33. In his *Briefe and true report*, Hariot also notes that among the natives of Virginia "set battels are very rare." More often, he claims, they conduct their wars "by sudden surprising one another . . . or els by ambushes or some subtile devises" (p. 187).

47. *Settling with the Indians*, p. 127. See also Hulme, *Colonial Encounters*, p. 163.

48. Morrell, *New England or a Briefe Enarration*, p. 17. Cf. Levett's observation in *A Voyage into New England* that "they are very bloody-minded and full of treachery. . . . Therefore I would wish no man to trust them" (p. 53).

49. *Generall Historie*, pp. 144–45, 165.

50. Ibid., p. 32. See also DiSalvo, " 'In narrow circuit', " pp. 24–25.

51. On Adam and Eve's vulnerability to "security" see my article "Mortals' Chiefest Enemy," pp. 111–26.

52. *Voyage into New England*, p. 53.

53. *Day-Breaking*, p. 14. See also the reference to the Indians' "darke and despicable Tartarian Tents" in *Clear Sunshine*, p. 62, and other statements of the theory in Sir William Alexander, *Encouragement to Colonies*, pp. 40–41; Edward Brerewood, *Enquiries Touching the diversity of Languages, and Religions through the cheife parts of the world* (London, 1614), pp. 94–98; and *Purchas*

His Pilgrimage, p. 727. Pagden discusses Acosta's argument in *The Fall of Natural Man*, pp. 193–94. Morton, on the other hand, vehemently opposed Acosta's theory, arguing that the Indians derived from the ancient Trojans (see *New English Canaan*, pp. 16–18). The chief rival to the Tartarian hypothesis, in England at least, was Joannes Fredericus Lumnius's belief that the inhabitants of America descended from the ten lost tribes of Israel. See: White, *The Planters Plea*, p. 8; Winslow, *Glorious Progress*, pp. 72–73, 93–95; Whitfield, *Light Appearing*, 119–20, 127–28, Menasseh ben Israel, tr. Moses Wall, *The Hope of Israel* (London, 1650); Thomas Thorowgood, *Jewes in America* (London, 1650). The theory was opposed by Hamon L'Estrange in *Americans no Jews* (London, 1652). For a comprehensive discussion of the entire issue see Huddleston, *Origins of the American Indians*.

54. Perhaps coincidentally, the author of *A True Declaration* compares Powhatan to "a greedy Vulture" (p. 17).

55. Quoted in Sheehan, *Savagism and Civility*, p. 53. In Milton's own *Moscovia* the Tartars are the barbarous enemies of the Russians.

56. *Changes in the Land*, p. 33.

57. *New English Canaan*, pp. 38–39.

58. *A True Relation*, p. 142.

Chapter 5. The Narrator

1. Despite Ferry's claim that the narrator in *Paradise Lost* is "as deliberate an invention as the other characters in the poem" (*Milton's Epic Voice*, p. 20) I am persuaded by William G. Riggs's argument that he is "recognizably John Milton, blind and embattled in England's declining age" (*The Christian Poet in Paradise Lost* (Berkeley: University of California Press, 1972), p. 5). In what follows, therefore, I make no distinction between the narrator and Milton himself.

2. De Léry's claim occurs in the preface to his *History of a Voyage*. Milton's topic, on the other hand, had been "attempted" not only in Genesis itself but in countless poems, plays, and commentaries based on the biblical text.

3. See, for instance, Cheyfitz, *The Poetics of Imperialism*, and Greenblatt, *Learning to Curse* (New York: Routledge Kegan Paul, 1990).

4. Wood, *New Englands Prospect*, "To the Reader." See also: Higginson, *New-Englands Plantation*, p. 5; de Léry, *History of a Voyage*, p. lx.

5. *Coming Over*, p. 2. Hariot, for instance, commented ruefully that some of those returning from the Roanoke colony "have spoken of more then ever they saw, or otherwise knew to be there" (Hakluyt, *Principal Navigations*, p. 167).

6. *The first voyage* in Hakluyt, *Principal Navigations*, pp. 123–28.

7. *A True Declaration*, p. 14.

8. Pp. 54–55. It sounds as if Levett had been reading Jonson's "To Penshurst." See lines 29–38 in particular.

9. *Leah and Rachel*, pp. 7–10.

10. "To the Reader."

11. Richard Rich, *Newes from Virginia*, sig. A3–A3v. In similar terms, Hamor informs readers of *A True Discourse* that he has been for "almost six yeeres a Sufferer and eye-witness" (sig. A4v) of the Virginia colony's development, and early in *Leah and Rachel*, Hammond also emphasizes that he has lived there twenty-one years and that his account is based "on experience, not hearsay" (p. 7).

12. Smith, *Generall Historie*, p. 3.

13. *Mourt's Relation*, sig. B4v. Morton, *New English Canaan*, p. 5. Wood, *New Englands Prospect*, p. 19. Cf. *Mourt's Relation* sig. B1r. "Experimental" was a favorite word in the titles and subtitles of colonial tracts; see the subtitles to Wood's *New Englands Prospect*, Underhill's *Newes from America*, and Morton's *New English Canaan*.

14. Pagden, *European Encounters*, p. 55.

15. *Good Newes From Virginia*, sigs. B3–B3v. Cf. Waterhouse who, having admitted that the facts of the Virginia massacre have been "varied and misreported," offers readers of *A Declaration of the State of Virginia* "the collection of the truth hereof, drawne from the relation of some of them that were beholders of that Tragedie" (sigs. A3r–A3v).

16. *CW* 10.331, 382.

17. *Marvelous Possessions*, p. 123; *European Encounters*, p. 51.

18. See D. F. Hawke's introduction to the *Generall Historie* in *Captain John Smith's History of Virginia* (Indianapolis: Bobbs-Merrill, 1970), pp. vii–ix.

19. *The English-American*, title page.

20. *Discoverers, Explorers, Settlers*, p. 6. In *The Machine in the Garden*, Leo Marx argues that the design of the "classic American fable" consists of a redemptive voyage of discovery.

21. The editor of *The Day-Breaking* attempted to forestall such criticism by calling attention to the exemplary character of the author, "so eminently godly and faithfull, that what he here reports, as an eye or an eare witnesse, is not to be questioned" (To the Reader, p. iv).

22. See: Hulme, *Colonial Encounters*, chap. 4; Jennings, *The Invasion of America*, chap. 5.

23. *Marvelous possessions*, p. 122.

24. P. 3. As Pagden remarks, "suffering is the inevitable fate of the author in the New World, but it is also that suffering which authenticates and ennobles the text he will finally be able to write" (*European Encounters*, p. 66).

25. Satan also misinterprets the prohibition on the tree of knowledge after hearing Adam repeat it to Eve in Book 4.

26. *Milton's Epic Voice*, pp. 56–67.

27. *History of a Voyage*, pp. lx–lxi. Cf. *Purchas his Pilgrimage*: "A new World it may be also called, for that World of new and unknowne Creatures, which the old World never heard of, & heere onely are produced" (p. 717). Hakluyt has a rather different explanation. The New World is so called, he writes, because it is "New in regard to the new and late discovery thereof made by Christopher Colon . . . World in respect of the huge extension thereof, which to this day is not thoroughly discovered" (*Ep. Ded.* to volume 3 of the *Principal Navigations*). The title of Vespucci's first pamphlet was *Mundus Novus*. Peter Martyr called his biography of Columbus *De Orbe Novo*.

28. *History of the Indies*, p. 6.

29. Sig. Er.

30. *Nova Britannia*, p. 14. See also *The New Life*, p. 7.

31. *Good Newes from New England*, pp. 24–25; Eburne, *A Plaine Pathway*, p. 28. See also p. 7. In *Good Newes from Virginia*, on the other hand, Whitaker emphasized the civilizing power of the Christian religion. "Oh remember," he exhorted his readers, "what was the state of England before the Gospell was preached in our Countrey? How much better were we then, and concerning our soules health, then these now are?" (pp. 24–25).

32. By the same token, as I suggested in Chapter 2, to read an account of the garden of Eden was to come face to face with the historical equivalent of the New World.

33. Wayne Franklin, *Discoverers, Explorers, Settlers*, p. 23.

34. *A Sermon*, sig. F1r.

35. *A Key into the Language of America*, p. 204. See also pp. 99, 104.

36. *History of a Voyage*, pp. 131–33. Cf. Montaigne's essay "On Cannibals."

37. *Marvelous Possessions*, p. 20.

38. *Discoverers, Explorers, Settlers*, p. 23.

39. *A Briefe and True Relation*, p. 41.

40. *History of a Voyage*, p. lx. See Elliott's discussion in *The Old World and the New*, pp. 20–23. In the context of *Paradise Lost* this problem resolves itself into two diametrically opposed issues: how to describe the unfallen world to a fallen reader (the narrator's problem) and how to describe evil deeds to an innocent audience (Raphael's problem).

41. Pedro de Quiroga quoted in Pagden, *European Encounters*, p. 40.

42. *A briefe and true report* in Hakluyt, *Principal Navigations*, pp. 193–94. Cf. Brereton's *A Briefe and true Relation*, p. 40, and Higginson, *New-Englands Plantation*, p. 7.

43. See Giamatti, *The Earthly Paradise and the Renaissance Epic*, chap. 6.

44. Sig. B2r.

45. " 'Their Sex Not Equal Seem'd': Equality in *Paradise Lost*," in P. G. Stanwood, *Of Poetry and Politics: New Essays on Milton and His World* (Binghamton, N.Y.: Medieval and Renaissance Texts and Studies, 1995), pp. 171–85.

46. Wood's "true, lively, and experimentall description" of New England might be regarded as a partial exception to this generalization, but as Alden T. Vaughan reminds us in his introduction, despite his apparent objectivity Wood's real purpose was "enticing other Englishmen to America. For *New Englands Prospect* was not merely description; it was also promotional literature" (p. 11).

47. The phrase "purse or person" runs through the colonial literature of the seventeenth century like a refrain. See: *Nova Britannia*, p. 6; *A Good Speed to Virginia*, sigs. C1r, C2r; *Good Newes From Virginia*, sig. C4r; *Mourt's Relation*, sig. B1v; *Good Newes from New England*, p. 596; *New Englands Prospect*, chap. 1; and *A Description of New England*, p. 24.

48. Robert Johnson, *The New Life*, p. 17.

49. I am thinking in particular of the studies of New England thought by Perry Miller.

50. Hakluyt, *Principal Navigations*, pp. 151–61.

51. *Nova Britannia*, pp. 3–4; and *Good Newes From Virginia*, p. 23; *Perfect Description*, p. 11. See also Waterhouse, *A Declaration*, p. 20.

52. *Generall Historie*, pp. 42, 44, 49, 77, 107. The final quotation appears in almost identical form in the Virginia Company's *True Declaration*, p. 19.

53. Sig. A4v. John Cotton also claimed in his sermon on *Gods Promise to His Plantations* that the Almighty was "our planter" (p. 11).

Conclusion

1. "Invisible Bullets: Renaissance Authority and its Subversion," *Glyph* 8 (1981), 40–57. Greenblatt's description of "the containment of a subversive force by the authority that has created that force in the first place" (p. 55) applies precisely to the relationship between God and Satan in *Paradise Lost*.

2. *A Brief History of Moscovia*, *CW* 10. 363–64.

3. For a detailed discussion of the connections between the two ventures see Nicholas P. Canny, "The Ideology of English Colonization: From Ireland to America," *WMQ* 30 (1973), 575–98.

4. *Reason of Church Government*, *CW* 3.1.228.

5. "Milton's *On the Articles of Peace*: Ireland under English Eyes" in David Loewenstein and James G. Turner, eds., *Politics, Poetics, and*

Hermeneutics in Milton's Prose (Cambridge: Cambridge University Press, 1990), p. 123.

6. *Observations upon the Articles of Peace with the Irish Rebels, CW* 6. 243–48.

7. *Defensio Secunda, CW,* 8.219.

8. Corns, "Milton's *On the Articles of Peace,*" p. 123.

9. *Epic and Empire: Politics and Generic Form from Virgil to Milton,* p. 265.

10. Ibid, p. 8.

11. *Of Reformation, CW* 3.1.49–50.

Bibliography

Useful information about many of the primary sources contained in this bibliography can be found in the following essays: Richard Dunn's survey of seventeenth-century historians of America in James M. Smith, ed., *Seventeenth-Century America* (Chapel Hill: University of North Carolina Press, 1959); Jarvis M. Morse's comprehensive treatment of the first English accounts of North America in *American Beginnings: Highlights and Sidelights of the Birth of the New World* (Washington, D.C.: Public Affairs Press, 1952); David Cressy's analysis of early descriptions of New England in *Coming Over: Migration and Communication between England and New England in the Seventeenth Century* (Cambridge: Cambridge University Press, 1987), chap. 1; and Louis B. Wright's discussion of early promotional literature in *Religion and Empire: The Alliance between Piety and Commerce in English Expansion, 1558–1625* (Chapel Hill: University of North Carolina Press, 1943).

Primary Sources

Abbot, George. *A briefe description of the whole world*. London, 1599, repr. 1656.

Acosta, José de. *Historia natural y moral de las Indias*. Seville, 1590. Tr. Edward Grimeston. *The naturall and morall historie of the East and West Indies*. London, 1604.

Alexander, Sir William. *An Encouragement To Colonies*. London, 1624.

Bacon, Sir Francis. "Of plantations." In *The Essayes or Counsels Civill and Morall.* London, 1625. Reprint. *Francis Bacon: A Selection of His Works.* Ed. Sidney Warhaft. Toronto: Macmillan, 1965.

The Banners of Grace and Love Displayed in the farther Conversion of the Indians in New England. London, 1657.

Barlowe, Arthur. *The first voyage made to the coasts of America.* London, 1584. In Richard Hakluyt, *Principal Navigations,* vol. 6.

Benson, George. *A Sermon Preached at Paules Cross.* London, 1609.

Bishop, George. *New England Judged.* London, 1661.

Bland, Edward. *The Discovery of New Brittaine.* London, 1651. March of America Facsimile Series, No. 24. Ann Arbor, 1966.

Bradford, William. *Of Plymouth Plantation.* Ed. Samuel E. Morison. New York: Alfred A. Knopf, 1953.

[Bradford, William, Robert Cushman, and Edward Winslow]. *A Relation or Iournall of the beginning and proceedings of the English Plantation Setled at Plimoth in New England (Mourt's Relation).* London, 1622. March of America Facsimile Series, No. 21. Ann Arbor, 1966.

Brereton, John. *A Briefe and true Relation of the Discoverie of the North part of Virginia.* London, 1602. In George P. Winship, *Sailors' Narratives of Voyages Along the New England Coast 1524–1624.* Boston: Houghton, Mifflin, 1905. March of America Facsimile Series, No. 16. Ann Arbor, 1966.

Brerewood, Edward. *Enquiries Touching the diversity of Languages, and Religions through the chiefe parts of the world.* London, 1614.

Bullock, William. *Virginia Impartially Examined.* London, 1649.

Carew, Thomas. *Coelum Britannicum.* Westminster, 1634.

Castell, William. *A Petition of W.C. Exhibited to the High Court of Parliament now assembled, for the propagating of the Gospel in America and the West Indies; and for the setling of our Plantations there.* London, 1641. In *American Colonial Tracts Monthly.* Rochester, New York: G.P. Humphrey, 1898. i. 12. In Peter Force, *Tracts,* vol. 1.

——. *A Short Discoverie of the Coasts and Continent of America.* London, 1644.

Chapman, George, Ben Jonson, and John Marston. *Eastward Ho. The Revels Plays.* Ed. R. W. Van Fossen. Manchester: Manchester University Press, 1979.

Childe, John. *New England's Jonas Cast up at London.* London, 1647. In Peter Force, *Tracts,* vol. 4.

Clarke, John. *Ill Newes from New-England.* London, 1652. In *CMHS,* 4th ser., vol. 2, 1854.

Columbus, Christopher. *Letter to Santangel.* Barcelona, 1493. Tr. Lionel C. Jane. London: Blond, 1968.

——. *The Journal.* Tr. Lionel C. Jane. London: Blond, 1968.

Copland, Patrick. *Virginia's God be Thanked*. London, 1622.

Cotton, John. *Gods Promise to His Plantations*. London, 1630. *Old South Leaflets*, vol. 3, no. 53. Boston: Directors of the Old South Work, 1896.

——. *The Bloody Tenent, washed, And made white in the bloud of the Lambe*. London, 1647.

Council for New England. *A Briefe Relation of the Discovery and Plantation of New England*. London, 1622.

Council for Virginia. *A True And Sincere declaration of the purpose and end of the Plantation begun in Virginia*. London, 1610.

——. *A True Declaration of the estate of the Colonie in Virginia*. London, 1610. In Peter Force, *Tracts*, vol. 3.

——. *A Declaration of the State of the Colonie and Affaires in Virginia*. London, 1620. In Peter Force, *Tracts*, vol. 3.

Crakanthorpe, Richard. *A Sermon at the Inauguration of King James*. London, 1609.

Crashaw, William. *A Sermon Preached in London*. London, 1610.

Cushman, Robert. *A Sermon Preached in Plimmoth in New-England*. London, 1622.

——. *The Sin and Danger of Self-Love, a Discourse delivered at Plymouth in New-England. (The First Sermon Ever Preached in New England)*. New York: J. E. D. Comstock, 1858.

Dante Alighieri. *The Divine Comedy*. Tr. Paolo Milano. *The Portable Dante*. New York: Viking, 1947.

A Declaration of the Lord Baltimore's Plantation. London, 1633.

Donne, John. *A Sermon Upon The VIII Verse Of The I Chapter Of The Acts Of The Apostles*. London, 1622.

——. *Poems by John Donne with Elegies on the Author's Death*. London, 1633.

Drayton, Michael. "To Master George Sandys." 1622. *The Works of Michael Drayton*. Ed. W.J. Hebel and Basil Blackwell. Oxford: Shakespeare Head Press, 1961.

——. "To the Virginian Voyage." In *The Works of Michael Drayton*.

Eburne, Richard. *A Plaine Pathway to Plantations*. London, 1624.

Eliot, John. *A Late and Further Manifestation of the Progress of the Gospel amongst the Indians in New-England* London, 1655. In *CMHS*, 3d ser., vol 4, 1834.

Eliot, John, and Thomas Mayhew. *Tears of Repentance*. London, 1653. In *CMHS*, 3d. ser., vol 4, 1834.

Eliot, John, et al. *A further Accompt of the Progresse of the Gospel amongst the Indians in New-England*. London, 1659.

Frampton, John. *Joyfull newes out of the newe founde worlde*. London, 1577.

Gage, Thomas. *The English-American his Travail by Sea and Land*. London, 1648.

Gardyner, George. *A Description of the New World. Or, America Islands and Continent.* London, 1651.

Gómara, Francisco López de. *Historia general de Las Indias.* 1552. Tr. Thomas Nicholas. *The pleasant historie of the conquest of the Weast India.* London, 1578.

Good news from New-England. London, 1648. In *CMHS*, 4th ser., vol. 1, 1852.

Gorges, Sir Ferdinando. *A Briefe Narration of the Originall Undertakings of the Advancement of Plantations Into the parts of America.* London, 1658. In *Collections of the Maine Historical Society*, vol. 2. Portland: The Society, 1847.

———. *America Painted to the Life.* London, 1659.

Gorton, Samuel. *Simplicities Defence.* London, 1646. In Peter Force, *Tracts*, vol. 4.

Gray, Robert. *A Good Speed to Virginia.* London, 1609. In Wesley Craven, *Early Accounts of Life in Colonial Virginia.* New York: Scholars' Facsimiles and Reprints, 1976.

Hakluyt, Richard (the elder). *Discourse on Western Planting.* London, 1584. In *Documentary History of the State of Maine*, vol. 2. Ed. Charles Deane. Cambridge: John Wilson and Son, 1877.

———. Hakluyt, Richard. *The Principal Navigations, Voyages, Traffiques, and Discoveries of the English Nation.* London, 1598–1600. Vol. 6. London: J. M. Dent and Sons, 1907; repr. 1910.

Hammond, John. *Hammond versus Heamans.* London, 1655.

———. *Leah and Rachel, or the Two Fruitful Sisters Virginia and Maryland.* London, 1656. In Peter Force, *Tracts*, vol. 3.

Hamor, Ralph. *A True Discourse of the Present Estate of Virginia.* London, 1615. Repr. Richmond: The Virginia State Library, 1957.

Hariot, Thomas. *A briefe and true report of the new found land of Virginia.* London, 1588. In Hakluyt, *Principal Navigations*, vol. 6.

Hartlib, Samuel. *The Reformed Virginian Silk Worme.* London, 1655. In Peter Force, *Tracts*, vol. 3.

Haye, Edward. *A report of the voyage . . . by Sir Humphrey Gilbert.* In Hakluyt, *Principal Navigations*, vol. 6.

Heamans, Roger. *An Additional Brief Narrative of a Late Bloody Design Against the Protestants in . . . Maryland.* London, 1655.

Heylyn, Peter. *Cosmographie.* London, 1652.

Higginson, Francis. *New-Englands Plantation, or, A Short and True Description of the Commodities and Discommodities of that Countrey.* London, 1630. In Peter Force, *Tracts*, vol. 1. In Alexander Young, *Chronicles of the First Planters.*

————. *A True Relation of the Last Voyage to New-England.* In Alexander Young, *Chronicles of the First Planters.*

Hooke, William. *New Englands Teares for Old Englands Feares.* London, 1641.

————. *New Englands Sence of Old-England and Irelands Sorrowes.* London, 1645.

[Hugh, Peter, and Thomas Weld]. *New Englands First Fruits.* London, 1643. In *CMHS*, 1st ser., vol. 1, 1792.

The Humble Request. London, 1630.

Israel, Mannaseh ben. *Spes Israelis.* Tr. Moses Wall. *The Hope of Israel.* London, 1650. Ed. Henry Méchoulan and Gérard Nahon. Oxford: Oxford University Press, 1987.

Johnson, Edward. *Wonder-Working Providence of Sions Saviour in New England.* London, 1653. Ed. J. Franklin Jameson. Original Narratives of Early American History. New York: Barnes and Noble, 1910; repr. 1959.

Johnson, Robert. *Nova Britannia, Offring Most Excellent fruites by Planting in Virginia.* London, 1609. In Peter Force, *Tracts,* vol. 1.

————. *The New Life of Virginea.* London, 1612. In Peter Force, *Tracts,* vol. 1.

Langford, John. *A Just and Cleere Refutation.* London, 1655.

Las Casas, Bartolomé de. *Historia de las Indias.* 1527–59. Tr. Andreé M. Collard. New York: Harper and Row, 1971.

————. *Brevíssima relación de la destrucción de las Indias.* 1552. Tr. M. M. S. *The Spanish Colonie.* London, 1583. Tr. John Philips. *The Tears of the Indians.* London, 1656.

Lechford, Thomas. *Plain Dealing: or, Newes from New-England.* London, 1642. In *CMHS*, 3d ser., vol. 3, 1833. Reprinted as *New Englands Advice to Olde-England.* London, 1644.

Léry, Jean de. *Histoire d'un voyage faict en la terre du Brésil.* Tr. Janet Whatley. *History of a Voyage,* Berkeley: University of California Press, 1991.

L'Estrange, Hamon. *Americans no Jews.* London, 1652.

Levett, Christopher. *A Voyage into New England.* London, 1628. In Maine Historical Society, *Maine in the Age of Discovery.* Portland: The Maine Historical Society, 1988.

Lord Baltimore's Case. London, 1653. In Clayton C. Hall, *Narratives of Early Maryland, 1633–84. Original Narratives of Early American History,* vol. 10, New York: Charles Scribner's Sons, 1910.

Martyr, Peter d'Anghiera. *De Orbe Novo.* Tr. Richard Eden. *The Decades of the Newe Worlde.* London, 1555. In Edward Arber, *The First Three English Books on America.* Birmingham: Turnbull and Spears, 1885. Ed. Francis A. McNutt. New York: Burt Franklin, 1912; repr. 1970.

Milton, John. *The Works of John Milton.* Ed. Frank A. Patterson. New York: Columbia University Press, 1932–38.

Monardes, Nicolás. *Primera y segunda y tercera parte de las historia medicinal de las cosas que se traen de nuestras Indias occidentales que sirven en medicina.* Seville, 1565. Tr. John Frampton. *Joyfull newes out of the newe founde worlde.* London, 1577.

Montaigne, Michel de. *Essays.* Tr. J. M. Cohen. London: Penguin Books, 1958.

More, Henry. *Conjectura Cabbalistica.* London, 1653.

[Morrell, William]. *New-England or A Briefe Ennaration of the Ayre, Earth, Water, Fish and Fowles of that Country.* London, 1625.

Morton, Thomas. *New English Canaan.* London, 1632. In Peter Force, *Tracts,* vol. 2.

New-England's Ensigne. London. 1659.

Ovid, Publius Naso. *The Metamorphoses.* Tr. G. S[andys]. *Ovid's Metamorphoses Englished.* London, 1626. Tr. Mary M. Innes. *The Metamorphoses of Ovid.* Harmondsworth, Middlesex: Penguin Books, 1955.

Oviedo, Gonzalo Fernández de. *Historia general y natural de las Indias.* Seville, 1535. Tr. Richard Eden. *The Natural History of the West Indies.* London, 1555.

Peckham, George. *A true Reporte of the late discoveries.* London, 1683. In Hakluyt, *Principal Navigations,* vol. 6.

A Perfect Description of Virginia. London, 1649. In Peter Force, *Tracts,* vol. 2.

Plantagenet, Beauchamp. *A Description of the Province of New Albion.* London, 1648. In *American Colonial Tracts Monthly.* Rochester, New York: G.P. Humphrey, 1898, vol. 2.

Price, Daniel. *Sauls Prohibition Staide . . . with a reproofe of those that traduce the Honourable Plantation of Virginia.* London, 1609.

Purchas, Samuel. *Purchas his Pilgrimage.* London, 1613.

——. *Purchas his Pilgrim.* London, 1619.

——. *Purchas His Pilgrimes.* London, 1625.

R. G. *Virginia's Cure.* London, 1662. In Peter Force, *Tracts,* vol. 3.

Rastell, John. *Interlude of the Four Elements.* London, 1515. *A Select Collection of Old English Plays.* Ed. W. C. Hazlitt. London: Reeves and Turner, 1874.

A Relation of Maryland. London, 1635. In Clayton C. Hall, *Narratives of early Maryland.*

A Relation of the Successfull Beginning of Lord Baltimore's Plantation in Maryland. London, 1634.

Rich, R. *Newes from Virginia. The lost Flocke Triumphant.* London, 1610. In Wesley Craven, *Early Accounts of Life in Colonial Virginia.*

Rosier, James. *A True Relation of the most prosperous voyage made this present year 1605 by Captaine George Waymouth.* London, 1605. In George P. Winship, *Sailors' Narratives.* Also March of America Facsimile Series, No. 17. Ann Arbor, 1966.

Rous, John. *New England A Degenerate Plant.* London, 1659.

Scott, Thomas (?). *The Spaniards' Cruelty and Treachery to the English in the time of Peace and War Discovered.* London, 1656.

Sepúlveda, Juan Ginés de. *Democrates segundo, o de las justas causas de la guerra contra los indios.* Seville, 1544.

Shepard, Thomas. *New England's Lamentation for Old England's Present Errors.* London, 1645.

———. *The Cleare Sunshine of the Gospell Breaking forth Upon the Indians in New-England.* London, 1648. In *CMHS,* 3d ser., vol 4, 1834.

Smith, Capt. John. *A True Relation of such occurrences and accidents of noate as hath hapned in Virginia since the first planting of the Collony.* London, 1608.

———. *A Map of Virginia.* London, 1612.

———. *A Description of New England.* London, 1616. In Peter Force, *Tracts,* vol. 2.

———. *The Generall Historie of Virginia, New England, and the Summer Isles.* London, 1624. Reprint. Ed. D. F. Hawke. *Captain John Smith's History of Virginia.* Indianapolis: Bobbs-Merrill, 1970.

———. *Advertisements for the unexperienced Planters of New-England, or anywhere. Or, the Pathway to experience to erect a Plantation.* London, 1631.

———. *The Complete Writings of Captain John Smith.* Ed. Philip L. Barbour. 3 vols. Chapel Hill: University of North Carolina Press, 1986.

[Strachey, William]. *For the Colony in Virginea Britannia.* London, 1612.

Strachey, William. *Historie of Travaile Into Virginia Britannia.* Ed. R. H. Major. 1849.

Strong, Leonard. *Babylon's Fall in Maryland.* London, 1655. In Clayton C. Hall, *Narratives of Early Maryland.*

Symonds, William. *Virginia, a Sermon Preached at White-Chappel.* London, 1609.

Thevet, André. *Les Singularités de la France Antarctique autrement nomé Amérique.* 1557. Translated as *The New found worlde.* London, 1568.

Thorowgood, Thomas. *Jewes in America.* London, 1650.

Tynley, Robert. *Two Learned Sermons.* London, 1609.

Tyranopocrit Discovered. London, 1649.

Underhill, John. *Newes from America.* London, 1638. In *CMHS,* 3d. ser., vol. 6, 1837.

Vespucci, Amerigo. *Letter to Piero Soderini, The Four Voyages.* Tr. George T. Northrup. Princeton, 1916.

———. *Mundus Novus.* Tr. George T. Northrup. Princeton, 1916.

Vincent, Philip. *A True Relation of the late Battell fought in New-England.* London, 1637. In *CMHS,* 3d. ser., vol. 6, 1837.

Virginia and Maryland. London, 1655. In Clayton C. Hall, *Narratives of Early Maryland.*

Vitoria, Francisco de. *De indis,* 1557.

Ward, Nathaniel. *The Simple Cobler of Aggawam in America.* London, 1647. Ed. P. M. Zall. Lincoln: University of Nebraska Press, 1969.

Waterhouse, Edward. *A Declaration of the State of the Colony and Affaires in Virginia.* London, 1622.

Weld, Thomas. *A Short Story of the Rise, Reign, and Ruin of the Antinomians, Familists and Libertines.* London, 1644.

Wheelwright, John. *Mercuris Americanus.* London, 1645.

Whitaker, Alexander. *Good Newes From Virginia.* London, 1613. In Wesley Craven, *Early Accounts of Life in Colonial Virginia.*

White, John. *The Planters Plea. Or, the Grounds of Plantations Examined, And usuall Objections answered.* London, 1630. In Peter Force, *Tracts,* vol. 2.

Whitfield, Henry. *The Light appearing more and more towards the perfect Day.* London, 1651. In *CMHS,* 3d ser., vol. 4, 1834.

Whitfield, Henry, et al. *Strength Out Of Weaknesse; Or a Glorious Manifestation Of the further Progresse of the Gospel among the Indians in New-England.* London, 1652. In *CMHS,* 3d ser., vol. 4, 1834.

Williams, Edward. *Virgo triumphans, or Virginia in General.* London, 1650. In Peter Force, *Tracts,* vol. 3.

Williams, Roger. *A Key into the Language of America.* London, 1643. Ed. John J. Teunissen and Evelyn J. Hinz. Detroit: Wayne State University Press, 1973.

[Wilson, John]. *The Day-Breaking if not the Sun-Rising of the Gospel with the Indians in New-England.* London, 1647. In *CMHS,* 3d ser., vol. 4, 1834.

Winslow, Edward. *Good News from New-England.* London, 1624. In Edward Arber, ed. *The Story of the Pilgrim Fathers, 1606–1623 A.D.* London: Houghton, Mifflin, 1897.

——. *Hypocrisie Unmasked.* London, 1646. Ed. H. M. Chapin. New York: Burt Franklin, 1968.

——. *New Englands Salamander.* London, 1647. In *CMHS,* 3d. ser., vol. 2, 1830.

——. *The Glorious Progress of the Gospel Amongst the Indians in New-England.* London, 1649. In *CMHS,* 3d. ser., vol. 4, 1834.

Winthrop, John. *A short story of the rise . . . of New-England.* London, 1644.

Wood, William. *New Englands Prospect.* London, 1634. Ed. Alden T. Vaughan. Amherst: University of Massachusetts Press, 1977.

Collections

Craven, Wesley, ed. *Early Accounts of Life in Colonial Virginia* New York: Scholars' Facsimiles and Reprints, 1976.

Deane, Charles, ed. *Documentary History of the State of Maine.* Cambridge: John Wilson and Son, 1877.

Directors of the Old South Work, ed. *Old South Leaflets.* Boston: Directors of the Old South Work, 1896.

Force, Peter, ed. *Tracts and Other Papers, Relating Principally to the Origin, Settlement, and Progress of the Colonies in North America, From the Discovery of the Country to the Year 1776.* 4 vols, Washington, D.C., P. Force, 1836–46.

Goetzmann, William H., ed. *The Colonial Horizon: America in the Sixteenth and Seventeenth Centuries.* Reading, Mass.: Addison Wesley, 1969.

Hall, Clayton C., ed. *Narratives of Early Maryland, 1633–84. Original Narratives of Early American History,* vol 10. New York: Charles Scribner's Sons, 1910.

Maine Historical Society. *Collections.* Portland, Maine: The Society, 1847.

Massachusetts Historical Society. *Collections.* Boston: The Society, 1809–.

Winship, George P., ed. *Sailors' Narratives of Voyages along the New England Coast, 1524–1624.* New York: B. Franklin, 1968.

Wright, Louis B., ed. *The Elizabethans' America.* Cambridge: Harvard University Press, 1965.

Young, Alexander, ed. *Chronicles of the Pilgrim Fathers of the Colony of Plymouth, 1602–25.* New York: Da Capo, 1841.

——. *Chronicles of the First Planters of the Colony of Massachusetts Bay, 1623 to 1636.* Boston: Charles C. Little and James Brown, 1846.

Secondary Sources

Andrews, Kenneth R. *Trade, Plunder, and Settlement, 1480–1630.* Cambridge: Cambridge University Press, 1984.

Andrews, Kenneth R., et al. *The Westward Enterprise 1480–1650.* Liverpool: Liverpool University Press, 1978.

Armstrong, John. *The Paradise Myth.* London: Oxford University Press, 1969.

Axtell, James. "The White Indians of Colonial America." *WMQ* 33 (1975): 55–88.

——. *The European and the Indian: Essays in the Ethnohistory of Colonial North America.* New York: Oxford University Press, 1981.

Barker, Francis, et al., eds. *Europe and Its Others.* Proceedings of the Essex Conference on the Sociology of Literature, vol 2. Colchester: University of Essex Press, 1985.

Blessington, Francis. *"Paradise Lost" and the Classical Epic* London: Routledge and Kegan Paul, 1979.

Bremer, Francis J. *Puritan Crisis: New England and the English Civil Wars, 1630–1670.* New York: Garland, 1989.

Bridenbaugh, Carl. *Vexed and Troubled Englishmen, 1590–1642.* New York: Oxford University Press, 1968.

Broadbent, John B. *Some Graver Subject.* London: Chatto and Windus, 1960.

Calder, Angus. *Revolutionary Empire: The Rise of the English-Speaking Empires from the Fifteenth Century to the 1780's.* London: E. P. Dutton, 1981.

Canny, Nicholas P. "The Ideology of English Colonization: From Ireland to America." *WMQ,* 3d. ser., 30 (1973): 575–98.

Canny, Nicholas P., and Anthony Pagden. *Colonial Identity in the Atlantic World, 1500–1800.* Princeton: Princeton University Press, 1987.

Carr, Helen. "Woman/Indian: The American and his Others." In Francis Barker et al., *Europe and Its Others,* pp. 46–60.

Carroll, P. N. *Puritanism and the Wilderness: The Intellectual Significance of the New England Frontier, 1629–1700.* New York: Columbia University Press, 1969.

Cave, Alfred A. "Canaanites in a Promised Land: The American Indian and the Providential Theory of Empire." *AIQ* 12 (1988): 277–97.

Cawley, Robert R. *The Voyagers and Elizabethan Drama.* Boston: D. C. Heath, 1938.

———. *Milton and the Literature of Travel.* Princeton: Princeton University Press, 1951.

Cheyfitz, Eric. *The Poetics of Imperialism.* Oxford: Clarendon Press, 1991.

Chiappelli, Fredi, ed. *First Images of America: The Impact of the New World on the Old.* Berkeley: University of California Press, 1976.

Comito, Terry. *The Idea of the Garden in the Renaissance.* New Brunswick, N.J.: Rutgers University Press, 1978.

Corns, Thomas. "Milton's *Observations on the Articles of Peace:* Ireland under English Eyes." In David Loewenstein and James G. Turner, ed., *Politics, Poetics, and Hermeneutics in Milton's Prose,* pp. 123–34. Cambridge: Cambridge University Press, 1990.

Craven, Wesley F. *The Southern Colonies in the Seventeenth Century 1607–89.* Baton Rouge: Louisiana State University Press, 1949.

Cressy, David. *Coming Over: Migration and Communication between England and New England in the Seventeenth Century.* Cambridge: Cambridge University Press, 1987.

Cronon, William. *Changes in the Land: Indians, Colonists, and the Ecology of New England.* New York: Hill and Wang, 1983.

Davies, K. G. *The North Atlantic World in the Seventeenth Century.* Minneapolis: University of Minnesota Press, 1974.

DiSalvo, Jackie. " 'In narrow circuit strait'n'd by a Foe': Puritans and Indians in *Paradise Lost.*" In Ronald G. Shafer, ed. *Ringing the Bell Backward:*

The Proceedings of the First International Milton Symposium, pp. 19–33. Indiana, Penn.: Indiana University of Pennsylvania Press, 1982.

Duncan, Joseph. *Milton's Earthly Paradise*. Minneapolis: University of Minnesota Press, 1972.

Elliott, J. H. *The Old World and the New, 1492–1650*. Cambridge: Cambridge University Press, 1970.

Evans, J. M. *"Paradise Lost" and the Genesis Tradition*. Oxford: The Clarendon Press, 1968.

——. "Mortals' Chiefest Enemy." *MS* 20 (1984): 111–26.

Fallon, Robert T. "Milton's Epics and the Spanish War: Towards a Poetics of Experience." *MS* 15 (1981): 3–28.

——. *Captain or Colonel: The Soldier in Milton's Life and Art*. Columbia: University of Missouri Press, 1984.

Fanon, Frantz. *The Wretched of the Earth*. Tr. Constance Farrington. New York: Grove Press, 1966.

Ferry, Ann D. *Milton's Epic Voice*. Cambridge: Harvard University Press, 1963.

Franklin, Wayne. *Discoverers, Explorers, Settlers: The Diligent Writers of Early America*. Chicago: University of Chicago Press, 1979.

Giamatti, A. Bartlett. *The Earthly Paradise and the Renaissance Epic*. Princeton: Princeton University Press, 1966.

Greenblatt, Stephen J. *Renaissance Self-Fashioning*. Chicago: University of Chicago Press, 1980.

——. "Invisible Bullets: Renaissance Authority and Its Subversion." *Glyph* 8 (1981): 40–57.

——. "Learning to Curse: Aspects of Linguistic Colonialism in the Sixteenth Century." In Fredi Chiappelli, ed., *First Images of America*, 2: 561–80.

——. *Learning to Curse*. New York: Routledge Kegan Paul, 1990.

——. *Marvelous; Possessions: The Wonder of the New World*. Chicago: University of Chicago Press, 1991.

Greene, J. P. *Great Britain and the American Colonies, 1606–1763*. Columbia: University of South Carolina Press, 1970.

Hanke, Lewis. *Aristotle and the American Indians: A Study in Race Prejudice in the Modern World*. London: Hollis and Carter, 1959.

Hobson, J. A. *Imperialism, A Study*. London: George Allen and Unwin, 1902.

Honour, Hugh. *New Golden Land*. New York: Random House, 1975.

Huddleston, Lee E. *Origins of the American Indians: European Concepts, 1492–1729*. Austin: University of Texas Press, 1967.

Hulme, Peter. *Colonial Encounters: Europe and the Native Caribbean, 1492–1797*. London: Methuen, 1986.

Hunt, John D. "Milton and the Making of the English Landscape Garden." *MS* 15 (1979): 81–105.

Jennings, Francis. "Virgin Land and Savage People." *AQ* 23 (1971): 519–41.

——. *The Invasion of America: Indians, Colonialism, and the Cant of Conquest.* Chapel Hill: University of North Carolina Press, 1975.

Jones, Howard Mumford. "The Colonial Impulse: An Analysis of the 'Promotion' Literature of Colonization." *PAPS*, 90, no. 2 (1946): 131–61.

——. *O Strange New World.* New York: Viking, 1964.

Kerrigan, William, and Gordon Braden. "Milton's Coy Eve: *Paradise Lost* and Renaissance Love Poetry." *ELH* 53 (1986): 27–51.

Knapp, Jeffrey. *An Empire Nowhere: England, America, and Literature from Utopia to the Tempest.* Berkeley: University of California Press, 1992.

Knott, John R. *Milton's Pastoral Vision.* Chicago: University of Chicago Press, 1971.

Kolodny, Annette. *The Lay of the Land.* Chapel Hill: University of North Carolina Press, 1975.

Kupperman, Karen O. *Settling with the Indians.* Totawa, N.J.: Rowman and Littlefield, 1980.

Levin, Harry. *The Myth of the Golden Age in the Renaissance.* Bloomington: Indiana University Press, 1969.

Lewalski, Barbara K. *"Paradise Lost" and the Rhetoric of Literary Forms.* Princeton: Princeton University Press, 1985.

Lieb, Michael. *The Dialectics of Creation.* Amherst: University of Massachusetts Press, 1970.

Lockyer, Roger. *Tudor and Stuart Britain, 1471–1714.* New York: St. Martin's Press, 1964.

Loewenstein, David, and James G. Turner. *Politics, Poetics, and Hermeneutics in Milton's Prose.* Cambridge, Cambridge University Press, 1990.

MacLaren, I. S. "Arctic Exploration and Milton's 'Frozen Continent.' " *NQ* 31 (1984): 325–26.

Maltby, Walter S. *The Black Legend in England: The Development of Anti-Spanish Sentiment, 1558–1660.* Durham, N. C.: Duke University Press, 1971.

Martindale, Charles. *John Milton and the Transformation of Ancient Epic.* London: Croom Helm, 1986.

Marx, Leo. *The Machine in the Garden: Technology and the Pastoral Ideal in America.* New York: Oxford University Press, 1964.

Memmi, Albert. *The Colonizer and the Colonized.* Tr. Howard Greenfeld. Boston: Beacon Press, 1991.

Miller, Perry. *Errand into the Wilderness.* Cambridge: Harvard University Press, 1964.

Morison, Samuel E. *Builders of the Bay Colony.* Boston: Houghton Mifflin, 1930.

——. *Christopher Columbus, Mariner.* Boston: Little, Brown, 1955.

——. *The European Discovery of America.* New York: Oxford University Press, 1971.

Morse, Jarvis M. *American Beginnings: Highlights and Sidelights on the Birth of the New World.* Washington, D.C.: Public Affairs Press, 1952.

Nash, Gary B. *Red, White, and Black: The Peoples of Early America.* Englewood Cliffs, N.J.: Prentice Hall, 1974.

O'Gorman, Edmundo. *The Invention of America.* Bloomington: Indiana University Press, 1961.

Pagden, Anthony. *The Fall of Natural Man: The American Indian and the Origins of Comparative Ethnology.* Cambridge: Cambridge University Press, 1982.

———. *Spanish Imperialism and the Political Imagination.* New Haven: Yale University Press, 1990.

———. *European Encounters with the New World.* New Haven: Yale University Press, 1993.

Parker, John. *Books to Build an Empire.* Amsterdam: N. Israel, 1965.

Parker, Patricia. "Rhetorics of Property: Exploration, Inventory, Blazon." In *Literary Fat Ladies: Rhetoric, Gender, Property,* pp. 126–54. London: Methuen, 1987.

Parker, William R. *Milton: A Biography.* Oxford: The Clarendon Press, 1968.

Parry, J. H. *The Age of Reconnaissance.* Cleveland: World Publishing Company, 1963.

Patrides, C. A. "*Paradise Lost* and the Theory of Accommodation." In W. B. Hunter et al., *Bright Essence: Studies in Milton's Theology,* pp. 159–63. Salt Lake City: University of Utah Press, 1971.

Pearce, Roy Harvey. *The Savages of America: A Study of the Indian and the Idea of Civilization.* Rev. ed. Baltimore: Johns Hopkins Press, 1965.

Pomfret, John E., and Floyd M. Shumway. *Founding the American Colonies, 1583–1660.* New York: Harper and Row, 1970.

Porter, H. C. *The Inconstant Savage: England and the North American Indian, 1500–1660.* London: Duckworth, 1979.

Quinn, David B., and A. N. Ryan. *England's Sea Empire, 1550–1642.* London: G. Allen and Unwin, 1983.

Quint, David. *Epic and Empire: Politics and Generic Form from Virgil to Milton.* Princeton: Princeton University Press, 1993.

Rowse, A. L. *The Elizabethans and America.* London: Macmillan, 1959.

Salisbury, Neal. "Red Puritans: The 'Praying Indians' of Massachusetts Bay and John Eliot." *WMQ,* 3d. ser., 31 (1974): 29–38.

Sheehan, Bernard W. *Savagism and Civility: Indians and Englishmen in Colonial Virginia.* Cambridge: Cambridge University Press, 1988.

Shuffleton, F. "Indian Devils and Pilgrim Fathers." *NEQ* 49 (1976): 108–16.

Smith, Abbott E. *Colonists in Bondage: White Servitude and Convict Labor in America, 1607–1776.* Chapel Hill: University of North Carolina Press, 1965.

Smith, James M., ed. *Seventeenth-Century America*. Chapel Hill: University of North Carolina Press, 1959.

Sosin, J. M. *English America and the Restoration Monarchy of Charless II*. Lincoln: University of Nebraska Press, 1980.

Spengemann, William C. *A New World of Words: Redefining Early American Literature*. New Haven: Yale University Press, 1994.

Stavely, Keith. *Puritan Legacies: Paradise Lost and the New England Tradition, 1630–1890*. Ithaca: Cornell University Press, 1987.

Steele, Colin. *English Interpreters of the Iberian North West from Purchas to Stevens*. Oxford: Dolphin, 1975.

Stout, Harry S. "The Morphology of Remigration: New England University Men and Their Return to England, 1640–69." *JAS* 10 (1976): 151–72.

Todorov, Tzvetan. *The Conquest of America: The Question of the Other*. Tr. Richard Howard. New York: Harper and Row, 1984.

Vaughan, Alden T. *New England Frontier: Puritans and Indians, 1620–75*. Boston: Little Brown, 1965.

Waldock, A. J. A. *"Paradise Lost" and Its Critics*. Cambridge: Cambridge University Press, 1947.

Washburn, Wilcombe E. "The Moral and Legal Justifications for Dispossessing the Indians." In James M. Smith, ed., *Seventeenth-Century America*. pp. 15–27.

———. *Red Man's Land, White Man's Law*. New York: Scribner, 1971.

Wilding, Michael. " 'Thir Sex Not Equal Seem'd': Equality in *Paradise Lost*." In P. G. Stanwood, ed., *Of Poetry and Politics: New Essays on Milton and His World*, pp. 171–85. Binghamton, N.Y.: Medieval and Renaissance Texts and Studies, 1995.

Wright, B. A. *Milton's "Paradise Lost."* London: Methuen, 1982.

Wright, Louis B. *Religion and Empire: The Alliance between Piety and Commerce in English Expansion, 1558–1625*. Chapel Hill: University of North Carolina Press, 1943.

Zuckerman, Michael. "Pilgrims in the Wilderness: Community, Modernity, and the Maypole at Merry Mount." *NEQ* 50 (1977): 255–77.

———. "Identity in British America: Unease in Eden." In Nicholas Canny and Anthony Pagden, *Colonial Identity in the Atlantic World, 1500–1800*, pp. 115–57.

Index